Responsible Organizations in the Global Context

Annie Bartoli
Jose-Luis Guerrero • Philippe Hermel
Editors

Responsible Organizations in the Global Context

Current Challenges and Forward-Thinking Perspectives

Foreword by Andrew M. Pettigrew

Editors
Annie Bartoli
University of Versailles
Versailles, France

Georgetown University
Washington, DC, USA

Philippe Hermel
University of Versailles
Versailles, France

Georgetown University
Washington, DC, USA

Jose-Luis Guerrero
Georgetown University
Washington, DC, USA

Foreword by
Andrew M. Pettigrew
University of London
London, UK

ISBN 978-3-030-11457-2   ISBN 978-3-030-11458-9 (eBook)
https://doi.org/10.1007/978-3-030-11458-9

Library of Congress Control Number: 2018968422

© The Editor(s) (if applicable) and The Author(s), under exclusive licence to Springer Nature Switzerland AG 2019
This work is subject to copyright. All rights are solely and exclusively licensed by the Publisher, whether the whole or part of the material is concerned, specifically the rights of translation, reprinting, reuse of illustrations, recitation, broadcasting, reproduction on microfilms or in any other physical way, and transmission or information storage and retrieval, electronic adaptation, computer software, or by similar or dissimilar methodology now known or hereafter developed.
The use of general descriptive names, registered names, trademarks, service marks, etc. in this publication does not imply, even in the absence of a specific statement, that such names are exempt from the relevant protective laws and regulations and therefore free for general use.
The publisher, the authors and the editors are safe to assume that the advice and information in this book are believed to be true and accurate at the date of publication. Neither the publisher nor the authors or the editors give a warranty, express or implied, with respect to the material contained herein or for any errors or omissions that may have been made. The publisher remains neutral with regard to jurisdictional claims in published maps and institutional affiliations.

This Palgrave Macmillan imprint is published by the registered company Springer Nature Switzerland AG.
The registered company address is: Gewerbestrasse 11, 6330 Cham, Switzerland

Foreword: Business and Society Approached Inclusively, Globally, and Historically

The study of the modern corporation in its social, political, economic, and global context is one of the most important scholarly and policy issues of our age. In this introductory essay, I offer a personal and therefore partial view of how to approach research in this avowedly interdisciplinary field of study. There are three essential points to be made. Firstly, the need to frame any productive research agenda in inclusive terms. Here my preference is to express this research agenda in the inclusive phrase "business and society relationships" rather than the narrower domain of corporate social responsibility (CSR) or the responsible firm. Secondly, I believe it is essential to address business and society relationships in context and to examine a context which is dramatically changing. Globalization is driving many fundamental changes in the modern corporation which is often referred to now as the rootless corporation (Davis et al. 2006) or even the rootless cosmopolitan (Wolf 2004). As changes in globalization are impacting the liberal democratic ethos of many societies in North America and Europe, the relationship between business and society is changing. These changes should be at the heart of any corresponding research agenda. My third core observation is that the changing contours of business and society relationships need to be studied over retrospective and real time. Here the historical perspective and method are crucial both to contextualize what is going on and to appreciate the temporal development of business and society relationships. In so doing, I shall not just be arguing that history is about the past but acknowledging that the past is very much alive in the present and in shaping the emerging future. If our aim is to develop a practical and evidence-based theory about how to change the systems in and around business and society relationships, then we need to approach this research area inclusively, contextually/globally, and dynamically.

Why do I take the view that business and society relationships are a more fruitful and inclusive intellectual term than the more familiar languages of the responsible firm or the study of corporate social responsibility (CSR)? The term CSR has been a useful rallying cry in the development of this research field. See, for example, the notable review papers and chapters by Carroll (1999, 2008). But notwithstanding the excellent research progress made in CSR, there is a continuing sense that CSR as a rallying cry and a value crusade has both distorted and narrowed the development of that field of study. So, for some, CSR has acquired a legacy of partiality, value contamination, and exclusivity. Meanwhile a host of other titles have appeared in this research field, for example, corporate social performance, business ethics, corporate citizenship, and sustainability (Carroll 2015). This proliferation of languages and sub-groupings has not helped to build a robust research field and agenda. CSR started as and remains a contested intellectual terrain.

With this intellectual legacy, what are the virtues of adopting the term "business and society relationships"? One crucial advantage is that "business and society relationships" is a more value-neutral term than CSR. In building a research agenda, this is crucial. Secondly, "business and society relationships" is a more inclusive term which helps capture together the many meta-level issues of how and why corporations impact on society and vice versa. Thirdly, the term "business and society relationships" bridges easily into and across the social sciences where much of the available theory lies to develop the study of business and society relationships.

But what are elements of a more inclusive analytical vocabulary that can help uncover key features of business and society relationships? We can advance the field by addressing five key themes and issues and their interconnections.

The power of the modern corporation
The legitimacy of the modern corporation
The responsibility of the modern corporation
The governance of the modern corporation
The regulation of the modern corporation

In this introductory essay, there is not space to explore all five of these themes. This has been attempted in an earlier publication, Pettigrew (2009). Here I will focus specifically on the power of the modern corporation and address some of the issues associated with the relationship between globalization and the potential power of some large corporations of today.

Acquiring and using power, whether individual and/or corporate, is one of the essential engines of human existence. But we all know that it is one thing to acquire power, but quite another matter to hold on to it over time.

The misuse of power of corporations can bring legitimacy challenges which threaten corporate reputation and loss of market power. Just think of BP and its Gulf of Mexico disaster with its corresponding loss of market and financial power in the USA and beyond. Senior executives are constantly taking actions with powerful consequences for themselves, their companies, and others. In common parlance, we think of firms having the potential for market power, financial power, and even sociopolitical power (Mizruchi 2004; Scherer and Palazzo 2011; Ciepley 2013).

In the context of globalization, there is now clear recognition of the need to challenge the power of the rootless corporation with its far-flung value chains, decentralized governance, internationally dispersed manufacturing, and constantly churning executive cadre. Davis et al. (2006) quote Tommy Hilfiger prior to going private in 2006 as the archetypical rootless corporation. Prior to 2006, Tommy Hilfiger had its corporate headquarters in Hong Kong, its legal incorporation in the British Virgin Islands, and its shares on the New York Stock Exchange, held its AGM in Bermuda, and carried out most of its manufacturing in Mexico and Asia.

Similar questions are being raised on a daily basis about the exercise of power by the so-called big data companies, such as Amazon, Facebook, Google, Apple, and Microsoft. Facebook has been at the center of recent controversies about the breach of personal data. Amazon has been regularly challenged about the salary levels and employment conditions of its employees. Nation states have struggled to deal with the power of these rootless corporations as they relate to matters of terrorist-inspired data on the internet. But where does power lie between states and the big data companies across international boundaries? At the moment, there are too few large-scale empirical studies of power relationships between nation states, non-governmental organizations (NGOs), and international bodies such as the European Union (EU), and the ongoing activities of corporations. Another key area of study is the analysis of the activities of global firms and their relationships with so-called failing, weak, and repressive nation states.

Some scholars are asking if there is a role for the business corporation that goes way beyond mere compliance with legal standards and conformity with moral rules and expectations (Scherer and Polazzo 2011). If we want globalizing firms to exceed the standards of responsible behavior, then we need to understand:

1. How, where, when, and why those standards are defined?
2. Who has the power to uphold the standards?
3. And what is the price in legitimacy/reputational terms of corporate non-compliance?

A big thematic research question in an age of globalization and the rootless corporation is how are the limits of social responsibility be defined, implemented, and monitored?

Answering these kinds of meta-level questions inevitably requires us to look at the inter-relationship between our five key themes of power, legitimacy, responsibility, governance, and regulation of the modern corporation. The misuse of corporate power can lead to the delegitimization of the corporation. But under what circumstances, when, why, and how? What challenges do regulatory and state bodies face in responding to corporate excesses? Is regulation a more certain path to a responsible corporation than CSR strategies by the corporation itself?

Such researchable questions will need to be holistic in character by examining the links between our five key themes of power, legitimacy, responsibility, governance, and regulation. Those studies in a globalizing world will need to be designed to examine the cross-border relationships of firms and states and regulatory bodies. Crucially, the studies will need to be temporal, looking at the origins of power, legitimacy, and regulation and the consequences and outcomes deriving from the misuse of power and the failures of governance and regulation. Such studies will require outstanding intellectual leadership and the recruitment of sustainable teams of scholars to pursue the big researchable themes over time. This kind of aspirational scholarship represents a counter-cultural challenge to the present risk-adverse academic culture in many countries throughout the world (Pettigrew and Starkey 2016).

Let me now briefly examine the third and final issue signaled in the opening paragraphs of this short essay. I am referring to the importance of time and history in studying the dynamics of business and society relationships. The kinds of questions just posed on business and society relationships have been explicitly processual in character. Process research is the dynamic study of behavior within and between organizations and focusing on context, activities, and actions that unfold over time (Pettigrew 1997, 2012). Process questioning involves the analysis of some phenomena over time using the language of what, who, where, why, and how. Process scholars explore antecedent questions, evolution and development questions, sequencing questions, pace questions, and consequence and outcome questions. This kind of analysis demands capturing reality in flight and requires temporal analyses often made up of retrospective and real-time data. Here the historical perspective and method play a significant role (Buckley 2009; Jones et al. 2012).

But what are some of the virtues of the historical perspective and method? First, historical appreciation can help avoid the spurious labeling of some phenomena as "new". To read some accounts of CSR, the impression is that as a phenomenon it might have been invented in the 1950s and 1960s, or if one is lucky, during the period of the industrial revolution in the late eighteenth and early to mid-nineteenth centuries (Carrol 2008). But recent publications by Pettigrew and Smith (2017) and Smith and Pettigrew (2017) demonstrate that the history of social responsibility stretches way back to the early seventeenth century. So, history can also expand the domain of enquiry to the very long term as Pettigrew and Smith (2017) demonstrate the changing reciprocal relationships between corporations and their various social obligations over the period of 1600–1950.

To take history seriously is to take time seriously. Historians can go beyond identifying patterns in the evolution and development of some phenomena to examine when and how things happen in order to explain why something is happening. So, we need process scholarship and the historical perspective and method for our inclusive research agenda on business and society relationships. These forms of scholarship can help us explore the different patterns of development of business and society relationships in different countries, regions, cultures, and eras. We can then explore the implications of such developmental patterns for the use and misuse of power by corporations, and the implications and consequences for the legitimacy, governance, and regulation of the corporation. The changing patterns of globalization and the rise of the transnational and rootless corporation can also be explored in historical and processual terms. With this kind of ambitious research agenda, we will be much better informed than we are now about responsible organizations in their global context.

University of London   Andrew M. Pettigrew
London, UK

References

Buckley, P. J. (2009). Business History and International Business. *Business History, 51*(3), 307–333.
Carroll, A. B. (1999). Corporate Social Responsibility: Evolution of a Definitional Construct. *Business and Society, 38*, 268–295.
Carroll, A. B. (2008). A History of Corporate Social Responsibility: Concepts and Practice. In A. Crane, A. McWilliams, D. Matten, J. Moon, & D. S. Siegel (Eds.), *The Oxford Handbook of Social Responsibility*. Oxford: Oxford University Press.
Carroll, A. B. (2015). Corporate Social Responsibility: The Centre Piece of Competing and Complementary Frameworks. *Organizational Dynamics, 44*, 87–96.

Ciepley, D. (2013). Beyond Public and Private: Towards a Political Theory of the Corporation. *American Political Science Review, 107*(1), 139–158.

Davis, G. F., Whitman, M. N., & Zald, M. (2006, April). *Political Agency and the Responsibility Paradox: Multi-National Firms and Corporate Social Responsibility* (Ross School of Business, Paper No. 1031). University of Michigan.

Jones, G., Van Leeuwen, M., & Broadberry, S. (2012). The Future of Economic, Business and Social History. *Scandinavian Economic History Review, 60*(3), 225–253.

Mizruchi, M. S. (2004). Berle and Means Revisited: The Governance and Power of large US Corporation. *Theory and Society, 33*, 579–617.

Pettigrew, A. M. (1997). What Is a Processual Analysis? *Scandinavian Journal of Management, 13*, 337–348.

Pettigrew, A. M. (2009). Corporate Responsibility in Strategy. In N. C. Smith & E. Lenssen (Eds.), *Mainstreaming Corporate Responsibility* (pp. 12–20). Chichester: Wiley.

Pettigrew, A. M. (2012). Context and Action in the Transformation of the Firm: A Reprise. *Journal of Management Studies, 49*(7), 1304–1328.

Pettigrew, A. M., & Starkey, K. (2016). The Legitimacy and Impact of Business Schools: Key Issues and a Research Agenda. *Academy of Management Learning and Education, 15*(4), pp. 649–664.

Pettigrew, W. A., & Smith, D. C. (2017). *A History of Socially Responsible Business c. 1600–1950*. London: Palgrave Macmillan.

Scherer, A. G., & Palazzo, G. (2011). The New Political Role of Business in a Globalized World: A Review of New Perspective on CSR and Its Implications for the Firm, Governance and Democracy. *Journal of Management Studies, 48*(4), 899–931.

Smith, D. C., & Pettigrew, W. A. (2017). The History of Corporate Social Responsibility: Towards a Comparative and Institutional Contribution. In W. A. Pettigrew & D. C. Smith (Eds.), *A History of Socially Responsible Business c. 1600–1950* (pp. 1–31). London: Palgrave Macmillan.

Wolf, M. (2004). *Why Globalization Works*. New Haven: Yale University Press.

Contents

1 **Introduction: What Does Responsibility Mean to Organizations in the Current Global Context?** 1
Annie Bartoli, Jose-Luis Guerrero, and Philippe Hermel

Part I Ethics and Human Resource Management as Key Parts of Organizational Responsibility 19

2 **The Ethical and Responsible Organization: Organizational Due Process, Employee Voice, and Procedural Justice in Human Resource Management** 21
Douglas M. McCabe

3 **Continual Improvement Concepts Applied to Organizational Responsibility** 39
Holly Duckworth

4 **CSR, Employee Commitment, and Survival During Crisis Period: The Case of Tunisia** 51
Menel Ben Mlouka and Rafla Hefaiedh

Part II Communication and Reputation Related to Social Responsibility   77

5 Classifying Ethics Codes Using Natural Language Processing   79
   Zachary Glass and E. Susanna Cahn

6 Because It's Worth It? A Critical Discourse Analysis of Diversity: The Case of L'Oréal   97
   François Goxe and Michaël Viegas Pires

7 Aesthetic CSR Communication: A Global Perspective on Organizational Art Collections   117
   Angela Bargenda

8 Making Multinational Corporations Aware of Their Social Responsibility: Law Versus Reputation?   133
   Benoît Petit

Part III Representations and Practices of Responsibility in the European Context   151

9 Corporate Social Responsibility in Europe: Discourses and Practices   153
   Sofia Imane Bouterfas, Stela Raytcheva, and Gilles Rouet

10 CSR Practices: The Case of Veolia in Three European Countries   175
    Jana Marasova, Anna Vallušová, Elka Slavcheva Vasileva, and Delphine Philip de Saint Julien

11 Social Costs of Non-Responsible Research   199
    Sylvie Faucheux, Caroline Gans Combe, Catherine Kuszla, and Martin O'Connor

Part IV New Forms of Responsibility to Address Societal Challenges   221

12 Social Networks and Professional Communities: A Fair Governance?   223
Christophe Assens and Jean-Pierre Bouchez

13 Corporate Social Responsibility in Times of Internet (In)security   237
Anna Tarabasz

14 Integration and Coordination of Care and Social Services as a Responsible Way of Handling Psychiatric Disability   251
Annie Bartoli, Christelle Perrin, and Jihane Sebai

15 Postface and Conclusion: Current Challenges and Forward-Thinking Perspectives on Responsibility in Organizations   275
Mile Terziovski

Index   287

Notes on Contributors

Christophe Assens is Professor of Strategy at the ISM-IAE Graduate School of Management, University of Versailles. He is the deputy director of LAREQUOI Research Center in Management. His research specializes in the management of networks, which escape the regulation of the state or the market, outside the traditional strategies of outsourcing and internalization. He is the laureate of the French Syntec Prize and the ManpowerGroup—HEC Paris Foundation Prize, for his book *The Management of Networks* published by De Boeck (2013). His most recent book is entitled *Networks Social, All Ego? Free or Hostage from the Eyes of Others*, De Boeck (2016).

Angela Bargenda is Professor of Marketing, Communication, and Management at ESCE International Business School in Paris. She is the head of the Master's Program International and Digital Marketing: Communication, Luxury and Prestige Products. She holds a PhD and her current areas of research include aesthetic marketing, corporate social responsibility (CSR), heritage branding, brand identity, marketing semiotics, and corporate art and architecture. She regularly contributes on these topics to international journals and conferences.

Annie Bartoli is Professor of Management at the University of Versailles and research Professor at Georgetown University (Washington, DC), Center for International Education and Development (CIED). She is the co-founder of the LAREQUOI Research Center in Management, ISM-IAE Graduate School of Management in St-Quentin-en-Yvelines (France). Her research and teaching areas include public and non-profit management, change management, research methods, and cross-cultural management. She has published 7 books, more than 20 book chapters, and dozens of articles in peer-reviewed journals. She also has been chairing several international scientific conferences in various countries.

Menel Ben Mlouka holds a PhD in Management Science and is Assistant Professor of Management at the ESSEC Tunis, and the Director of the 4C ISLAIB Béja Center, a career and skills certification center whose goal is to improve the employability of young graduates by proposing a personalized support program, coaching, training, and certifications.

She is also a member and coordinator of the CSR Chair (IHEC Carthage) and a member of the research laboratory Ecstra, IHEC Carthage, in Tunisia.

Jean-Pierre Bouchez holds a PhD in Management Science and is a Research Supervisor at the research center in management LAREQUOI at the University of Versailles. He is also creator of Planet S@voirs. He has worked as a consultant and lecturer for a hundred organizations in France and abroad and has previously been vice president (human resources) in large companies. He is author or co-author of several dozens of publications of scientific and professional nature. His most recent books are *The Company in the Digital Age. New Collaborative Practices* (2016) and *The Knowledge Economy: Construction, Issues and Perspectives* (2012).

Sofia Imane Bouterfas is a PhD student at the LAREQUOI Research Center in Management at the University of Versailles, France. She works on corporate social responsibility (CSR) strategies and applied ethics. More specifically, her research project is focused on the process of making efficient CSR strategies.

E. Susanna Cahn is Professor of Management and Management Science at Pace University, Lubin School of Business. She holds a PhD from Columbia University. Her research on business ethics and decision models ranges from business applications of quantitative models drawn from decision theory, queuing, and forecasting to development of codes of business ethics and pedagogy of business ethics education.

Holly Duckworth is Vice President and Chief Learning Officer for Kaiser Aluminum. She is a founding board member of the Sherpa Sustainability Institute. Holly has published two books: *Social Responsibility: Failure Mode Effects and Analysis* and *A Six Sigma Approach to Sustainability: Continual Improvement for Social Responsibility*. She has a BS in Mechanical Engineering, an MS in Management, and a PhD in Industrial and Organizational Psychology. Holly is an ASQ certified Six Sigma Black Belt and certified Manager of Quality and Organizational Excellence, and a certified Sustainability Associate with the International Society of Sustainability Professionals.

Sylvie Faucheux is Professor of Economics and Director of IFG Executive Education and of Academic Innovation for the INSEEC U higher education group based in Paris. A specialist in ecological economics, she has published extensively in such fields as sustainability indicators, corporate social responsibility, social foresight, and eco-innovation. Her current research interests include green growth, climate change economics, education partnership building for sustainability, corporate social responsibility (CSR), and responsible innovation. She was coordinator of the EC-funded DEFORM project (*Define the Global and Financial Impact of Research Misconduct*) during 2016–2018 with teams from the University of Crete and INSEEC U.

Caroline Gans Combe is an analyst specializing in business value, data, and strategy. With the PME Reihoo, she has for several years focused on evaluation tools and methodologies to make visible in business accounts the financial value of virtuous practices and non-monetary assets (e.g., data and responsibility). She managed the H2020 *DEFORM* Project (coordinated by INSEEC U) on cost models of research fraud and is now working in the H2020 "*ProRes*" project to implement guidelines from *DEFORM*. She is business and data adviser for the *HPSCREG* project and an independent expert for the ERC, EUROSTARS, and the Innovative Medicine Initiative.

Zachary Glass holds a BSE from Princeton University in Mechanical and Aerospace Engineering. His research has focused on using natural language processing for domain-specific term extraction. He is also a licensed CPA with an interest in blockchain applications for business.

François Goxe is Associate Professor of Strategy and International Business at the University of Versailles, France. His research interests include international business and entrepreneurship with an emphasis on emerging countries, networks of international entrepreneurs and managers, and critical sociological perspectives on those issues. He has received several awards and nominations for his research, including *Paris Universities' Chancery Award* for Economics and Management Research (2012) and (Asia Pacific Division) *Best Paper Award* from the International Council for Small Business (ICSB) (2011).

Jose-Luis Guerrero is a tenured Associate Professor at the Georgetown University McDonough School of Business. He holds a PhD in Industrial and Mechanical Engineering and a Master of Sciences in Statistics from the University of Illinois. He is also an economics statistician from Rosario University, Argentina. He was awarded Doctor Honoris Causa in Administration by Ovidius University (Romania) and was elected fellow at the Judge Business School, Cambridge University (England). He got awards from the International Institute for Applied Knowledge Management and from the International Industrial Engineering and Operations Management. His research areas include big and small data, international business, social responsibility, and quality.

Rafla Hefaiedh holds a PhD in Management Science. She is Assistant Professor of Management and the Director of Training and External Relationship at the ESSEC Tunis, where she is in charge of the relationship with students, companies, universities, and all external partners. She is also a co-founder and co-responsible of a Research Master in Management and of a Professional Master in Management and Marketing of Luxury Industries. Rafla is a member of research centers in France (LAREQUOI, UVSQ) and in Tunisia (Ecstra, IHEC).

Philippe Hermel is a tenured Professor, a Scientific Director at LAREQUOI Research Center, and Honorary Dean of ISM Graduate School of Management at the University of Versailles. He is research professor at Georgetown University, Center for International Education and Development (CIED), Washington, DC. He has published ten books, and about a hundred of articles and research reports, especially on strategic change and innovation, human resources, quality management, and international and intercultural management. He is or was a member of several peer-reviewed journals and committees and an associate editor of JIBS. He has been a chairholder for the United Nations Educational, Scientific and Cultural Organization (UNESCO).

Catherine Kuszla is Professor of Management Science at the University of Paris Nanterre, France. Her current research activities include governance structures and processes, strategic management and auditing systems, and value creation in organizations characterized by uncertainties, political games, and risk—including international institutions, R&D, and innovation processes. She teaches corporate governance, auditing, and quality management in business and follows closely the evolution of professional practice in the fields of auditing, regulation, and quality management. She was a member of the research team in the EC-funded DEFORM project (*Define the Global and Financial Impact of Research Misconduct*) during 2016–2018.

Jana Marasova is university Professor and researcher at the Faculty of Economics of Matej Bel University in Banská Bystrica, Slovakia. She teaches economic theory and business management. Her research is focused on human resources management and corporate social responsibility.

Douglas M. McCabe is Professor of Management at Georgetown University McDonough School of Business in Washington, DC. He is the recipient of numerous research, teaching, and service awards and is the author of numerous academic refereed journal articles (e.g., in *California Management Review* and the *Journal of Business Ethics*). He has appeared on television and radio over 200 times as the networks have sought his views on various management topics. His television credits include being interviewed on "ABC World News Tonight," "NBC Nightly News," "CBS Evening News," "CNN," and "CNN International."

Martin O'Connor is Professor of Economics at the University of Paris-Saclay in France. His main preoccupation is with the biophysical environment in the history of economic thought and in contemporary society. Active in the fields of ecological economics, environmental politics, and sustainability, he has published and taught in many interdisciplinary domains including complex systems, science and society, social sciences epistemology, KQA (knowledge quality assurance), technological and environmental risks, multi-criteria evaluation, environmental justice, knowledge partnerships, and deliberative approaches to evaluation and governance.

Christelle Perrin holds a PhD in Management Science from the University of Paris Pantheon-Assas. She is an associate professor at the ISM-IAE Graduate School of Management and a member of the LAREQUOI Research Center in Management at the University of Versailles. Her research focuses on management and governance in public and non-profit organizations, especially regarding non-governmental organizations (NGOs) and the social and welfare economy. She has published on the topics of private-public partnerships, associative management, and digitization processes in public organizations. She is the director of the master program in Territorial Public Management for civil servants.

Benoît Petit is Associate Professor of Law at the University of Paris-Saclay, attached to its Law School in University of Versailles. His fields of research mainly focus on Labor and Employment Law, Human Rights Law, legal implications of corporate social responsibility (CSR), as well as Sustainability Ethics and Theory of Law. He directs the master's degree on Human Resource and Social Welfare Law, as well as the "Observatory on Law, Ethics and CSR" that he has founded within his research laboratory (DANTE Lab). Since 2016, he also has been holding the position of vice president of the University of Versailles in charge of strategic issues.

Andrew M. Pettigrew is Emeritus Professor at the Said Business School University of Oxford and Professor of Strategy and Organization, School of Business, Economics and Informatics at Birkbeck College, University of London. His research has pioneered the use of contextual and processual analyses of strategy making, change, decision making, and power. He has been awarded many distinctions as a scholar, including Fellow of the British Academy and Distinguished Scholar of the (US) Academy of Management. His latest research is on system-wide change and the institutional development of business schools. He has been awarded Honorary Doctorates by the University of Linkoping, Copenhagen Business School, the University of Liverpool where he graduated in 1965, and the University of Liege. In 2008, he was awarded an OBE (Officer of the Order of the British Empire) by the Queen for his services to Higher Education.

Delphine Philip de Saint Julien is Associate Professor of Management and a Research Supervisor at the LAREQUOI Research Center in Management at the University of Versailles, France. She is also the head of a Master Program in Human Resources Management at the ISM-IAE Graduate School of Management of this university. Her research is focused on downsizings and their human consequences in organizations. She has published three books and a dozen of articles in peer-reviewed journals in these fields.

Stela Raytcheva is Associate Professor of Management at the University of Versailles, France, and a member of LAREQUOI, Research Center in Management. She is the head of a Master Program in Management and Communication and International Relations Director at the ISM-IAE Graduate School of Management of the University of Versailles. Her main research axes are intercultural management, discourse analysis, and change management. These three topics are interrelated and mobilized in the study of corporate social responsibility (CSR) and organizational ethics.

Gilles Rouet is Professor of Management, University of Versailles (France); Professor of International Relations, Matej Bel University, Banská Bystrica (Slovakia); and Head of the Graduate School of Management (ISM-IAE). He holds the *ad personam* Jean Monnet Chair "Identity and Culture in Europe". In the past, he was coordinator of European programs in Russia and Georgia, as well as Attaché at the Embassy of France in Slovakia, and in Bulgaria. He has published a dozen of books and hundreds of articles and papers, namely, about European integration, Bologna Process, Management of High Education Institutions, Public Management, and European Identities.

Jihane Sebai is Associate Professor at the ISM-IAE Graduate School of Management and member of LAREQUOI Research Center in Management at the University of Versailles in France. Her research focuses on the following areas: health management, health democracy, coordination structure, integration of care, mental health, and so on. In addition to her research and teaching activities, she works for expertise missions for communities and health organizations, and she has published numerous articles in this area.

Anna Tarabasz is Assistant Professor at SP Jain School of Global Management in Dubai (UAE) and faculty member of the Marketing Department, University of Lodz (Poland). Previously, she was coordinator for Marketing and E-commerce at the American University in the Emirates, Dubai. She served as a visiting professor in France (Grenoble University) and Kazakhstan (Zhetysu State University). She has published scientific articles in English, Polish, and French. She got her PhD in Economics at the University of Lodz, with prior education in marketing, management, and e-commerce (University of Lodz and University Jean Moulin Lyon 3, France).

Mile Terziovski is a tenured Professor, Department Chair, and Director of the Master of Entrepreneurship and Innovation Program at the Department of Business Technology and Entrepreneurship, Swinburne University of Technology, Melbourne, Australia. He formerly was the Dean of the Curtin Graduate School of Business and tenured Professor of Innovation. Previously, he was head of the International Graduate School of Business at the University of South Australia (UniSA) and held a tenured Professorial Chair in Strategy and Innovation. His research specializes in innovation and entrepreneurship.

Anna Vallušová works as a researcher and a professor at the Matej Bel University in Banská Bystrica, Slovakia. In the Faculty of Economics, she covers courses of micro- and macro-economics. Her research is focused on the interaction of human resources management with corporate social responsibility in the context of post-socialist countries.

Elka Slavcheva Vasileva is Professor in the Department of Economy of Natural Resources, University of National and World Economy, Sofia, Bulgaria, where she lectures on standardization, quality, and environmental management. Her research is focused on sustainable consumption and production and on consumers' policy.

Michaël Viegas Pires is Associate Professor of Strategy and International Business at the University of Versailles, France. His research interests include the intercultural dimension of strategy and the discursive dimension of international management. His work about the intercultural dynamics of mergers and acquisitions and multinational corporations has been published in international publications, such as the *Journal of World Business* and *Thunderbird International Business Review*.

List of Figures

Fig. 3.1	Comparison of process improvement methods. (Source: Author)	46
Fig. 5.1	Bag of words example document	86
Fig. 5.2	Hypothetical graph of a support vector machine, with observed documents containing only the words "financial" and "moral"	89
Fig. 6.1	The two sides of rationalistic discourse	108
Fig. 14.1	ICCE framework. (Source: Authors)	253
Fig. 14.2	Process of patient empowerment. (Source: Authors)	265

List of Tables

Table 4.1	Description of case studies	60
Table 4.2	Summary of results	68
Table 5.1	Word frequency scores for example document	87
Table 5.2	Classification accuracy	93
Table 6.1	Summary of empirical material	104
Table 6.2	Dimensions of diversity	106
Table 6.3	Labels for individuals suffering from disability	107
Table 6.4	Frequency of disability-related words and expressions (general vs specific)	107
Table 7.1	Studied cases	122
Table 9.1	Summary—CSR among the four studied companies	166
Table 11.1	Framework for analysis of responsibility in and around research	203
Table 12.1	An illustrative example: the originally "self-organizing" CoP of maintenance technicians at Xerox	228
Table 13.1	List of possible cyber threats awaiting individuals	241

1

Introduction: What Does Responsibility Mean to Organizations in the Current Global Context?

Annie Bartoli, Jose-Luis Guerrero, and Philippe Hermel

Within the large, heterogeneous body of studies on management and organization, the question of responsibility linked to company actions has been approached more or less explicitly. Over time, too, the sensitivity to the theme of organizational responsibility has largely evolved. While it is not a new trend, a number of authors have long emphasized the relationship between responsibility, organizations, and management. Drucker (1973), in particular, believed that managers of major institutions, and especially of business, must be accountable for the common good; otherwise, no one else would take on this task. Reflecting on his 1977 notes, Prahalad (2010) recalls that a responsible manager must "assume responsibility for outcomes as well as for the processes and people you work with." Such considerations seem even more crucial in this era of profound uncertainty, large-scale globalization, and somewhat contradictory expectations regarding the social, economic, environmental and political responsibilities of major corporations.

A. Bartoli (✉) • P. Hermel
University of Versailles, Versailles, France

Georgetown University, Washington, DC, USA
e-mail: agb39@georgetown.edu; hermelp@georgetown.edu

J.-L. Guerrero
Georgetown University, Washington, DC, USA
e-mail: guerrerj@georgetown.edu

Some Challenging Questions Regarding Organizations' Responsibility

All organizations, whether public or private, are expected to be managed in order to carry out their mission in accordance with the expectations and interests of their main stakeholders. If management can be defined as a set of processes and methods used to pilot any form of organization (Fayol 1949; Mintzberg 1973; Thietart 2012), it can also be broken down into a wide variety of modalities, from comprehensive and meaningful approaches to technocratic and dehumanized tools that likely cause a loss of meaning or dignity for workers (Kostera and Pirson 2017). All of these different approaches could be considered forms of management, with some being quite responsible and others more unaccountable. Furthermore, they can be found in market enterprises and in public and non-profit activities.

The managerial vocabulary used to discuss the issues of corporate responsibility, and more broadly the responsibility of all organizations, is plural and fluctuates according to the time period and the country (Hermel and Bartoli 2013). Current discussions appear to focus on the umbrella term of corporate social responsibility (CSR). The idea of CSR generally depicts the following: beyond their mission and the specific behavior of their employees, organizations must also consider the external consequences of their behaviors and activities on society as a whole. In general, CSR covers principles relating to human rights, labor and employment practices, environmental issues, and anti-corruption policies. The social responsibility of an organization is then expressed vis-à-vis all stakeholders who may be affected by its activity. Even if it is inclusive and open, CSR has become standardized and results in some supposedly universal objectives and criteria.

In time, these notions have become norms taken up in the speeches and activities of companies. They are implicitly considered to be "good practices," actions that are necessary to meet the challenges and stakes of contemporary societies. But they are not always based on simple, fundamental reflections that consider why and for what the organization needs to be "responsible." Indeed, why should any organization take on more responsibility beyond the sum responsibilities of its members, and particularly its leaders?

The very essence of what constitutes an organization implies collective responsibility. To function smoothly, organizations require the coordination of employees' actions toward a common goal, thus allowing for an organization's actions to exceed the value of individual actions. In turn, a company's collective character dilutes the possibility of individual culpability, and its responsibility to society mainly derives from its character as a collective actor.

Identifying Some Origins of the Concept of Responsibility for Organizations

Even though the subject has become a certain fad as of late, in reality the reasoning is not as new as it appears. It is necessary to consider social responsibility alongside two types of older organizational philosophies—one related to social concerns in the industrial sector, the other to the societal roles of companies.

Regarding the social considerations of the business world, Gond and Igalens (2018) return to historical literature on corporate philanthropy during the late nineteenth and early twentieth centuries. The culture among some American businessmen evoked a type of "industrial paternalism" whereby employers sought to create a loyal and peaceable workforce through social policies close to the philosophy of CSR. One can also link these themes to the work of Hyacinthe Dubreuil (1934), who advocated organizational methods that could lead workers to assume broader and more rewarding responsibilities within their workplace.

The other consideration is the societal role of companies, that is, their place and impact in society. The work of Howard Bowen (1953) is often regarded as the cornerstone of this approach. He developed the idea of "the obligations of businessmen to pursue those policies, to make those decisions, or to follow those lines of action that are desirable in terms of the objectives and values of our society" (Bowen 1953). Subsequent scholars began to favor a more holistic notion of corporate responsibility. For instance, Archie B. Carroll (1979) proposed a comprehensive take on CSR through the four levels of a "pyramid." The base represented the economic responsibilities of a business and its obligation to be productive and profitable. The second level referred to the legal responsibilities of companies to fulfill their economic duties in accordance with the law. The third level described ethical responsibility, or established and fair codes of conduct. And finally, the fourth and top level denoted philanthropic responsibilities, which reflected the involvement of companies in improving the overall wellbeing of society.

During the 1970s, many governments and companies implemented social policies in line with these theories. For instance, several legislations led to the creation of environmental protection procedures and occupational safety organizations in the US and Europe. Among the most notable examples include the Environmental Protection Agency (EPA) and the Occupational Safety and Health Administration (OSHA) in the US. Some large companies, like Danone in France, began to implement socio-economic strategies in order to combine profitability with safe working conditions (Riboud 2014).

Heeding this movement, R. Edward Freeman (1984) coined the famous notion of "stakeholder." Developed in reference to the term "shareholder," the term "stakeholder" attempts to account for all of the socio-economic and political actors of the business environment. It expands a business's typical economic and financial reach to social, political, and societal sectors. Such sectors are arguably supposed to contribute to the economic and social performance of the company and must be taken into account in the company's strategic management process (Ansoff 1980). In this regard, the company acts as a socio-political organization engaged in ongoing conflict-cooperation relationships with its internal and external stakeholders (Martinet 1984).

Concurrently, in different parts of the world, ecological problems presented scholars with an opportunity to consider the larger impact of organizations on society and on future generations. In 1987, the World Commission on Environment and Development convened to formulate the concept of "sustainable development," a term that referred to the "development that meets the needs of the present without compromising the ability of future generations to meet their own needs." With sustainable development, people and policy makers could address their concerns over the environment, economy, and social equity while likewise formulating any necessary actions to protect the future (World Commission on Environment and Development 1987).

Decades later, the expression "sustainable development" remains paramount in discussions of social responsibility. It generally concerns the "macro" scale of countries and the planet, but it is also found in speeches concerning the "micro" level of a company or public organization. In the latter case, it is often used in the sense of CSR, and more particularly as an environmental management policy. For example, companies may put in place an environmental management system, or EMS, to accomplish CSR. Through a distinct set of activities and policies, an EMS will "enable an organization to reduce its environmental impacts and increase its operating efficiency" (EPA 2017).

Responsibility in the Global Context

Given the intensifying pressures of international competition, it is essential to analyze the various dimensions of responsible organizations in a global perspective. Indeed, socio-economic and political systems are facing many societal challenges, and management methods are more and more suspected of serving particular corporate interests instead of the public (Hambrick 1995; Pirson 2014). Consequently, more accountable, integrated processes of organizational management might be better for the present and future stakes of our society in the global context (Bartoli and Hermel 1989).

But to what extent does globalization accentuate these issues of organizational responsibility? Actually, the relative blurring of borders linked to globalizing economies and international business exchange is likely to transform company situations. If the impact of organizations is no longer only to be considered at the local level but also at the global level, their responsibility must also become and remain global. Besides, over the last decades, economic globalization has been strongly impacted by countries (such as China, India, and Brazil) that were different from the main drivers of internationalization in the twentieth century (Leisinger 2016). Therefore, western managerial paradigms might have no universal legitimacy in a cross-cultural world.

Responsible management in the global context thus includes cross-cultural management: It strives to take into account the various dimensions of the world. As Ghemawat (2001) elucidates, distance is certainly a key factor for global organizations, but geographical considerations should not be the sole issue at stake. Culture, economy, legal jurisdictions, administrative characteristics, and political tendencies are sources of differences and specificities that are critical to what makes an organization. Therefore, dealing with questions of responsible organizations cannot have the same meanings and the same implications everywhere in the world.

In some countries, the incentive to be global in focus is also of state and legislative origin. In France, the government recognizes CSR as a concept in which companies integrate social, environmental, and economic concerns into their in-house activities and their interactions with their stakeholders. Several pieces of French legislation have legalized incentives for companies to partake in CSR. For instance, a law dated August 17, 2015, relating to the transition to green energy, and its implementing decree, dated August 19, 2016, reinforced the obligations of companies to report issues of climate, energy, food waste, and the circular economy. These and other themes related to CSR appear in the French Commercial Code.

Since 2014, a European directive concerning the publication of non-financial information and diversity data requires large companies to publish annual reports on environmental and social issues. Companies must provide data concerning the results and risks to which they are subject, including non-financial performance indicators on environmental, social, and personnel issues, as well as human rights and anti-corruption policies. Interestingly, this regulation is linked to the 2005 Green Paper policy from the European Commission, which defined CSR as "the voluntary integration of the social and ecological concerns of companies in their activities and relations with their stakeholders" (European Commission 2018). This initial definition has since then become "the responsibility of enterprises for their impact on society" (European Commission 2018).

These incentives are obviously not present in all countries or geographical areas—far from it. In fact, it is questionable whether the introduction of government incentives or obligations is a relevant approach for developing responsibility. The issue of responsibility can be seen as a subject of philosophical reflection that could become misguided if it is too regulated.

Definitions and Contours of Responsible Organizations

Within this framework, the concept of responsible organizations can include, on the one hand, several dimensions of corporate social responsibility within ethical, societal, and environmental policies (Schwartz and Carroll 2003) and, on the other hand, some internal management processes (Mintzberg 1989; Hammer and Champy 1993) such as the quality of human resource policies and leadership skills (Pfeffer 1994). The possible synergy between diverse stakeholders—employees, shareholders, governments, customers, partners, sponsors, communities, society, and so on—and corporate performance offers an intriguing look at the current stakes of responsible management (Freeman 1984; Waddock and Graves 1997).

The theories and practices of organizations generally lead to a distinction between responsibility and accountability (Lindkvist and Llewellyn 2003). Responsibility refers to one who assumes the charge of something or someone, and accountability connotes the need to report or explain one's actions (Backman 1975). In the same vein, Bivins (2006) states: "If responsibility is defined as a bundle of obligations, functional and moral, associated with a role, then accountability might be defined as 'blaming or crediting someone for an action' – normally an action associated with a recognized responsibility." In reality, though, the two concepts seem somewhat necessary and complementary and help to seize the contours of a responsible organization, either at the company level or for the whole society (Martinet and Reynaud 2004).

The following chapters approach the subject of "responsible organizations" from several perspectives: an international perspective, through analyses made in different countries or via comparative approaches; an institutional perspective, studying both commercial businesses and public or non-profit organizations; and a scientific and professional perspective, by including the outlooks of practitioners in the works of researchers. Topics such as business ethics, big data, and the role of governments are also discussed, since they are essential elements of organizational processes and missions and can be considered as "the primary ingredients to be infused into the four elements of the managerial process: planning, organizing, leading, and controlling" (Laasch and

Conaway 2015). Some of these particular parameters of application deserve a deeper focus in this introductory chapter. As such, the subsequent paragraphs shed light on responsibility and ethics, responsibility and big data, responsibility and inclusion, and responsibility in government and public affairs.

Responsibility and Ethics

Recent studies on business ethics have highlighted the various dimensions of integrity and accountability among managers (Brenkert 2004). For instance, an organization's ability to secure human rights for employees or for all stakeholders is just one of the issues that scholars probe. These subjects also concern, of course, organizations' compliance with laws and regulations. In concrete terms, a number of "scandals" of international significance (i.e. Enron, WorldCom, Tyco, and Madoff) and also the "leaks" (i.e. The Panama Papers) have highlighted the issue of ethics with a particular focus on the legality and transparency of the actions of top executives. The list of these unethical cases is extensive, and here we will only mention a few.

The American company Enron is a prime example. Enron rose to prominence in the field of natural gas, for which it set up a brokerage system to buy and sell electricity largely in California. In 2001, it went bankrupt as a result of losses from its speculative operations—actions that had been concealed through unethical accounting manipulations.

Similarly, in early 2002, Tyco fell into disrepute. A company specializing in the production of electronic and medical supplies, Tyco committed tax and accounting fraud. Its ex-executives have since been sentenced to 25 years in prison. The company is still in operation today. In June 2002, news spread that US telephone operator WorldCom also committed accounting fraud. The company auditor reportedly manipulated profit numbers to keep up the appearance of ever-increasing profits. WorldCom filed for bankruptcy on July 21, 2002.

At the end of 2008, the Madoff case revealed the enormous amount of fraudulent transactions incurred worldwide (The Wall Street Journal 2009). For nearly 30 years, Bernard "Bernie" Madoff, an American financier and stockbroker, managed a fund that offered investments with seemingly exceptional yield. In reality, he secretly operated a gigantic "pyramid" swindle where the interest was paid with the funds provided by the new clients. Tens of billions of dollars have been lost by banks, charities, and individual investors around the world. Madoff is now serving 150 years in prison for his Ponzi scheme.

Yet a series of massive data leaks have likewise revealed the fraudulent tax strategies of governments, political figures, artists, athletes, and large companies. From the 2007 Clearstream case to the 2016 publication of the Panama Papers, the leaks unearthed the best-kept secrets of tax havens, where wealthy people or multinationals hid their money to escape national tax systems. Most of these leaks relied on the same kind of process: a whistleblower decides to copy confidential data from his or her company and then forwards the information to journalists.

The Panama Papers affair involved 11.5 million disclosed documents that contained detailed information on the finances and agents of more than 214,000 tax havens. The documents, some dating back to the 1970s, were created by the Panamanian law firm and service provider Mossack Fonseca and were leaked by an anonymous source "John Doe." The documents contained personal financial information from wealthy individuals and politicians. Although offshore business entities are legal, some of the shell companies were used for illegal purposes, including fraud, tax evasion, and failure to comply with international sanctions.

The press has played a major role in all instances of document leaks. They are often coordinated within networks of journalists conducting their investigations jointly and confidentially across borders. Arguably, then, this international diffusion of topics on ethics appears to indicate the public's growing awareness of responsibility among socio-economic actors. Such international investigative work thus confirms the entry of journalism into globalization and the necessity of journalists to highlight the concerns of stakeholder responsibility in our societies (Prieur 2016).

These scandals have shaken the public's confidence toward economically minded businesses. They also highlight the importance and the impact of information in today's societies—a phenomenon that is all the more complex with the increase of digitalization and use of data in all its forms.

Responsibility and Big Data

With the growth of big data and data mining come new questions on ethics, responsibility, and inclusion. Indeed, big data and digital tools can bring significant benefits to both individuals and organizations, but at the same time, they question the meaning of privacy in our society, and they highlight the risk of manipulation oriented on profit for the shareholders rather than on the stakeholders' interests (Smith 2003). For example, the data-gathering company Acxiom processes more than 50 trillion data transactions per year. It contains information about 500 million active consumers worldwide, with about 1500 data points per person regarding age, race, sex, weight, height, marital status, education level, politics, and buying habits (Singer 2012; Barocas and Selbst 2016). Given this context, various government reports have expressed concerns about consumer privacy, endangered by the purchase and sale of information (Federal Trade Commission 2012).

Indeed, the abundance of data and the concept of big data have created more concerns for consumers' and citizens' private information. While the expression "big data" comes from unknown sources, the *Oxford English Dictionary* (OED) introduced the term in 2013 and has defined it as such: "computing data of a very large size, typically to the extent that its manipulation and management present significant logistical challenges; (also) the branch of computing involving such data" (Oxford English Dictionary 2018). For specifying original works that quote this expression, the OED mentioned the work of the sociologist Charles Tilly, who described a new approach to cope with the recurring changes in social history. His approaches to big data discerned certain forthcoming changes as he explained how "…investigators tend to lose their wit, grace, and sense of proportion in the pursuit of statistical results, that none of the big questions has actually yielded to the bludgeoning of the big-data people…" (Tilly 1984). However, Tilly may have used this term in a very different context than it is used today. In the American business culture, some authors also refer to Roger Mougalas from O'Reilly Media, who used the term "Big Data" in 2005 (Halevi and Moed 2012).

Yet as organizations continue to collect more data to understand their customers and citizens, big data has helped them expand customers' reach, understand customers' behavior, and embark on the fourth industrial revolution. In particular, a group of multinational organizations, known as GAFA (Google, Apple, Facebook, and Amazon), has changed the paradigm of conducting business. An incredible number of free applications, which allow these companies to explore business opportunities, may have seduced many customers into freely revealing sensitive information.

Problems eventually began to emerge regarding the security of the supplied information. In the years since the apps were developed, data breaches have plagued private corporations such as AOL (92 million records lost in 2004), TK-TJ (94 million records lost in 2007), Maxx Heartland (130 million records lost in 2009), Sony (77 million records lost in 2011), and Target (110 million records lost in 2013) (Horovitz 2014; Cluley 2018). The cost associated with these breaches trickled down to the customers and shareholders. For example, the Target breach cost the company $17 million in net expenses and an insurance claim of $44 million. The consulting company Gartner puts the costs of the breach between $400 million and $450 million. But hackers are not the only problem in big data. Since 2015, a vulnerability within 438 applications helped to unlock the private information of 500,000 users of Google+ (Newman 2018). It took three years for the behemoth company Google to discover the data breach. Indeed, the incredible size of these companies makes them unaware of how to protect their customers and the consequences that might arise from a data breach.

Moreover, Cambridge Analytica's extraction of data from 85 million Facebook users sheds light on the concept of data veracity within responsible organizations. The company's work focused on manipulating citizens for political purposes and the expansion of fake news. As stated by the European Data Protection Supervisor (EDPS), an independent institution of the EU, this kind of online manipulation raises new forms of accountability and ethical concerns in the modern world: "Online manipulation is also a symptom of the opacity and lack of accountability in the digital ecosystem. […] At the root of the problem is partly the irresponsible, illegal or unethical use of personal information" (EDPS 2018). In this context, the use of data veracity becomes an important element of responsible organizations. While often overlooked in mining information, data veracity can be succinctly defined as conformity to the truth (Yin et al. 2008). If a source is reliable when it provides many pieces of true information, then a piece of information is likely to be true if it is provided by many reliable sources (Li et al. 2014). The opposite of verifiable truth—deception—takes many forms, most recently in the form of "fake news" or articles that deliberately mislead readers to advance an agenda.

These disturbing cases of data loss created an urgent need for organizations to be responsible with the private information of their customers. In a report from the Boston College Center for Corporate Citizenship, which examines business leaders' perceptions of corporate citizenship, the areas that are currently prioritized for increased resource investment are consumer data protection and privacy (BCCCC 2018). Interestingly, this study notes that programs to increase the diversity and inclusion of employees are the leaders' second priority.

Responsibility and Inclusion

Inclusion refers to "equal opportunity for participation." Although it is increasingly used in the fields of management, political science, and economics, it was initially developed in the discipline of educational science to consider all students, including students with special needs, as full members of the education system (Ford 2013).

In the context of organizational development, Miller and Katz (2002) consider how "the process of inclusion engages each individual and makes people feeling valued essential to the success of the organization." In the same vein, Smith and Lindsay (2014) write how inclusion is "a state in which all organizational members feel welcome and valued for who they are and what they bring to the table." For its part, the Global Diversity Practice defines inclusion as organizational efforts and practices in which different groups or individuals, all having different backgrounds, are culturally and socially accepted, welcomed, and equally treated (GDP 2017).

From the social to the economic to the financial, inclusion thus describes many aspects of responsible corporate efforts (Thompson 2017). But we live in an era of automation and data exchange, when digital inclusion becomes an element of progress and knowledge but also of challenges and new questions. According to the Institute of Museum and Library Services (2011), digital inclusion describes the ability of individuals and groups to access and use information and communication technologies. It is based on some basic principles, including availability and affordability, adoption and digital literacy, consumer education and protection, and accessibility for people with disabilities.

As such, digital inclusion takes on a dual role: the social programs that give people access to computing and information technology, and the economic imperative for various communities to benefit from the industry. As of 2018, 28 million people in the US do not use the Internet at home and may be excluded from financial and economic innovations that occur online (NTIA 2018). Indeed, the existence and risks of the digital divide mean that every population stands to benefit from digital use, and institutions and governments cannot truly innovate if their only innovations are available online. The digital divide can also create or increase difficulties in economic and financial inclusion, the latter being defined as the regular use of formal financial services, which may not be accessible for many low-income households (Demirgüç-Kunt and Klapper 2013).

Topics of diversity and inclusion must therefore be considered essential to the policies of responsible organizations, whether private, not for profit, or public.

What Is Responsibility for Public Organizations?

Given the current proliferation of corporate responsibility within academic literature and business practice, one question that arises is whether these attempts to conceptualize certain moral or ethical obligations relate exclusively to companies, or more broadly to merchant and non-market organizations. In other words, is this concept applicable to all types of companies? (Larat and Bartoli 2018).

In 2010, the International Organization for Standardization (ISO) published a standard that approaches this issue in a broad way: "This International Standard is intended to be useful to all types of organizations in the private, public and non-profit sectors, whether large or small, and whether operating in developed or developing countries" (ISO 2010). The ISO also states: "Governmental organizations, like any other organization, may wish to use this International Standard. However, it is not intended to replace, alter or in any way change the obligations of the state" (ISO 2010). In this way, government institutions appear to be somewhat excluded from the scope of CSR, insofar as these institutions would be, by nature, responsible to society.

However, if we explore the question of social responsibility in the public context, the connection between action and responsibility of stakeholders is critically important, for government action is itself the result of changing configurations. It is no longer enough to consider public organizations as opaque groups serving an abstract political mission. We must also address their concrete actions—and especially the consequences of these actions—as the result of operating modes, anticipation processes, and problem-solving operations (Duran 2013). The political, administrative, and social dimensions of responsibility must then be approached in their complementarities for any kind of organization.

Genesis and Objectives of the Book

The book aims to spur critical thought on the various dimensions and impacts of "responsibility" for organizations, including companies, institutions, and governments, while considering international differences and similarities and global challenges. The team of contributors strives to analyze to what extent responsibility is becoming a crucial issue for all kinds of organizations.

The original conception of this book dates to an international conference "Responsible Organizations in the Global Context" held on June 15 and 16, 2017, in Washington, DC (US), co-organized by the LAREQUOI Research Center in Management of the University of Versailles (France) and the Center for Intercultural Education and Development (CIED) of Georgetown University (US). One hundred thirty participants from 29 different nations shared their research and reflections during this event. From these discussions, select papers became the basis of this book, to which other complementary contributions were added.

Responsible Organizations in the Global Context: Current Challenges and Forward-Thinking Perspectives is composed of 14 chapters divided into four parts. The first part considers ethics and human resources management as key factors of organizational responsibility. The second part is devoted to deepening the themes of communication and reputation, which are often major motifs in CSR policies. The third part presents conceptual analyses and practical examples from Europe. Lastly, the fourth part discusses new forms of responsibility that address societal challenges. In addition, Professor Andrew Pettigrew of the University of Oxford, England, has authored the foreword in order to open discussions on the historical and global context of the relationship between business and society. A concluding chapter in the form of a postface, written by Professor Milé Terziovski of Swinburne University of Technology, Australia, presents a summary of the entire book and highlights the challenges and opportunities for responsible organizations in the global context.

The first merit of the book is its very international character. The authors hail from a dozen different nations around the world, and several chapters focus on comparisons between countries or cross-cultural logics. Indeed, conceptions and practices regarding the responsibility of organizations vary considerably according to national cultures and contexts. Therefore, the distinctive ambition of this book is to analyze and illustrate the worldwide diversity of approaches to responsibility and accountability.

A second originality of the book is to take a holistic perspective to the issue of organizational responsibility. Contemporary scholarly literature is generally fragmented in its discussion of corporate responsibility, and many publications focus only on a few particular details: for instance the theme of CSR, the topic of individual responsibility, and the legal or ethical issues raised by current developments in the digital and global economy. The aim of this book is to consider how a responsible organization is not only a company or an institution that implements CSR policies but also a community that seeks to question the multiple dimensions of its responsibility. Indeed, how do organizations want and are able to confront the various dimensions of responsibility in a more comprehensive way? Even if the gaps between intentions and practices are inevitable across space and time, they do not prevent organizations to develop new practices and succeed to make an intention a reality.

References

Ansoff, H. I. (1980). Strategic Issue Management. *Strategic Management Journal, 1*(2), 131–148.

Backman, J. (Ed.). (1975). *Social Responsibility and Accountability*. New York: New York University Press.

Barocas, S., & Selbst, A. D. (2016). Big Data's Disparate Impact. *California Law Review, 104*(3), 671–732.

Bartoli, A., & Hermel, P. (1989). *Le développement de l'entreprise. Nouvelles conceptions et pratiques*. Paris: Economica.

Bivins, T. (2006). Responsibility and Accountability. In K. Fitzpatrick & C. Bronstein (Eds.), *Ethics in Public Relations: Responsible Advocacy* (pp. 19–39). Thousand Oaks: SAGE Publications.

Boston College Center for Corporate Citizenship (BCCCC). (2018). *State of Corporate Citizenship*. Available from https://ccc.bc.edu/content/ccc/research/reports/state-of-corporate-citizenship.html

Bowen, H. R. (1953). *Social Responsibilities of the Businessman*. New York: Harper & Row.

Brenkert, G. (Ed.). (2004). *Corporate Integrity and Accountability*. Thousand Oaks: SAGE Publications.

Carroll, A. B. (1979). A Three-Dimensional Conceptual Model of Corporate Performance. *The Academy of Management Review, 4*(4), 497–505.

Cluley, G. (2018, July 12). Average Cost of a Data Breach Exceeds $3.8 Million, Claims Report. *Trip Wire*.

Demirgüç-Kunt, A., & Klapper, L. (2013). Measuring Financial Inclusion: Explaining Variation in Use of Financial Services across and Within Countries. *Brookings Papers on Economic Activity, 44*(1), 279–340.

Drucker, P. (1973). *Management: Tasks, Responsibilities, Practices*. New York: Harper & Row.

Dubreuil, H. (1934). *A chacun sa chance. L'organisation du travail fondée sur la liberté*. Paris: Éditions Bernard Grasset.

Duran, P. (2013). La responsabilité administrative au prisme de l'action publique. *Revue française d'administration publique, 147*(3), 589–602.

Environmental Protection Agency (EPA). (2017). *Learn About Environmental Management Systems*. Available from https://www.epa.gov/ems/learn-about-environmental-management-systems

European Commission. (2018). *Corporate Social Responsibility (CSR)*. Available from https://ec.europa.eu/growth/industry/corporate-social-responsibility_en

European Data Protection Supervisor (EDPS). (2018). *Opinion 3/2018 EDPS Opinion on Online Manipulation and Personal Data*. Available from https://edps.europa.eu/sites/edp/files/publication/18-03-19_online_manipulation_en.pdf

Fayol, H. (1949). *General and Industrial Management* (C. Storrs, Trans.). London: Sir Isaac Pitman & Sons.

Federal Trade Commission. (2012). *Protecting Consumer Privacy in an Era of Rapid Change: Recommendations for Businesses and Policymakers*. Available from https://www.ftc.gov/sites/default/files/documents/reports/federal-trade-commission-report-protecting-consumer-privacy-era-rapid-change-recommendations/120326privacyreport.pdf

Ford, J. (2013). Educating Students with Learning Disabilities in Inclusive Classrooms. *Electronic Journal for Inclusive Education, 3*(1), 1–20.

Freeman, R. E. (1984). *Stakeholder Management: A Strategic Approach*. New York: HarperCollins Publishers.

Ghemawat, P. (2001). Distance Still Matters: The Hard Reality of Global Expansion. *Harvard Business Review, 79*(8), 137–140, 142–147, 162.

Global Diversity Practice (GDP). (2017). *What Is Diversity & Inclusion?* Available from http://www.globaldiversitypractice.co.uk/what-is-diversity-inclusion/

Gond, J.-P., & Igalens, J. (2018). *La Responsabilité sociale de l'entreprise*. Paris: Presses Universitaires de France.

Halevi, G., & Moed, H. F. (2012). The Evolution of Big Data as a Research and Scientific Topic: Overview of the Literature. *Research Trends, 30*, 3–6.

Hambrick, D. (1995). Fragmentation and Other Problems CEOs Have with Their Top Management Teams. *California Management Review, 37*(3), 110–127.

Hammer, M., & Champy, J. (1993). Reengineering the Corporation: A Manifesto for Business Revolution. *Business Horizons, 36*(5), 90–91.

Hermel, P., & Bartoli, A. (2013). Responsabilité Sociale et Développement Intégré des Organisations: Écarts entre Discours et Pratiques. In P. Hermel & P. Corbel (Eds.), *Management des évolutions technologiques, organisationnelles et stratégiques* (pp. 17–52). Paris: Éditions L'Harmattan.

Horovitz, B. (2014, February 26). Data Breach Takes Toll on Target Profit. *USA Today*. Available from https://www.usatoday.com/story/money/business/2014/02/26/target-earnings/5829469/

Institute of Museum and Library Services, University of Washington Technology & Social Change Group, International City/County Management Association. (2011). *Building Digitally Inclusive Communities: A Guide to the Proposed Framework*. Washington, DC: Institute of Museum and Library Services.

International Organization for Standardization (ISO). (2010). *ISO 26000: 2010 Guidance on Social Responsibility*. Available from https://www.iso.org/standard/42546.html

Kostera, M., & Pirson, M. (Eds.). (2017). *Dignity and the Organization*. New York: Palgrave Macmillan.

Laasch, O., & Conaway, R. N. (2015). *Principles of Responsible Management: Global Sustainability, Responsibility, and Ethics*. Stamford: Cengage Learning.

Larat, F., & Bartoli, A. (2018). *L'action publique responsable: tautologie ou problématique émergente? To be published in Revue Française d'Administration Publique (RFAP)*. Available from http://www.larequoi.uvsq.fr/articles-2018-349360.kjsp

Leisinger, K. M. (2016). Corporate Leadership in Times of Public Distrust. In M. C. Coutinho de Arruda & B. Rok (Eds.), *Understanding Ethics and Responsibilities in a Globalizing World* (pp. 15–42). Cham, Switzerland: Springer International Publishing.

Li, Q., Li, Y., Gao, J., Zhao, B., Fan, W., & Han, J. (2014). Resolving Conflicts in Heterogeneous Data by Truth Discovery and Source Reliability Estimation. In *Proceedings of the ACM SIGMOD International Conference on Management of Data, Snowbird, June 22–27* (pp. 1187–1198). New York: ACM Publications.

Lindkvist, L., & Llewellyn, S. (2003). Accountability, Responsibility and Organization. *Scandinavian Journal of Management, 19*(2), 251–273.

Martinet, A. C. (1984). *Le management stratégique. Organisation et politique.* Paris: McGraw-Hill.

Martinet, A. C., & Reynaud, E. (2004). *Management stratégique et écologie.* Paris: Economica.

Miller, F., & Katz, J. (2002). *The Inclusion Breakthrough. Unleashing the Real Power of Diversity.* San Francisco: Berrett-Koehler Publisher, Inc.

Mintzberg, H. (1973). *The Nature of Managerial Work.* New York: Harper & Row.

Mintzberg, H. (1989). *On Management: Inside Our Strange World of Organizations.* New York: Free Press.

National Telecommunications and Information Administration (NTIA). (2018). Digital Nation Data Explorer. Available from https://www.ntia.doc.gov/data/digital-nation-data-explorer#sel=noInternetAtHome&demo=&pc=count&disp=both

Newman, L. H. (2018, August 10). Google's Privacy Whiplash Shows Big Tech's Inherent Contradictions. *Wired.*

Oxford English Dictionary. (2018). Available from http://www.oed.com/view/Entry/18833#eid301162178

Pfeffer, J. (1994). Competitive Advantage Through People. *California Management Review, 36*(2), 9–28.

Pirson, M. A. (2014). Reconnecting Management Theory and Social Welfare: A Humanistic Perspective. *Academy of Management Annual Meeting Proceedings, 2014*(1), 12245.

Prahalad, C. K. (2010, January–February). The Responsible Manager. *Harvard Business Review.* Available from https://hbr.org/2010/01/column-the-responsible-manager

Prieur, C. (2016, April 13). Panama papers, la revolution du journalism collaboratif. *Le Monde.*

Riboud, A. (2014). L'entreprise: un double projet économique et social. *L'Économie politique, 62*(2), 50–59.

Schwartz, M. S., & Carroll, A. B. (2003). Corporate Social Responsibility: A Three-Domain Approach. *Business Ethics Quarterly, 13*(4), 503–530.

Singer, N. (2012, June 16). Mapping, and Sharing, the Consumer Genome. *The New York Times.* Available from https://www.nytimes.com/2012/06/17/technology/acxiom-the-quiet-giant-of-consumer-database-marketing.html

Smith, H. J. (2003, July 15). The Shareholders Vs. Stakeholders Debate. *MIT Sloan Management Review.* Available from https://sloanreview.mit.edu/article/the-shareholders-vs-stakeholders-debate/

Smith, J. G., & Lindsay, J. B. (2014). *Beyond Inclusion: Worklife Interconnectedness, Energy, and Resilience in Organizations.* New York: Palgrave Macmillan.

The Wall Street Journal. (2009). The Madoff Case: A Timeline. Available from https://www.wsj.com/articles/SB112966954231272304

Thietart, R.-A. (2012). *Le Management.* Paris: PUF.

Thompson, S. (2017). *Defining and Measuring 'Inclusion' Within an Organisation.* Brighton: Institute of Development Studies.

Tilly, C. (1984). The Old New Social History and the New Old Social History. *Review* (Fernand Braudel Center), *7*(3), 363–406.
Waddock, S., & Graves, S. B. (1997). The Corporate Social Performance-Financial Performance Link. *Strategic Management Journal, 18*(4), 303–319.
World Commission on Environment and Development. (1987). *Our Common Future*. New York: Oxford University Press.
Yin, X., Han, J., & Yu, P. S. (2008). Truth Discovery with Multiple Conflicting Information Providers on the Web. *IEEE Transactions on Knowledge and Data Engineering, 20*(6), 796–808.

Part I

Ethics and Human Resource Management as Key Parts of Organizational Responsibility

2

The Ethical and Responsible Organization: Organizational Due Process, Employee Voice, and Procedural Justice in Human Resource Management

Douglas M. McCabe

Introduction

A key employee right has emerged over the period of the past decade—that is, an employee's right to receive an impartial review of one's grievances and to be treated fairly in the context of the employment relationship. In essence, the concept of due process involves the rights of employees to have impartial third parties such as peer review panels or arbitration to review the personnel decisions that may adversely affect them. Therefore, organizational decisions must be fair and align themselves with procedural justice and ethical due process (Carroll et al. 2018). Thus, the purpose of this chapter is to integrate and analyze the research findings of the author's previous studies dealing both directly and tangentially with the strategic human resource management issues involved in alternative dispute resolution procedures and systems found in nonunion employment. Particular attention will be given to one of the most significant issues in this area at the operating and tactical level of individual companies: the procedural techniques with respect to the processing of the complaints and grievances of employees in nonunion companies.

D. M. McCabe (✉)
Georgetown University, Washington, DC, USA
e-mail: mccabed@georgetown.edu

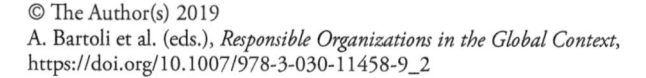

Furthermore, this chapter will analyze from a theoretical and applied perspective the bilateral development of current justice initiatives regarding employee voice in a variety of organizational settings. Particular attention will be paid to the following topics, among others: How are procedural fairness and substantive justice institutionalized? How is conflict management utilized for improving organizational effectiveness through its integration with other management processes? How does control over the institutionalization of voice matter in how employees react to the process and ultimate outcomes, particularly in terms of perceptions of fairness? How are ethical concerns addressed in order for the processes to be fair for employers and employees? How are corrective justice concerns treated in the debate over organizational justice? Finally, this chapter will contain an extensive overview of the case studies conducted to date by the author.

Strategic Overview

The intention of this overview is to stimulate awareness in scholars and management—and particularly among the employee relations and human resource management personnel who write companies' employee-relations manuals—of the inherent complexity of the process resolving employees' grievances. The preparation of the grievance section of a manual is not a task which the person who is assigned to it may deem to be secondary to his or her other duties, and similarly top management, when it approves the prepared draft, may not deem it a project meriting only perfunctory attention. All concerned must be acutely conscious that what is at issue is ethical employer-employee relations, worker satisfaction, and, from management's self-interest viewpoint, the paramount factor of the morale of that group of men and women whom all companies in theory, and some in practice, define as "our most important asset." And underlying all of this is a concept that is very simple to define yet very difficult to administer—justice (McCabe and Rabil 2002a, b).

It is reasonable to conjecture in some instances that a grievance resolution procedure is primarily not a system established for the benefit of employees but rather a means for management to correct its own mistakes, even though in some instances the problem is a misunderstanding of company policy or rules on the part of employees. Credence is furnished for such a conjecture by the plausibility of observers who assert that business executives do not generally submit their proposed actions to an ethical test. What is being proposed here is that what inspires some companies to install grievance resolutions procedures is not a sense of ethical obligation to employees but rather management's self-interest in maintaining a body of employees whose morale is high as a consequence of being well-treated by management. It is a truism that it is mandatory for the success of a business enterprise that the morale of the organization's members be at a high level (Blancero et al. 2010).

The question raised by this discussion is whether the effectiveness of a grievance resolution procedure is independent of the motive which established it, either the motive of a felt ethical obligation toward employees or the motive of management's self-interest. The importance of this question is in the fact that the motive for doing something is the inspiration that generates energy in accomplishing it, especially in the fact that in the case in which the motive of felt ethical obligation toward employees conflicts with the motive of management's self-interest, the stronger motive will prevail.

The point being developed here is the conclusion that companies' obvious need for formal procedures for resolving employee's grievances is a consequence of companies' failure to avoid the situation that generates the grievances.

This discussion would be incomplete if it did not stress the importance of the prevention of employees' grievances. If management could have prevented a certain grievance, then it is unethical for it to claim that its conscience is clear because it decided the grievance in the employees' favor. It is questionable whether management's decisions regarding legitimate grievances are generally fully compensatory of the damage done to the employees. If a rendered decision is not appealed by the employee to higher management, this fact does not certify that full compensation has been accomplished. It may be that the employee thinks it is the best decision he or she can obtain, or the employee may be dissuaded from appealing by some felt disinclination to intensify the battle for his or her perceived rights.

Nonunion Procedures for Due Process

The importance of adequate procedures for processing employees' grievances is in the fact that an employee's grievance lowers their morale, and sometimes the morale of their fellow employees, and low morale among one or more employees is the proverbial "monkey-wrench" in the smoothly functioning gears of a company. When employees know that there is a well-organized, fair-and-square procedure for resolving their grievances, management's struggle to minimize the quantity and intensity of their complaints is already half-won (Masucci et al. 2012).

In a unionized company, employees' grievances are processed pursuant to procedures established at the collective bargaining table, with, in addition, an employee being represented by his union steward. In a nonunion company, in contrast, the procedures, if any, are unilaterally established by management.

Over the past two decades, this author has surveyed numerous nonunion companies varying in size for the purpose of analyzing and reporting their grievance resolution systems, some rather simple but many of them quite complex.

Somewhat surprisingly, this writer noted a lack of effort among these companies to devise the most practicable procedures by means of inter-company coordination in which the experiences of companies can be built upon. Additionally, many companies do not define the word "grievance" in their personnel manuals. One observed company avoided using the words "complaint" and "problem" as synonyms, while another stated in its manual that an employee's "problem" becomes a "grievance" only when it is submitted to management in writing in the prescribed form. In any event, everyone recognizes an employee as being more or less dissatisfied with his company when they listen to him.

Inasmuch as an employee agrees, by virtue of accepting employment, to abide by the provisions of the company's personnel manual and other regulations applicable to his conduct and management's treatment of them, they may not enter a grievance against a management policy or practice which conforms with the manual and the other regulations, with the exception that he may enter a grievance against what he deems an improper interpretation thereof by management personnel, a case of management violating its own rules.

There are two types of grievance resolution procedures in nonunion companies: informal and formal. In some companies the two types are inter-mixed.

Informal Procedure

The informal type is the so-called "open door" policy, common in many companies, which states that an employee is welcome at any time to approach any management official from a foreman up to the president for a private, that is, "off the record," discussion of a grievance, the hope of management being that this will suffice to resolve the grievance.

The critical question is how wide open the "open door" actually is in practice. This depends not on the policy as officially stated but rather on whether management personnel, up to the president, give it merely "lip service" or wholeheartedly practice it. It is obvious that many employees will be fearful of approaching management personnel at any level with their problems if they are uncertain of the friendliness of the reception that they will receive.

Regardless of the quality of a company's "open door," this writer found that the concept is widely practiced in nonunion companies and that some publicize it with considerable pride.

Formal Procedures

The remainder of this section is concerned with the formal type of grievance resolution procedures in nonunion companies. They may be classified as follows:

- Arbitration at the request of an employee or management.
- A system of appeal steps upward through management at an employee's option.
- A "grievance appeal board," available at an employee's option, with authority to overrule a decision usually at any management level, consisting usually of a mixture of employees and management personnel, generally a total of five.
- Availability of personnel department officials to assist employees in processing their grievances.
- A combination in various forms of some or all of the above items.

As a general rule, an employee may not hire an attorney to represent him in negotiations with management in a grievance case and may not resort to court action after having invoked and gone through the company's established grievance resolution procedure. Management is naturally allergic to having outsiders interfere in its internal "family problems."

Arbitration

Among the companies surveyed, only a few provided for binding arbitration by an outside professional arbitrator. The explanation is undoubtedly, as indicated above, that companies are allergic to having outsiders interfere in their internal "family problems," and that is assuredly the case when management has reason to anticipate that an arbitrator will rule against it. These companies should be commended for their magnanimity.

It is noteworthy that an arbitrator must consider a company's rules, as stated in the personnel manual and other regulations, "as written," that is, interpreting what they appear to state on the basis of impartial and reasonable judgment, but without authority to change them. The personnel manual of one company states, in cases in which a written company policy or practice is challenged by an employee, the following: "The arbitrator's decision will be limited to questions involving the *application* or *interpretation* of the company policy at issue. The arbitrator will not decide on the reasonableness or propriety of the policy itself. However, he should recommend any obviously advisable clarification or change."

One wonders whether that employee is competent to appraise arbitrators. In any event, arbitration, which is binding on the parties, is acknowledged to be a just, speedy, and inexpensive method of settling employment relations disputes, certainly those involving employees' grievances (McCabe and Rabil 2002a, b).

System of Appeal Steps Upward Through Management

It is a common practice among many of the surveyed companies by the author to provide a system whereby an employee who is dissatisfied with their immediate supervisor's decision in a grievance case may appeal to higher management. There are many variations in the steps provided, with the final step often being as high as the president. The general principles found among these companies are that the immediate supervisors must not penalize employees who "go over their heads," an employee must engage in each stipulated step when making two or more appeals up through higher management unless authorized by the procedure to skip a certain step, and the human resource department may assist the employee in making his presentation.

The basic concept behind the provision of an appeal system for employees' grievances is that grievances are inevitable and employees' dissatisfaction with the decisions of their immediate supervisors is also inevitable, with it being important for management to resolve that dissatisfaction. Nevertheless, it is generally accepted in business that one of the responsibilities of immediate supervisors is to resolve employees' grievances, and therefore an excessive number of appeals over a supervisor may indicate incompetence on their part. Also, a provision is made in some companies for an employee to bypass his immediate supervisor in processing a grievance if for any reason it would be very embarrassing for the employee or in some other manner inappropriate.

A series of appeal steps takes time. Personnel manuals stipulate the maximum number of days an employee is permitted in making each step, and the days allotted to the manager to render a decision. The maximum total time, if the final decision favors the employee, is subject to the dictum that "justice delayed is justice denied," if it was management which was tardy.

Confidentiality is an important consideration in employees' grievances, because an employee has a right to personal privacy. Some companies insist that confidentiality be maintained by all management personnel involved, while a few prefer a degree of exposure. It is arguable than an employee's right to privacy outweighs a company's desire to accumulate statistics regarding grievances.

It is interesting that, in very large companies, the principle of decentralization operates to have differing grievance resolution procedures in a company's various plants or divisions, with, in this writer's observation, differences in terminology and procedural details making it obvious that there was little or no coordination among the authors, a violation of the principle that "two heads are better than one." If an appeal procedure was issued by a unit of a company, appeals may not go higher than its top man, whereas one issued by a corporate headquarters sometimes provides that the final appeal may be to an official at that level. Furthermore, human nature being as it is, it is logical to assume that when an employee's appeal reaches steps among higher-level managers, they will consult in an "off-the-record" basis with whatever decisions the lower managers rendered in the case.

The numerous ways in which an appeal procedure may be devised are indicated by the company in which the official at each level meets separately with the next lower official who rendered a decision and the employee, and then jointly with both, "to gather all facts." If the grievance reaches the senior vice president and is not resolved to the employee's satisfaction, the former refers the case in writing to the human resource department. That department interviews the employee "to further define the complaint and the employee's requested solution," and submits all information to the president, who renders a final decision after discussing the matter with each member of management who reviewed the grievance, including the employee's immediate supervisor, and with the employee being the last person interviewed by the president. In a case of a "very" personal nature, the employee may bypass the prescribed appeal steps and deal exclusively with the president. Such demands on the time of a president are practical only in a company in which employees' grievances are generally disposed of at low management levels.

Grievance Appeal Boards

Many companies which were surveyed by the author provide for an internal tribunal, consisting generally of about five persons, some management personnel, and the other employees, with authority to render final decisions in employees' grievance cases, usually as the final step at an employee's option in the system of appeal steps discussed above. Many names are used for such tribunals, but this writer recommends grievance appeal boards, which describe the function.

Associated with the concept of such boards is the additional concept—very popular among companies which desire a democratic image in the view of their employees—of so-called peer review of a grievance by the employee's "peers," that is, his fellow employees, in contrast with review only by management personnel, and this explains the presence of employees together with management personnel on a board.

Who can be expected to be more lenient or more stern in judging an employee's grievance, management personnel or the employee's "peers"? It is interesting that this writer was told by a friend who has been the president of an Army courts-martial board in World War II that enlisted men had told him that, in their opinion, a board consisting of officers would be more lenient in judging an accused enlisted man than would one consisting of enlisted men.

It is exceptional for a grievance appeals board to consist only of management personnel, an indication of the popularity of the "peer review" concept. There is, however, no general principle in operation dictating whether a board's majority should be management personnel or employees, other than the implementation of a "peer review" policy by employees being in the majority.

A peculiar situation is unavoidable in the situation in which, with three employees and two management personnel on a board, two of the employees vote in favor of the employee's grievance and the third employee votes with the two management personnel against it. That is, of course, very legitimate, and the peculiarity is that one employee on the board can be deemed to be in the position of a "swing vote" deciding a tie vote between two employees and two management personnel. This writer does not know the frequency with which, in a board of three employees and two management personnel, a vote of the nature here described would occur, and in this writer's opinion the important point is to preserve the concept of "peer review" by having employees being a majority of a grievance appeals board.

It is common practice in a number of companies to have a member of the human resource department serve on a grievance appeals board. There are various differences among such companies. In some, that person has merely advisory status regarding the company's personnel rules and regulations. In others, they serve as the chairman of the board, sometimes as a voting member. It is obviously an advantage to have available a person knowledgeable about the company's policies and procedures applicable to employees and their grievances. This is especially important in most companies due to the common practice of having grievance appeals boards only on an ad hoc basis, that is, the assembling of newly selected members of a board for each grievance case.

In other words, grievance appeals boards are not, like a company's standing committees, permanent boards with permanent members. The basic reason for that appears to be the fact that a board's membership, like the membership of a jury, is subject to veto both by the employee and by management—although not in all cases the management members of a board—the intent being that the membership of a board be as acceptable to both sides in the dispute as possible. Sometimes, however, the management members of a board serve more or less permanently.

It is obvious that the employee members of a grievance appeals board should have at least some training in their function. There are two extremes in this matter. Some companies provide, on a voluntary basis, a cadre of employees from which board members for a single grievance case are drawn but this writer found only one company which provided what may be called comprehensive or intensive training. In most companies, employee members of a board are selected literally "on the spur of the moment," always on voluntary basis and without any training, and then, at the beginning of the board's meeting, subject to veto by the grieving employee or management.

Summation

Among the common elements in employee handbooks is a so-called "open door" policy under which management encourages employees to informally discuss problems and grievances with management personnel at all levels, up to and including the president.

The success of that policy depends upon it being real and not merely "window dressing." It depends on all managers, including foremen, being conscientious in fulfilling the policy. It depends on an employee not fearing undesirable consequences of his bypassing his immediate superior and higher managers. And it depends on the employee realizing that, aside from the opportunity to "let off steam," a grievance may not be considered settled until there is mutual agreement between themselves and their immediate superior, unless, of course, the manager consulted induces the employee to drop the matter.

Another common element in some companies is what is called peer review panels or internal corporate tribunals. An internal tribunal is a committee in a company with authority to dispose of employee grievances. Peer review is a characteristic of such a committee when employees, as well as managerial personnel, serve on it. Thus, in nonunion organizations a recent development is internal tribunals established by management for the disposition of employee grievances. A tribunal usually consists of five persons. As the word "tribunal" implies, it is a panel made up of members of the organization who combine the functions of jury and judge with authority to hear and dispose of an employee's grievance. It is customary for companies to have formal procedures for disposing of grievances which permit an employee to appeal in prescribed steps to members of higher management, in some cases up to the president. In some companies a tribunal, such as the one described above, is added as a special feature. This writer likes to call this tribunal a "grievance appeal board" (GAB), a designation which describes its function. Many different terms are used for such tribunals.

When a company has a GAB, a company may make it either mandatory or voluntary as one of the grieved employee's steps of appeal. A typical system would be a first appeal to the immediate superior's manager and, perhaps, depending on the size of the company, a second higher appeal through management before reaching the GAB. The types of grievances which an appeals system may handle are usually stipulated in a company's employee handbook and a decision by a GAB is generally final, because if it is subject to change by management, employee confidence in the GAB is diminished.

Finally, the employee handbooks of some nonunion companies state the circumstances in which grievances may be referred for a decision by a "neutral arbitrator." (An arbitrator is "neutral" by definition.) The most important feature of arbitration is that the arbitrator renders a final and binding decision. The arbitrator must also determine, when examining an employee's grievance, whether management acted in a fair and reasonable manner in accordance with its established policies and practices, but he or she may not rule on whether the policies and practices are themselves fair and reasonable.

The logic of this is that an employee may not challenge, nor a person outside a company change, the way a company conducts its business. If such results were possible in arbitration, management would not submit to it. An arbitrator may, however, recommend changes, and an employee may do the same through the employee voice mechanisms being reviewed in this chapter. While it is customary for larger companies to publish their policies and operating practices in employee handbooks, an arbitrator may have difficulty where they are not published or are vaguely worded. A carelessly worded oral promise made to an employee by the human resource department or a supervisor may also be troublesome. The answer to all these situations is that the employee and management have both, with rare exceptions, agreed to the arbitration with its final and binding decision.

Underlying organization processes for the fair and reasonable solution by management of employees' grievances is the concept, borrowed from the 14th Amendment of the United States Constitution, of "due process." It is a concept of political philosophy which is often applied in other phases of society, including human resource management. In the areas of nonunion employer-employee relations, increasing emphasis is being given to the fact that not only management, but also employees, have rights. Consequently, "due process," meaning in this study the formal, fair, and reasonable processing by management of employees' grievances, is a concept that should be institutionally adopted (Ebisui 2016; Johnson 2015).

Policy Recommendations for Ethical Procedural Justice

A characteristic of the development of due process practices in employee handbooks has been the unpredictability of their suitability. Based upon the study and analysis of selected employee handbooks of some nonunion firms garnered by the author, the following actions should be taken where appropriate by human resource managers in a multiplicity of firms. Hence, a summary of general principles should be considered when preparing a company's employee handbook.

First of all, ambiguity in the phraseology of an employee handbook should be no more tolerated than it is in an engineer's blueprint.

Second—before you begin writing your employee handbook—one should examine the handbooks of a number of other companies to reflect on their thinking of the topics to be covered and to inquire as to their experience living under such a document.

Third, it is advisable to state in the introduction of an employee handbook that your company's philosophy is that "Our employees are our most important asset," together with an explanation for this assertion.

Fourth, consider the advisability—as some companies do—of providing a specific definition of what constitutes a grievance as your management desires employees to understand the word.

Fifth, it is essential to delineate in the employee handbook a formal four-step grievance process for nonunion employees.

Sixth, if you are a participative management company—that is, one in which fresh ideas are generated in employee-management committees—the employees should be allowed to make recommendations to management as to the provisions of an employee handbook. If they are involved, they will be more likely to accept such a document.

Seventh, if you are an extremely decentralized company with highly and substantially autonomous divisions, it might be prudent to have a different handbook for each division.

Eighth, before any detailed provisions of the employee handbook are written, a decision should be made regarding the enforcement participation by human resource managers.

Ninth, you will probably desire—as most companies do—to announce in your employee handbook that your firm has an open-door policy. Its primary advantage is undoubtedly social-psychological in nature; that is, giving employees a sense of intimate relationship with management as contrasted with a sense of isolation from management.

Tenth, a decision should be made regarding the employee handbook's policy of whether grievances should be confidential or not.

Eleventh, serious consideration should be given to the practice of stipulating in employee handbooks that employees may feel secure from retribution against them by a supervisor or manager because of an initiation of a grievance.

Twelfth, procedural justice and interactional justice issues regarding discipline and discharge should be well-formulated in the employee handbook.

Thirteenth, executives must comply with organizational procedures and policies delineated in employee handbooks. Procedures should never be short-circuited for the sake of expediency.

Fourteenth and finally, companies should adopt a contingency philosophy toward employee handbooks. They should realize that there is no one single and best handbook for all companies and all organizations and that no two firms should have identical employee handbooks for the sake of uniformity.

Recommendations for Future Research

An additional purpose of this chapter is to delineate research that is still needed in particular organizational sectors to be pursued by scholars. Those opportunities are indicated here by the following very succinct descriptions of current organizational due process issues.

Nonunion Grievance Mechanisms in Academic Institutions

Interest in mediation and other alternative ways of solving employee complaints—what some term "alternative dispute resolution"—is receiving greater attention in universities. Some universities are studying the idea to see if it can viably work to settle faculty and staff complaints and grievances. Can academic institutions utilize some form of mediation to supplement existing nonunion grievance procedures? The idea here is to get employees to sit down in a very nonconfrontational and nonlitigious atmosphere and merely talk, the essence of mediation—that is, the effort by a neutral third party to assist disputants in resolving their conflict. This technique might go a long way in solving employees' complaints and problems. Various colleges and universities, in their role as employers, have nonunion grievance systems which include the feature of mediation, an appropriate area for additional research.

Measuring the Effectiveness of the Nonunion Grievance Process

Some scholars believe that we should rechannel our research energies toward attempting to measure grievance effectiveness as an outcome of the grievance process. What constitutes a satisfactory measure of effectiveness needs to be answered by marching into the organizations and questioning the parties themselves. What may be judged an effective grievance system by the employer may be viewed quite differently by the employees. The expectations and definitions of an effective procedure may vary among employees and within the membership even of a single division of a company. Finally, it should be noted that many factors may influence grievance resolution effectiveness in any given individual employer-employee relationship. In this matter, future research might well include longitudinal methodological designs to capture the effects of changes in the idiosyncrasies of employee relations.

Mediation of Employee Rights Disputes in Corporations

Mediation can be a very appropriate part of the grievance process in nonunion corporations. Mediation can be used in settling disputes concerning ethical issues of working life and can provide alternative means for institutionalizing the protection of employee rights in the corporation. Should mediation occur at the first stage or at the final stage of the procedure? Can we develop a generalized model for handling grievances with mediation, which then can be tailor-made according to the employee-relations philosophy, size, and other normative characteristics of an organization? Can a proposed procedure include due process, administrative simplicity, and attention to financial costs?

Corporate Ombudsman Issues in Relation to the Nonunion Grievance Procedure

What are the most commonly asked questions by executives and human resource managers exploring the potential implementation of this idea? What is the working and operational definition of an ombudsman? What are the functions and purpose of an ombudsman? What can or should be his or her relationship with the complaint/grievance resolution process, procedure, or system? How can we use this technique to improve organizational employer-employee relations? How would a corporate ombudsman operate in a firm or organizational context? What are the major objections and concerns to a corporate ombudsman system?

Due Process Issues for Nonunionized Employees

Why are expectations about due process in organizations increasing? How are these expectations being exhibited? What is the nature of organizational justice and organizational due process in relation to nonunion grievance and complaint procedures? What human resource management devices can be utilized to enhance equity in companies? What is the nature of fair treatment of employees in relation to nonunion grievance procedures? What are the idiosyncrasies of institutionalized due process? In what various organizational ways can the concept of due process be assured?

Nonunion Grievance Procedures in Nonprofit Organizations

Employees working for nonprofit organizations do not necessarily have fewer grievances than those in profit-making organizations; in fact, they may have more because wages and other conditions of employment frequently are less satisfactory than those proposed by profit-making firms. Thus, it is becoming increasingly common to have formal grievance procedures established in charitable foundations, community service organizations, hospitals, and colleges. Even churches have grievance procedures for resolving disputes and differences of opinion occurring within their organizations. Future research can determine what demand there is for more democratic procedures in solving human resource management problems in these types of organizations.

Nonunion Grievance Procedures in Governmental Agencies

In most governmental jurisdictions, civil service systems provide procedures by which employees may appeal management decisions affecting them. Those procedures established by the governing body are referred to as statutory procedures. Employee input in determining the procedures usually is limited to what political influence they can bring to bear upon the governing body. Employee appeals terminate with an adjudication decision by an appeals body such as a civil service commission or by an adjudicator appointed by it. Additional research is needed regarding a comparison between various types of civil service appeals procedures and corporate nonunion grievance systems.

Nonunion Conflict Resolution in High Technology Firms

A number of research questions in relation to nonunion conflict resolution, according to a review of the literature, need further answering. A number of these questions are particularly important when studying the topic in nonunion high-technology firms. For example, how often are those nonunion grievance systems actually used? Which employees use these appeal systems and which ones do not? How does appeal activity affect employee and supervisor job performance, turnover, work attendance, and promotion? Do appeal filers and those against whom appeals are filed suffer in terms of subsequent performance and organizational rewards, compared to employees and supervisors/managers who are not officially in appeal activity?

International Human Resource Management Comparisons

There is a research need to examine foreign experience in the area of nonunion complaint procedures and systems. An examination of foreign experience is extremely important primarily because it would teach us to look at American problems from a somewhat different perspective. Foreign experience may suggest new or different approaches that merit our attention in the arena of alternative dispute resolution (Grenig 2016).

Summary and Conclusions

An examination of various employee handbooks by the author revealed three major trends in organizational due process systems: the utilization of arbitration, the use of peer review systems, and open-door policies, especially with formal appeals to top-level management at the presidential or vice-presidential level.

To begin with, the use of arbitration in the nonunion employment relationship was not as prevalent as one would expect. Nevertheless, arbitration remains a sensible option which executives and managers should always consider. The speed with which it functions is a definite asset for both parties, and its low cost is very attractive in comparison with the expense of dragging a dispute through a time-consuming civil court suit.

But what inducement is there for a firm to allow its employees to invoke this type of organizational due process? The inducement is that arbitration is just, speedy, and relatively inexpensive. Beyond that—and most important from a human capital competitive standpoint—is that its availability should assure employees that their company is fair-minded to the degree of willingness to have their complaint settled on neutral ground. The final consideration is that an employee's complaint can be the proverbial monkey-wrench in a company's otherwise smooth operations, especially if it affects the morale of other employees. Consequently, a firm should leave no stone unturned in its efforts to dispose of employees' complaints promptly with this type of organizational due process system (Berman and McCabe 2006).

Next, an examination of employee handbooks revealed that peer review systems as a structured format of organizational due process was more prevalent than anticipated. An increasingly large number of companies are establishing peer review panels to resolve conflicts as a form of institutionalized organizational due process. This trend represents an effort by companies to build an open, trusting atmosphere. Executives and employees see tangible benefits in this type of system. For example, peer review increases supervisor's awareness for the proper application of rules and procedures.

Another benefit of a peer review system as an organizational due process is its perceived justice by employees. Employees truly feel that a decision in which their fellow employees have fully participated guarantees a maximum amount of just and equitable treatment; provides employees with a tangible and legitimate voice; and meets a fundamental and basic employee desire for participative management. There is a fundamental principle at work here, namely, the ethical obligations of top management to do everything possible to achieve the imperative objective of a harmonious environment for the growth and maintenance of justice in the employment relationship. Thus, there is the justification for a company to install peer review systems based on an improved perception of fairness on the part of all employees about how people are treated at their company. Finally, every company should familiarize itself with the potential benefits of this type of organizational due process.

Finally, an examination of various employee handbooks revealed that formalized open-door systems of organizational due process were most prevalent. It is axiomatic that the internal human capital health of a company requires that its employees possess high morale, and this in turn requires that complaints—which are very destructive to morale—be dealt with as quickly as possible and, of course, as satisfactorily as possible from employees' viewpoints. The very first requirement, therefore, is the maintenance by management of a company environment which encourages employees to reveal their grievances to management instead of keeping them hidden.

From a human capital motivational standpoint, a just, fair, and legitimate open-door organizational due process framework is one in which executives are motivated by the desire for their employees to feel comfortable—and without fear of retribution—in going over the heads of their immediate supervisors in search of satisfying answers to personal problems, but inasmuch as management deems it impractical for all of its doors to be open at all hours and under all circumstances to employees, a more or less formally structured system is prescribed for an employee's appeals upward through management to the highest level authorized in the employee handbook. This author found this desideratum to be present in a number of organizational due process systems delineated in the surveyed employee handbooks.

In closing, it is a business axiom that a project will not be successful unless it is energized and monitored by the company's top executive. This is applicable to management's installation of various organizational due process mechanisms in employee handbooks in order to achieve better morale, productivity, and profits.

References

Berman, D., & McCabe, D. M. (2006). Compulsory Arbitration in Nonunion Employee Relations: A Strategic Ethical Analysis. *Journal of Business Ethics, 66*(2–3), 197–206.

Blancero, D. M., Del Campo, R. G., & Marron, G. F. (2010). Just Tell Me! Making Alternative Dispute Resolution Systems Fair. *Industrial Relations, 49*(4), 524–543.

Carroll, A. B., Brown, J. A., & Buchholtz, A. K. (2018). *Business & Society: Ethics, Sustainability, and Stakeholder Management* (10th ed.). Boston: Cengage Learning.

Ebisui, M. (2016). *Resolving Individual Employment Disputes: A Comparative Overview*. Geneva: International Labour Office.

Grenig, J. (2016). Evolution of the Role of Alternative Dispute Resolution in Resolving Employment Disputes. *Dispute Resolution Journal, 71*(2), 99–139.

Johnson, H. (2015). Adopting an Employment Arbitration Process. *Dispute Resolution Journal, 70*(4), 65–73.

Masucci, D., Miller, B. R., & Alvaraz, E. G. (2012). The Dispute Resolution Program: How Value-Added Corporate Strategies Secure Efficiency and Savings. *Dispute Resolution Journal, 67*(1), 40–47.

McCabe, D. M., & Rabil, J. M. (2002a). Administering the Employment Relationship: The Ethics of Conflict Resolution in Relation to Justice in the Workplace. *Journal of Business Ethics, 36*, 33–48.

McCabe, D. M., & Rabil, J. M. (2002b). Ethics and Values in Nonunion Employment Arbitration; A Historical Study of Organizational Due Process in the Private Sector. *Journal of Business Ethics, 41*, 13–25.

3

Continual Improvement Concepts Applied to Organizational Responsibility

Holly Duckworth

Introduction

Many organizations struggle with resources to apply to social and environmental responsibility performance improvement. Frequently, the function within organizations dedicated to social responsibility or sustainability (heretofore referred to as CSR leaders) is very small. In one case study, an organization with over a million employees has only two staff members focused on social responsibility (Duckworth 2010). This can make authentic responsibility performance improvement challenging. It can also lead to unauthentic actions, stagnate performance improvement, or untruthful communications to external stakeholders.

This chapter evaluates the means that responsible leaders can use to deploy existing resources, human resources that are already in their organizations, toward performance improvement. With just a few modifications of common performance improvement methods, important authentic and strategic sustainability improvements can be achieved without adding staff. Some organizations are turning to their Lean Six Sigma and Operational Excellence resources to participate in social and environmental responsibility performance. However, the process of utilizing these existing resources is

H. Duckworth (✉)
Sherpa Sustainability Institute, Durango, CO, USA
e-mail: holly@sherpabcorp.com

not completely straightforward. Standard Operational Excellence methods, designed for quality and productivity performance improvement, need to be modified to work well on responsibility targets.

In addition to limited resources for responsibility performance improvement, CSR leaders can struggle with having an impact during the development of business strategy (Bader 2015). Often, responsibility strategy can be an afterthought to the perceived "real" business strategy and objectives. To be done right, responsibility strategy must be linked to the larger organizational objectives. Regard for people and the planet is not to be made at the sacrifice of profit (Elkington 1998). Without a successful business, no responsibility performance improvement is needed. Sustainable profitability, people, and the planet are the end goal. Therefore, ensuring that all leaders speak the language of responsibility is imperative. And ensuring that CSR leaders are speaking the language of business objectives is imperative.

Methods for improving the complex, multidimensional challenges faced when pursuing social and environmental responsibility opportunities are needed. Methods for integrating responsibility improvement targets with business strategy are needed. Fortunately, the foundation of these methods already exists in the Operational Excellence and continual improvement function of the organization. This function has faced, and overcome, similar challenges. Adapting well-worn quality and innovation tools to the improvement of responsibility performance is one way to achieve authentic, integrated improvement with little, or no, added staff.

A Background of Continual Improvement Methods

Considering the continual improvement methods used, it reveals the tools applied toward the goal of zero-defect product quality levels and process capability. These efforts are deployed to minimize waste and inefficiency. Organizational programs such as Six Sigma, Lean Production, Design for Six Sigma, Process Re-Engineering, and Total Quality Management contain well-worn quality and innovation methods and tools. These quality methods contain a continual aspect, one that sets the expectation to never stop improving performance.

Quality, like responsibility, is an ideal state. With product or service quality, when one level of performance is achieved, the customer expects the next level of performance. Think back to the generally expected automotive quality and reliability levels in the 1950s. Breakdowns, component failures, and frequent heavy maintenance schedules were typical. Today, vehicles are sold with less than 10 defects per million units and reliability levels that require maintenance at 7000-mile intervals. This improved level of product quality did not happen overnight. Over many years, with a dedication to continual improvement of design and manufacturing processes, the automotive industry has improved vehicle quality. This has been an industry-wide improvement achieved through a steady, dedicated utilization of problem-solving, performance improvement, and innovation techniques. And the minute that customers receive a new level of quality and reliability, their expectations are set on an even better level of performance. And these ever-increasing expectations will continue. Thus, quality is an ideal state. There is always a little more on which to chip away; hence continual improvement methods are imperative.

This improvement aspect is differentiated from change. It's easy to change. It's much harder to improve. Improving implies that progress to goals can be measured and proven. Change, merely for change sake, is not the goal. Measuring baselines, developing achievable and strategically important goals, solving performance issues, improving the control of input factors, and starting all over again once a new level of process performance is achieved typify the continual improvement methods in the quality field. This level of performance improvement requires a technically rigorous methodology.

This ever-increasing set of expectations, accompanied by ever-increasing performance, has created the profession of quality. There are quality engineers, quality managers, and continuous improvement experts such as Six Sigma Black Belts and Green Belts. Each of these professions has bodies of knowledge and methodologies. There is recognition that a formal study of process analysis, process inputs and outputs, problem-solving methodologies, statistical process control, and other quality assurance methods is necessary to meet the expectations of customers. The maturity of the quality movement's impact on industry can be seen and studied. Greater standardization and professionalization have increased delivered quality to some extent and have increased expected quality a lot. As an example, in healthcare, the industry lags patient expectations; legal tensions ensue. A realization that quality methodologies need to be applied to stay ahead of customers' ever-increasing quality (and cost) expectations is happening. Ultimately, the quality movement is about culture change. It is about changing the beliefs, values, and behaviors of whole organizations, starting with management.

As customers' expectations increase, product quality responds, thus further increasing customers' expectations. Soon, high levels of product or service quality are required to compete in the market. This leads to the adoption of philosophies like "constancy of purpose," "drive out fear," and "improve constantly" (Deming 1986). The quality profession is born and management practices are permanently changed. Now that the quality movement is mature, artifacts like widely adopted management system standards, formal product and process improvement programs such as Total Quality Management, Six Sigma, and Lean Production, and Good Manufacturing Practices are organizational standards.

Perhaps the foundation of the quality movement came from the influence of W. Edwards Deming. Deming was degreed as a physicist and worked for the US Census Bureau (ASQ n.d.). Later, he worked with the War Department during World War II and was sent to Japan in 1946 by the Economic and Scientific Section of the War Department to help in the effort to rebuild the war-ravaged Japan. Prior to the war, Japanese manufacturing output was notorious for poor quality. As a consultant to many Japanese companies rebuilding after the war, he demonstrated, through his management principles, that an organizational culture devoted to product quality improvement could be built through specific management techniques.

It is important to note that Deming was a proponent of the "Plan–Do–Check–Act" (PDCA) methodology. This may be the first process improvement methodology of the modern era. The "Plan" and "Do" phases of his methodology require careful and intentional preparation and experimentation. Only after this "Check," or cause and effect analysis of experimentation results, should the process be adjusted or modified. Deming made this PDCA methodology a foundational element of his work, thus inventing the concept of continual improvement.

In the modern era of the quality movement, quality assurance is a credentialed profession; the American Society for Quality (ASQ), a professional society for those in the quality field, has more than 80,000 individual members. ASQ provides certification for 18 different professional levels (ASQ n.d.). One group of the quality profession that has experienced the fastest growth in the twenty-first century is that related to Six Sigma: Green Belt, Black Belt, and Master Black Belt. Six Sigma is the pinnacle of the current state of continual improvement.

Six Sigma began as a stretch goal of product quality; "sigma" represents the statistical term for standard deviation; "Six Sigma" represents six standard deviations better than customer specifications. In order to achieve near-perfect levels of performance, a new problem-solving methodology was needed. This sparked the define–measure–analyze–improve–control (DMAIC) problem-solving method within the Six Sigma methodology. DMAIC requires statistical proof, and carefully controlled processes focused on improving customer outcomes. An important innovation of Six Sigma is the concept of full-time performance improvement experts, called Black Belts. Most large companies around the world have adopted Six Sigma as a way of doing business. Six Sigma has become a way to achieve performance improvement in a way that business leaders can understand and sponsor.

Organizational Challenges with Social Responsibility

Quality is an ideal and social responsibility is an ideal. It has taken organizations over six decades of concerted effort to achieve modern product and service quality levels. There have been many mistakes along the way. Hopefully, CSR leaders learn from their quality counterparts. Unfortunately, many companies randomly attack social responsibility performance improvement opportunities without a methodology to follow. When the social responsibility movement achieves the same maturity as the quality movement, there will be global, auditable, management system standards of responsibility. Most high-performing companies will have a social responsibility performance improvement program in place. The good news for the social responsibility movement is that it will not have to start from scratch; it can stand on the shoulders of the quality movement.

So many similarities exist between quality and social responsibility, it would be unwise for CSR leaders not to learn from the quality movement. Starting from a goal of an ideal, the quality journey begins in full recognition that perfect quality will never be achieved. The potential, although perhaps small, always exists for a product failure or for customer dissatisfaction. Similarly, with CSR, there will always be some potential for negative environmental and social impact. Stakeholders will always demand just a little less impact, just a little more transparency and proactivity. The minute one level of performance is achieved, improvement to the next level of performance is expected.

There are similarities between quality and social responsibilities, and there are differences. One important difference is that, typically, CSR leaders have no direct staff (Duckworth 2010). Although those in quality and continual improvement are often in a position to lead process change with no direct authority over the process being changed, CSR leaders are always in this position. Additionally, heretofore, the CSR leader has had few formal methodologies or techniques that engage everyone in the organization. The CSR leader has no one to help. And even if he or she did, they wouldn't have a way in which to direct the help.

CSR leaders come from diverse backgrounds and have differing position levels and titles across organizations. CSR leaders may have the title of corporate affairs director and have a background in communications. CSR leaders may have the title of corporate compliance manager and have a background in environmental, health, and safety management. CSR leaders may have the title of chief sustainability officer and have a background in marketing or investor relations. Rarely do CSR leaders come from operations or quality management. They may not know the operations risks to irresponsibility.

Organizational structure is a significant challenge. Many progressive companies have a C-suite position for their CSR leader. However, due to an extremely small staff size, all authentic efforts to improve performance must come in collaboration with other business functions and units. Other functional and business unit leaders may prioritize their goals above any social responsibility performance improvement goals. They may be incentivized to prioritize short-term goals. This means that the CSR leader must lead with influence, not authority.

Without a whole-organization approach to continual improvement, social responsibility performance is without a systemic methodology. There may be some project accomplishments, policy developments, or product or service innovations that yield responsibility improvement. But this may be random or haphazard. Random methods may or may not include process operators, those front-line employees that are most important to responsible decision making. The CSR leader needs a method of continually working on the most important priorities of performance improvement and engaging everyone in the organization.

Organizational structure is working against the interests of responsibility performance improvement. Rigorous methodologies of risk prioritization, preventive action, problem-solving, and process improvement are needed. And because the CSR leader is practically staff-less, methodologies that allow broad involvement across the organization are desirable. Whole-organization solutions are needed.

Solutions for Organizational Structure and Action

In many cases, continual improvement programs are launched in order to change the culture of the organization. In organizations where customers are dissatisfied, or there has been a failure to gain new business, or perhaps, market share is decreasing due to innovation by competitors, culture change is needed. These issues might be externally motivated "burning platforms" on which an organizational culture change is launched. There might also be internally motivated reasons to launch an organizational culture change, such as employee attrition, poor decision making, or process risks. In either case, culture change does not happen easily or quickly. Changing organizational culture means changing the behavior of everyone in the organization, permanently. A critical mass of resources focused on social responsibility yields a culture where responsible behavior exists throughout the organization, all the time.

The CSR leader must have a rigorous methodology upon which everyone in the organization can focus in order to initiate culture change. Changing the culture of the organization isn't something done in addition to a "day job"; it is a full-time job. The CSR leader can benefit if the organization has a separate continual improvement (CI) department. The CI department can garner top leadership visibility and management support. Resources can be ramped up or down, extra resources can be deployed to surge an area of the company that might be struggling with irresponsible behavior.

Organizational support, clear roles and responsibilities, a rigorous methodology, linkage to the business strategy, and measurable outcomes are critical factors in the success of a CI program. These are the same elements needed by the CSR leader. Organizational support, as a critical success factor in a CI program, typically starts with top leadership's visibly communicated mandate for the culture change. Objectives need to be linked to real business issues or opportunities. All members of the organization need to be able to visualize the future state.

Continual improvement should be conceived of as a system. It is not a standalone department, or group of people, or methodology, or series of projects. It is a system. A CI program is a system in an organization (or a subsystem within a larger system) with the specific purpose to achieve performance improvement. The term continual refers to the repeating pattern of the activities within the program to achieve performance improvement. Once one level of performance is achieved, activities to achieve the next level of performance improvement are initiated. And this never ends. Customers and stakeholders will expect ever-increasing performance. There are a lot of moving parts in a CI program that could be focused on targeting responsibility improvement.

CI programs are important to all types of organizations. Organizations need a *strategy* of improvement, with improvement targets, with specific measures, or metrics, a time frame, and performance targets of focus. A continual improvement program starts with a cogent understanding of the organization's strategy and ends with a culture of performance improvement.

Examples of Continual Improvement for Social Responsibility

The CI program can integrate social responsibility performance improvement. One way that Continual Improvement for Social Responsibility (CISR®) (see Fig. 3.1) can be deployed in an organization is through the deployment of CI projects using the performance improvement method of Stakeholders & Subjects/Objective/Function & Focus/Analyze/Innovate & Improve/Report & Repeat (SOFAIR) (Duckworth and Hoffmeier 2016). SOFAIR is to CISR as DMAIC (Define/Measure/Analyze/Improve/Control) is to Six Sigma. SOFAIR is a method in which projects of performance improvement are targeted, using a problem-solving and process-improving methodology similar to Six Sigma.

As with other CI methods, it is important to remember the context in which CISR and SOFAIR are deployed. There should be full-time practitioners, as project leaders, devoted to continual improvement. Often, these are the Six Sigma Black Belts that are already working in the CI department. There should be a process that connects continual improvement efforts to business strategy. Then, performance improvement targets are developed and achieved through the completion of projects in a project portfolio. SOFAIR projects are deployed in consideration of an effective and integrated CISR program.

A SOFAIR project is started by gathering information. The first step of every SOFAIR project is engagement in dialogue with stakeholders. Performance improvement is defined by the stakeholders. Therefore, performance improvement is started by understanding what constitutes improvement in the eyes of the stakeholders. Engagement with the stakeholders, or gathering the "voice of the stakeholder," gives us the qualitative information to start social responsibility performance improvement. It gives us a

| Define | Measure | Analyze | Improve | Control |

Six Sigma D-M-A-I-C Model of project-oriented process improvement

| Stakeholders/Subjects | Objective | Function/Focus | Analyze | Innovate/Improve | Report/Repeat |

CISR® S-O-F-A-I-R Model of project-oriented process improvement

Fig. 3.1 Comparison of process improvement methods. (Source: Author)

depth of understanding of the issues that need to be resolved. The "S" in SOFAIR represents stakeholders and subjects.

The "O" in SOFAIR represents business objectives. The purpose of the objective phase of a SOFAIR project is to ensure that our responsibility improvement efforts are connected to organizational strategy. If there's no organizational success, the organization will not be sustained. After the S phase, stakeholder needs across all subjects are known. There is a system of dialogue with stakeholders. In the objective phase, there is synthesis of the stakeholder and subject information with business strategy. The goal at the end of the objective phase is to have a concise statement of mission, vision, goals, and objectives specific to the SOFAIR project being launched.

Next in SOFAIR is the "F" phase. The purpose of the function and focus phase is to make sure that the most important opportunities are the focus of improvement. Most organizations have limited resources and limited time to work on CISR. Therefore, efforts need to be targeted on improvements that are important to the organization and important to stakeholders. There should be an organized strategically targeted effort with resources working collaboratively to achieve objectives. Through the stakeholder and subject phase, it is understood what our stakeholders expect across a broad range of subjects. And through the objective phase, it is understood what is strategically important to the organization. The function and focus phase continues with the synthesis that is started on during the objective phase. This requires the application of systems thinking and the use of prioritization tools. Performance improvement happens at the process level. At the end of the function and focus phase, a focused goal statement for the project is developed. Through the function and focus phase of the SOFAIR project, a manageable scope of improvement for the project is created.

The analyze phase, "A", is when risk assessment and causal effects are studied. The relationships between process inputs and outputs are understood. By this time in the project, there is an understanding of stakeholder expectations across a broad range of interests from the "S" phase of the SOFAIR project. Now, there is a study of the process of interest. In the analyze phase, the detailed relationships between decisions and actions and how they impact stakeholders are studied. Causal analysis, for corrective action, and risk analysis, for preventive action, using a system view point, are the goals of the analyze phase.

In the innovate and improve phase, "I", process changes to improve outcomes are deployed. The goal is to change and control inputs to affect changes in outcomes through process improvement. Additionally, new processes with new inputs and outcomes through innovation may result. Methodological rigor to ensure that the process is only changed as much as needed, but changed intentionally and thoroughly to achieve improved results, is used.

Many less rigorous methods start with changes. And, in many cases, these changes do not result in improvement. Only through a rigorous method of study and understanding process relationships can the complexity of the targeted social systems be affected.

The final phase in a SOFAIR project is report and repeat, the "R" phase. Primary principles of responsibility include accountability and transparency. Accountability is the concept that an organization is responsible for its impacts on all stakeholders. It is the responsibility aspect of social responsibility. Transparency means that the decisions and actions that lead to impacts should be shared with stakeholders. Accountability and transparency are linked; transparency is the antecedent and accountability is the consequence. The use of reporting is one way of acting with accountability and transparency. Reporting is a key part of continual improvement for social responsibility, and thus a phase of the SOFAIR method. And, as a continual improvement methodology, the concept of repeating is a part of the SOFAIR method. There will always be increasing stakeholder expectations and new opportunities for performance improvement. The end of a SOFAIR project is marked by the beginning of the next round of improvement.

Top leadership must be willing to commit resources and support for CISR. There should be well-trained professionals educated in the SOFAIR method. Having many employees engaged in SOFAIR projects can result in culture change. As many people in the organization should be involved in SOFAIR as possible. Every SOFAIR project brings the organization closer and closer to a CISR culture. Through the repeated use of SOFAIR, embedded in a CISR program, project work eventually leads to a CISR culture. The end goal is not just projects or programs. The end goal is an organization that has core beliefs, values, and behaviors that result in sustainability and social responsibility. The end goal is a CISR culture.

Recommendations and Conclusion

Newspaper headlines are rife with social irresponsibility. The risk of actions and decisions, at all levels of an organization, causing negative impacts for stakeholders, is readily apparent. CSR leaders have very few direct resources in most organizations. And yet, many people throughout the organization need to better understand responsibility risks. Many people throughout the organization are needed to be engaged in social responsibility performance improvement. Most organizations are not going to incur the cost of large staffs reporting to the CSR leader.

A solution already exists in the organization. The CI professionals in the organization can be successfully directed to improve social responsibility performance. With just a few changes to standard quality methods, existing resources in the organization can become involved through participation in SOFAIR projects. This requires some skill development. This requires taking a whole-organization systems approach to continual improvement for social responsibility. It involves organizational members across the company and at all levels of leadership. It does not require adding resources; it does require the prioritization of social responsibility performance improvement as a business objective within the CI program.

The discourse in this chapter has explored one quality method—Six Sigma—that can be modified for application to responsibility performance. Other methods should be explored. For example, the Design for Six Sigma methodology could be explored as an innovation tool used for improvement systems to enhance responsible behavior. The Theory of Inventive Problem Solving (TRIZ) could be evaluated for use in innovation. It is recommended that additional quality assurance methods be investigated for application.

CSR leaders need help. The risks of irresponsibility exist throughout the organization. CSR leaders can fast-forward their organizational learning by studying the quality movement. Adaptation of quality techniques and broad engagement by organizational members can solve these problems. However, it is recommended that systems solutions be deployed before responsibility improvement opportunities become public predicaments.

References

Bader, C. (2015). What Do Chief Sustainability Officers Actually Do? *The Atlantic.* Available from http://www.theatlantic.com/business/archive/2015/05/what-do-chief-sustainability-officers-actually-do/392315

Deming, W. E. (1986). *Out of the Crisis.* Cambridge, MA: MIT Press.

Duckworth, H. (2010). *Social Responsibility: A Phenomenology of Perceived Successful Private Sector Leadership Experience.* Capella University, Doctoral Dissertation, UMI No. 3423856.

Duckworth, H. A., & Hoffmeier, A. (2016). *A Six Sigma Approach to Sustainability: Continual Improvement for Social Responsibility.* Boca Raton: CRC Press.

Elkington, J. (1998). *Cannibals with Forks: The Triple Bottom Line of 21st Century Business.* Stony Creek: New Society Publishers.

The American Society for Quality. (n.d.). *The Value of an ASQ Certification.* Available from http://asq.org/cert/control/

4

CSR, Employee Commitment, and Survival During Crisis Period: The Case of Tunisia

Menel Ben Mlouka and Rafla Hefaiedh

Introduction

Major changes have affected the world in general (e.g. 9/11, Arab revolutions, financial and economic crises, wars and tensions in different parts of the globe, etc.) and the managerial world more specifically (e.g. environmental nuisance, ill-treatment of workers, health problems, etc.). These upheavals are highlighted in the media (Ben Rhouma 2008), which has denounced the behavior of companies (Delallieux 2007) and the consequences of their environmental activities on their financial performance, reputation, and corporate legitimacy (Suchman 1995). This makes the concept of CSR a central position not only for the various actors who consider the role of the company in society (Pasquero 2006) but also in the strategic reflections of these companies (Reynaud et al. 2003). According to the proponents of an extended CSR, this strategy would mean responsibility toward employees, society, and the environment (Frimousse and Peretti 2015).

Indeed, the notion of responsibility carries a relational dimension between two entities, one of which is accountable to the other. Stakeholder theory (Freeman 1984) makes it possible to include the weight of these various groups which, according to Wood and Jones (1995), claim, test, and evaluate the behavior of the company in the context of CSR. That is why Aguinis and

---

CSR: Corporate Social Responsibility

M. Ben Mlouka (✉) • R. Hefaiedh
ESSEC Tunis, Tunis, Tunisia

Glavas (2012) propose to analyze stakeholder attitudes to better grasp the benefits of a CSR approach for an organization. Besides, as Ali et al. (2010) explain, CSR is mobilized by companies as a tool to consolidate their relationships with various stakeholders, including clients, investors, and employees.

With employees being stakeholders, Peretti (2012, p. 119) considers that their "commitment is based on reciprocity and therefore on the credibility of the company's commitments. A new social pact ensures the commitment of employees in response to commitments undertaken by the company."[1]

Moreover, in this context of globalization, instability, and widespread crisis, organizations are concerned about the behavior of their employees toward their work and their company, such as high turnover rates, absenteeism, decreased motivation, and negative attitudes toward the organization, making their commitment a strategic issue for them and influencing their performance (Ali et al. 2010). According to the resource-based theory, employees are strategic resources in which companies must invest by developing, retaining, and considering their demands.

In addition, research on employee behavior and corporate social responsibility has shown that using CSR as a strategic tool (Bouyoud 2010) would strengthen relationships with the company, thereby improving employee and organizational performance (Ali et al. 2010).

For all of these reasons, this chapter is dedicated to highlighting the contributions of companies' CSR practices toward their employees during periods of crisis, such as during the Tunisian revolution and post–revolution period. This period is characterized by a socio-economic instability and the widespread questioning of legitimacy regarding public and private institutions and political authorities. This climate of insecurity and uncertainty caused by social unrest no longer guarantees companies' stability and "license to operate."

This chapter is composed of three parts. The first part is dedicated to introducing the relationship between CSR and employee commitment through the stakeholders and commitment theories. In the second part, the research methodology is exposed. Finally, the third part presents the analysis and discussion of the results.

---

[1] "L'engagement des salariés repose sur la réciprocité et donc sur la crédibilité des engagements de l'entreprise. Un nouveau pacte social permet d'obtenir l'engagement des salariés en réponse aux engagements que prend l'entreprise" (translated by authors).

CSR and Employee Commitment

This part focuses on the reciprocity of the relationship between a company's commitment toward its employees through CSR and the employees' commitment in return.

CSR

According to Bowen (1953), CSR has emerged as a tool of regulation in a context of generalized crisis of national and international regulatory frameworks.

For Carroll (1979, p. 499), CSR is "the totality of the company's obligations to society (including) the economic, legal, ethical and discretionary categories."

Freeman (1984) refers to it as the satisfaction of the expectations of any group or individual likely to affect or be affected by the achievement of organizational objectives.

For Basu and Palazzo (2008), CSR expresses itself in the way managers conduct their relationships with stakeholders, engage in a lasting relationship with them, and act and behave in the face of the common good.

In return, Visser (2010) shows how companies have to make radical transformations in order to achieve a true "Age of Responsibility," as in CSR 2.0. This process should be systemic and must result in the creation of new economic models to combat the unsustainable phenomena generated by its activity. Furthermore, it must have a positive impact on the services of society.

Indeed, employees, as internal stakeholders, can be a source of pressure for the company to the extent that they may have claims contrary to the objectives of the organization. It would thus consist in guaranteeing their commitment and loyalty by adopting responsible behavior.

Employees' Organizational Commitment

The commitment theory has its origins in sociology (Becker 1960, mentioned by Paillé 2005; Kanter 1968) and in social psychology (Kiesler 1971). It has been important in literature on organizational behavior as a tool for assessing employees' turnover (Mowday et al. 1982).

O'Reilly and Chatman (1986) define organizational commitment as a psychological attachment of individuals to the organization.

Meyer and Herscovitch (2001, p. 301) define commitment as "a force that binds an individual to a course of action that is of relevance to a particular target."

This concept evolved from the 1960s to the 1990s and the model used in this chapter is the one developed by Meyer and Allen (1991). This model is based on three elements: "continuance commitment," "affective commitment," and "normative commitment."

According to Meyer and Allen (1991), "continuance commitment" is a form of reasoned commitment. It is motivated by the calculation of the perceived costs that the employee would have to assume if he decided to withdraw definitively from the organization. This follows the logic of Becker (1960, quoted by Paillé 2005), where commitment takes place when "the employee feels that he has made various investments in his company, which would be lost if he left"[2] (Paillé 2005, p. 713).

These investments cumulated during the employees' tenure at the organization are different in terms of number and content. As such, they can constitute a "professional rent"[3] (Paillé 2005), which would be difficult to transfer as it gains value with accumulated experience within the same organization. Thus, the more experience the employee accumulates, the more this rent will increase and the more he will see his commitment to the organization reinforced, lest he lose what he has invested for years if he were to leave definitely.

The second element developed by Meyer and Allen's model (1991) is that of "affective commitment." This type of commitment refers to the idea developed by Buchanan (1974), in which the attachment to the company is manifested in the desire to share its objectives and values instead of favoring considerations or more personal interests. Caldwell, Chatman, and O'Reilly (1990) thought of this type of attachment to be more stable for staff.

As for "normative commitment," it refers to the idea of Wiener and Vardi (1980, in Paillé 2005, p. 713) "that the employee feels obliged to develop loyal conduct towards his company, adhering to its standards."[4] Meyer and Allen (1991) find that this is due to a process of socialization and integration of the normative pressures experienced by the individual while serving within the organization. In their more recent works, Meyer and Herscovitch (2001) append the principle of reciprocity toward the organization to this element, when the employee feels valued by this organization.

---

[2] "L'employé éprouve le sentiment d'avoir effectué divers investissements dans son entreprise, qui seraient perdus s'il en partait" (translated by authors).

[3] "Rente professionnelle" (translated by authors).

[4] "Que le salarié se sent obligé de développer des conduites loyales envers son organisation, en adhérant notamment à ses normes" (translated by authors).

However, it should be noted that the "normative commitment" is a subject of controversy. On the one hand, some researchers argue that it does not distinguish itself from "affective commitment" (Paillé 2002). On the other hand, Meyer and Allen (1991) perceive it as an essential component of organizational commitment because it privileges its function of integrating the aims and values of the organization with the system of values of each of its members.

This distinction could be enriched by the antecedents of organizational commitment, which are linked to the individual and refer to the following variables (Rojot et al. 2014): (1) sociodemographic, including age, seniority in the organization, and seniority in the position (Mathieu and Zajac 1990; Meyer et al. 2002); (2) individual differences, including perceived competence, level of specialization, and Protestant work ethics (Mathieu and Zajac 1990); (3) culture and values, including collectivism versus individualism at the social level, hierarchical distance, the avoidance of uncertainty, and masculinity versus femininity (Hofstede 1980, 2001; Meyer et al. 2002).

Moreover, the antecedents of organizational commitment are related to work experience (Rojot et al. 2014) and are defined by two factors related to (1) the position and the role, including the degree of autonomy, the level of challenge, and the variety of tasks (Mathieu and Zajac 1990); (2) the organization, such as the perceived organization support and communication, perceptions of justice, human resource management, organizational climate, and employee perceptions of organizational values (Zayani 2016; Meyer et al. 2002; Meyer and Smith 2000; Reichers and Schneider 1990; Kalliath et al. 1999); and (3) the hierarchical superior, including quality of communication, participative leadership, expression of consideration and structuring behaviors, transformational leadership, and quality of exchanges between superior and employee (Mathieu and Zajac 1990; Meyer et al. 2002).

Those antecedents' variables of organizational commitment are correlated with job satisfaction (Rojot et al. 2014), work involvement, and commitment to the profession and career (Meyer et al. 2002; Paullay et al. 1994; Morrow 1983).

In fact, work involvement is affected by a set of traits related to the work itself (pay, promotion, career, etc.). According to Blau and Boal (1989) and Martin and Hafer (1995), the more the individual is committed and involved in his work, the greater his commitment to the organization will be and the less he will be thinking about leaving. It should be noted, however, that the departure of an employee may not be motivated solely by lack of commitment but simply by the career perspective (career commitment) (Blau and Boal 1989).

Other behaviors that are not directly related to commitment—but might affect it—are identified as good corporate citizenship behavior (Smith et al. 1983). An individual would have good citizen behavior when he/she knows that he/she would be rewarded in return, but it can also be a voluntary and deliberate act on his/her part and is by no means an obligation.

In this section, we have reviewed the concept of organizational commitment, its antecedents, and the factors that reinforce its existence in order to explore and understand the link between CSR practices and employee commitment, especially over a period of crisis.

The Impact of CSR on Employees' Commitment Over Crisis Period

Some authors suggest that corporate CSR actions, often actions to improve employee welfare, help to develop the level of commitment and sense of belonging (Moskowitz 1972; Albinger and Freeman 2000; Greening and Turban 2000; Backhaus et al. 2002; Peterson 2004; Dawkins 2004; Brammer et al. 2007; Ali et al. 2010; Hofman and Newman 2013).

Similarly, Ali et al. (2010) argue that employees who are strongly affected by CSR actions would see an increase in their organizational commitment and an improvement in their productivity. They consider "that organizations can enhance their employee organizational commitment through involving them in social activities such as identifying needs of the community and fulfilling them, working for better environment, involving employee welfare, producing quality products for customers, complying with government rules and regulations, and working within a legal atmosphere. All these activities influence in a significant and positive way employee commitment to organizations and improve organizational performance" (ibid, p. 2810).

According to Greening and Turban (2000), employees prefer to evolve in a company that respects the principles of social responsibility reflecting their image, values, and identity. Otherwise, they can mobilize trade unions or the media to preserve their rights and interests and to obtain better organizational justice (Aguilera et al. 2007), which will increase their sense of belonging. Moreover, the success of CSR approaches relies heavily on their participation and commitment.

The context of Tunisia—a country which experienced a revolution triggered in December 2010 and which has led to political, economic, and social instability—helps us understand how CSR practices can influence employee commitment and make the company survive during a period of crisis. By crisis, we mean economic, social, and political ones caused by the Tunisian Revolution (Boutiba et al. 2016).

Barabel and Meier (quoted by Peretti 2012) claim that to succeed during a crisis, companies require more involvement and commitment of employees to do better and to continue to consider the company as their own.

Barth (quoted by Peretti 2012) suggests that during a crisis, the company should have the means allowing employees to develop commitment to the company as a condition for them, to be satisfied with the job and to give it a meaning, to be recognized for their skills, and to have the feeling of controlling their action and their results.

According to Boyer (quoted by Peretti 2012), there would be no standard formula for a long-term commitment. Nonetheless, some practices can be mobilized for this purpose, in particular: (1) the creation of a corporate community and the development of a sense of belonging within the group, (2) the development of management by project, (3) the offer of a job that would allow the employee to feel a special dignity, through assigning him responsibilities in line with his skills (Davoine 2012, in Peretti 2012), (4) the training cycle opportunity for employees, (5) equity (Davoine 2012, in Peretti 2012), (6) employee coaching, and finally (7) accountability through CSR practices, including reminding the employee of the importance of what he is realizing for the organization and maintaining the image of a responsible employer (Davoine 2012, in Peretti 2012).

Thus, for Boyer (in Peretti 2012), it would be best to adopt everyday actions that will further strengthen the links between employees and their company over a crisis period. Davoine (2012, in Peretti 2012, p. 126) enriches this logic, saying that "managing commitment requires a multidimensional approach, which is both individual and collective."[5] Vazirani (2005) considers that leadership style impacts employees' commitment and that a leadership based on communication and employees' valorization enhances commitment more than an authoritative leadership style. An ethical leadership (Trevino et al. 2000; Chouaib and Zaddem 2013) makes employees more committed to CSR practices and thus to the company.

As for Frimousse (2012, in Peretti 2012), he believes that a strategy oriented toward human resources and based on the promotion of employability as well as continuous improvement of skills will maintain the commitment of employees. Thus, "the commitment of companies to encourage the development of skills and to guarantee the employability of employees meets the commitment of its employees, as a guarantee of its competitiveness"[6] (Frimousse 2012, in Peretti 2012, p. 125).

---

[5] "Gérer l'engagement nécessite une approche multidimensionnelle, à la fois individuelle et collective" (translated by authors).
[6] "A l'engagement des entreprises de favoriser le développement des talents et de garantir l'employabilité des salariés, répond l'engagement de ses salariés, gage de sa compétitivité" (translated by authors).

Research Methodology

Tunisia has experienced a change which has called into question several societal habits and which has come to lay new foundations within the Tunisian environment. Prior to 2011, even if all the structures and arrangements in place were favorable to the development of CSR, in reality the practices were different: regulation and sanctions were not or rarely applied, certain rights were violated, claims and societal injustices were suppressed. In public eye, however, the Tunisian context was distinguished by economic, political, and social stability.

During the old regime and its political context, there was little opportunity to protest against decisions or actions of organizations. This was often considered prohibited and firmly subdued. Today, several forms of demands are emerging because of the freedom of expression gained after the revolution. Consequently, these new pressures must be taken into consideration by companies.

Indeed, the disturbances that have emerged since 2010 shook this apparent stability, drove the regime in place, and established an uncertain climate characterized by new and numerous social movements, as well as media denunciations.

The social contract has been broken, and an oppressed, impoverished, and demanding society is increasingly expressing demands for an improvement in living conditions (increased wages, better working conditions, social justice, etc.). These new forms of collective action, which are more frequent, are constantly multiplying, and new stakeholders are emerging (Chaabouni and Véry 2015).

From now on, companies are exposed to increasingly numerous and intense societal pressures in Tunisia, to which they are called to provide an adapted societal response. Their threat is all the more pressing because public authorities are no longer enough, and these new claims or expressions of discontent are sometimes violently expressed. Companies are sometimes even forced to respond under duress and go against their goals (Chaabouni and Véry 2015; Turki 2015).

Since then, the business climate has been hampered and the socio-economic problems have emerged, such as rising unemployment and national debt, low growth, declining tourism, work stoppages, strikes, sit-ins, obstructions of public streets, disturbances of public order, sequestrations of bosses, and so on, signifying a real economic and social slump.

In view of this list of destabilizing actions, the internal stakeholders (employees) developed an "opportunistic" behavior of employees who take advantage of the fragility of companies and the environment to claim more (wage increase, bonuses, etc.).

Companies have had to and must manage these crises with previously unknown stakeholders, as the state is no longer able to address these concerns and ease tensions.

In addition, there is the disengagement of staff toward the company. Indeed, the research conducted by the Gallup Organization in 2013 has revealed that, with a disengagement rate of 54%, Tunisia has the most disengaged staff in the MENA region, closely followed by Algeria and Syria. The ranking of the Gallup Organization splits the degree of organizational commitment into three categories. As a result, Tunisian employees in 2013 were seen as committed up to 5%, disengaged up to 41%, and actively disengaged up to 54%. These results could be justified by the unemployment rate of graduates in the country, which has been steadily increasing since the revolution.

It should be noted that in 2010, according to the Gallup Organization, the rate of Tunisians' commitment in their organization was 21% with rates of disengagement at 44% and actively disengaged at 35%. This situation further justifies the interest of our research in understanding the extent to which corporate CSR practices could enhance organizational commitment for employees, especially over this crisis period.

In what follows, we present our approach of investigation, as well as four case studies (Eisenhardt 1989).

Access to Real Method: Four Case Studies

The cases studies are two multinational subsidiaries and two companies of Tunisian origin, all located in Tunisia and facing more or less the same pressures of revolution.

The description of the case studies is provided in Table 4.1.

The case studies were based on a series of interviews realized within each company, non-participatory observation, and document analysis.

Data Collection Methods

Our main variable is the individual and his perception of the research subject; we interviewed various profiles working within these companies (see Appendix 1).

These directional interviews were conducted using an open-ended interview guide (see Appendix 2). The collected data was analyzed adopting the thematic content analysis, using Nvivo10 software.

Table 4.1 Description of case studies

	CS Alpha	CS Beta	CS Gamma	CS Epsilon
Activity area	Call center	Textile	Petrochemical	Mechanical and metallurgical industry
Nationality	Tunisian	Tunisian	Anglo-Dutch	German
Exposure to revolution crises	Yes	Yes	No	Yes
CSR practices	Yes	Yes	Yes	Yes
Number of employees	400	500	500	14,000

Our observations allowed us to identify the phenomena and the behaviors taking place in an organization (Baumard et al. 2014, in Thiétart 2014; Savall and Zardet 2004) to understand how events occur. They also have allowed us to contextualize data. In addition, the collection and analysis of several types of documents related to our research topic and the studied companies were carried out in addition to observations and directional interviews.

All of the collected data, in accordance with the triangulation of tools (interviews, observation, and documentation), was analyzed, allowing us to carry out the within-case and cross-case analysis. The results from this analysis will be presented and discussed in the next section.

Results and Discussion

The data analysis (Miles and Huberman 2003) allowed the identification of the CSR practices of each of the case studies, the crisis impact, and how CSR practices impacted the employees' commitment.

CSR Practices

Different CSR practices with several origins were detected. Here, we present the most important ones:

– *Alpha:*

The Alpha CEO is aware of the importance of CSR and is behind its existence in his company. According to him, "now it is becoming increasingly important to have a CSR strategy. At Alpha we started to think about it in recent years."

Examples of CSR practices of the Alpha company: it has ISO 9001 version 2015 certification, is carrying transportation for employees, and is helping an orphan association.

Recent staff-only actions have been implemented through organized breakfasts every two weeks. The purpose is to create a friendly atmosphere and to get the staff out of their daily work pressure.

– *Beta:*

Beta has opted for the adoption of the ISO 14000 certification to distinguish itself from its Chinese competition, more than by top management CSR sensitiveness. Another reason was client conditions for the SA 8000 certification.

Another action realized after the revolution is the recruitment of a CSR consultant. The HR director said, "Recently we started work with a consultant who is specialist in sustainable development and who helps us set up the international certification standards with which we work. We also work with a consulting office which provides training in responsible citizen behavior to our staff…"

Beta offers better pay and more benefits than the ones required by this convention, along with some advantages such as transportation at night, health insurance, and training and awareness actions on saving energy and preserving equipment.

– *Gamma:*

The sensitivity of the chairman to CSR greatly influenced the dissemination of the principles and the development of a societal strategy within Gamma. According to the Health Safety Security and Environment (HSSE) official, "I can cite the example of Gamma where there were many actions made because there is an outpouring of solidarity."

Gamma follows a HSSE policy that deals with environment protection, individuals' safety, and the carrying out of social investment actions in favor of the community, in general, and of young people, in particular. It also has ISO 9001 and OHSAS 18001 certifications.

Other internal employee-oriented actions were established, such as safety, hygiene and health, club and tourist stays for employees, and team building activities. Their working conditions respect legal frameworks, values, and societal principles.

In addition, we had the opportunity to collect different types of documents (activity reports, CSR reports, press kits, press articles, brochures, internal journal, etc.) that confirmed the CSR practices mentioned by the interviewees.

– *Epsilon:*

The Tunisian general director is very sensitive to societal issues and explains that he has long been responsible for an association. He installs this state of mind in his teams. This is manifested through the various actions carried out within the social framework for internal employees, but also for the community and the country as a whole. Indeed, a social service was created to involve employees with a CSR program and execute the strategy and focus on financial and personal projects. The RH director reflects, "Our main resource is the workforce. It involves motivation; it is the same relationship as car and diesel." One of the CSR practices was a crisis committee set up to implement teamwork, find solutions, and mobilize people around joint projects. Epsilon has a kindergarten and a nursery for employees' children. Clubs, socio-cultural activities within production units, cultural and sports activities, and excursions and outings for employees have also been created. The subsidiary, like the other company of the sample, has ISO 14001 and 9001 certifications.

Some of the studied companies faced revolution pressures, but with more or less impact and gravity.

Revolution Crisis Impact

– *Alpha:*

The first crisis that was reported was linked to the wave of trade union demands that the country faced after the 2011 revolution. According to the HR director, in office since 2008, "There have been post-revolutionary demands, but they have been minimal. The staff did not really have any complaints to make; it was just mimicry. Moreover, at the time of the curfew that followed January 11, 2011, they were ready to spend the night on site not to stop production. A solidarity movement was set up between the staff. We did not stop working, even when there was no more public transport and the country was paralyzed."

In the past, the company has had to face a new union which, according to one of the telemarketers, "was trying to create problems and create a bad atmosphere at work when we were good" and is unrepresentative of the employees.

– *Beta:*

This company had to face the second wave of trade union demands that hit the country in 2012, following the revolution. Members of the trade union office stopped production at the Ben Arous factory for claims that were unfounded and more demanding than the ones under the convention. The company was obliged to give way and had to grant them certain advantages, even though the court rejected them. The CFO told us "we had to comply with the union's demands for exaggerated demands although we had won a trial."

Moreover, some of the Beta employees showed negative behavior, such as destruction of goods and equipment and unconsciousness in relation to waste of energy. This attitude became possible because of the liberty gained from the revolution and the irresponsible attitude that emerged. Indeed, when we were at Beta, we ourselves observed the "non-citizen" behavior of some employees. However, we also observed some employees who were unhappy with the behavior of their colleagues and who were trying to sensitize them with no avail.

– *Gamma:*

Gamma is one of the case study companies that was not impacted by the revolution. Its social policy and CSR practices protected it from social pressures and employees' demands.

According to the communication manager, speaking about employees: "They are extremely proud of what the company is doing. So, all this societal work is helping the positioning of the company as an attractive one for employment. When you know that you are going to work in a company and you know that it is making social investment projects that it is aware of, you will be 10,000 times more likely to work in a company like that than in a company that does not do that kind of effort."

– *Epsilon:*

Epsilon has a favorable social climate for work and strives to improve the working conditions of employees so that they become most productive. In a crisis situation, a crisis committee is set up to implement teamwork, find solutions, and mobilize people around joint projects. According to an employee, "Epsilon is considered as one of the best performing group sites for all social strategy. We are often visited by people from outside Tunisia who were interested in our strategy, our social activities and this social climate which is really very comfortable and where employees really feel at ease."

This company faced only one crisis because of the revolution and the subsequent right to strike. According to the subsidiary, the situation within the company was not in any way the result of legal or legitimate social or union demands or of blocking negotiations on the part of the employer. Rather, the crisis stemmed from post-revolutionary political calculations. For the general director, the sit-ins were wild, and the illegal strikes led to non-compliance with customer delivery deadlines and total disorder.

All these companies and their employees reacted more or less on different manners. Some of them were a source of pressure, while others were protecting their company and remained committed to it. What we try to study here is why these differences occurred and how to face them and make employees more committed (Meyers and Allen 1991) by using CSR.

CSR and Organizational Commitment Over Crisis Period

This study made it possible to identify a set of societal practices—sometimes common, sometimes specific—deployed by the companies on which this research was carried out. Indeed, all companies, whatever their nationality of origin, have revealed societal approaches oriented toward external stakeholders to improve their image and obtain their "license to operate" (Suchman 1995). They adopt CSR approaches to attract and retain staff (Ali et al. 2010).

– Congruence of Values

A company's commitment to society is a source of involvement and fosters a sense of belonging and pride for employees. They express a sense of satisfaction while working in an environment that respects their values and joins their vision of society. This finding is supported by Greening and Turban (2000); employees prefer to evolve within an organization that reflects their values and identity.

It is obvious to employees that a company with values and ethical citizenship has a duty to contribute to the welfare of communities. This culture of citizenship indirectly mobilizes the members of the organization around common projects, leading to better outputs in their work. In the collected testimonies, we find the use of the following terms to confirm our interpretation: "pride," "motivation," "belonging," "family," "gift," "duty," "role," "value," "culture," "involvement," and so on. Only Beta is struggling to mobilize its staff around this ethical citizenship, despite the different training sessions recently engaged on this type of topic. This can be explained by the late adoption of standards that respect working conditions and the protection of the environment. In this context, we find the results of the work of Story and Neves (2015), who consider that the behavior of the employee reflects the image of the company that employs him. If the company is irresponsible, the employee's attitude will be negative at work. If the company is perceived as responsible, the employee will behave positively, increasing his productivity at work (Rupp et al. 2006).

Epsilon employees developed a sense of belonging and pride through its societal culture. According to the communications manager, "Employees are extremely proud of what the company is doing... When you know that you are going to work in a company and you know that it is making social investment projects that it is aware of, you will be 10,000 times more likely to work in a company like that than in a company that does not do that kind of effort."

At the Gamma site, various elements confirming the attitude and feeling of pride expressed by the interviewees were observed.

The congruence of the norms and values of the organization with the values of the individual favors a normative commitment in the sense of Lee et al. (2001).

– Working Conditions

The climate (Reichers and Schneider 1990) and working conditions (pay, responsibility, role, etc.) (Mathieu and Zajac 1990) are also a source of motivation and satisfaction and hence of commitment (Porter et al. 1974; Golli et al. 2011). Indeed, companies where pay was perceived fair and where staff were valued, listened to, challenged, and involved (Barabel 2012) were the ones that best overcome the crisis. Perceived organizational justice has been one of the most cited factors of commitment. According to Beltaifa and Ben Ammar-Mamlouk (2009) and Colquitt et al. (2001), an equitable societal policy based on the principles of organizational justice could become a lever for positive employee behavior toward their organization. They become happier and more active (Aguilera et al. 2007). Here, Alpha, Gamma, and Epsilon were distinguished by the practices deployed on a daily basis and which abound in this sense. As a result, the response of employees during the crisis period was expressed through support and mobilization for the company.

It is true that Beta and Epsilon have been exposed to more pressures and societal demands on the part of their staff. In the case of Beta, this could be explained by the fact that the company was limited to what was required by the law. Only the post-revolution claims made it react and led it to grant more favors to its staff. Also, the nature of the activity and the staff profile (low level of education, low social class, etc.) could explain this disengagement behavior. The two companies were different in terms of the origin and motivation of the demands and also their ways of managing this crisis.

The first has simply yielded to claims, even illegitimate ones, to calm the pressures and avoid production stoppages. Only a few small maneuvers have been deployed (training and awareness on environment protection and the preservation of equipment). Epsilon had to face a regional crisis caused by a union representative, which was allowed by the freedom of expression that came as a consequence of the revolution. This company managed the crisis through awareness raising, accountability, inculcation of citizen awakening, and the development of a culture of belongingness. Another major reason was that employees will lose a lot if their company leaves Tunisia. After the revolution Epsilon has carried out community actions such as a kindergarten and a nursery for employees' children to enhance their commitment. Here we find the "continuance commitment" of Meyer and Allen (1991) and Lee et al. (2001), although the results of those authors have mainly revealed a negative correlation of working conditions with "continuance commitment" and that they would favor affective commitment. Indeed, employees have accumulated benefits throughout their career (age and seniority in the company) and risk losing their skills. Also, the fear of not finding another job in such a gloomy economic situation could be at the origin of this type of commitment. According to the Gallup Organization (2013), more than 46% of Tunisians prefer to work in the public sector, seeking employment stability instead of working in private companies or setting up their own business.

– Leadership and the relation with the manager

Even if the work on organizational commitment can be distinguished from the commitment to the leader, in our research this distinction has not been very marked. Leadership within managers is key in staff commitment (Mathieu and Zajac 1990; Meyer et al. 2002; Zayani 2016). Managerial leadership will determine employee's perceived support, the nature of the communication established, and the exchange relationship. It will affect the degree of commitment to the manager and thereby to the company. Indeed, the Tunisian economic fabric is characterized by the high number of family businesses, where the company is assimilated to its owner-leader, which gives it a certain kind of legitimacy. As such, he is considered by his staff to be the person whose approval and recognition would be sought most. This was observed in the two companies of Tunisian nationality.

Moreover, it is through leadership that social responsibility within the company could be most likely set up. With a well-established leadership, practices and their appropriation become easier to accept. As advanced by the Gamma key accounts director, "There were leaders who were charismatic enough to train their team. Now it has become a request; people tell you but nothing has been done." Indeed, even in the case of Beta, the few CSR actions decided by the owner-manager were well received.

As for the multinationals based in Tunisia, the leadership of CEOs appears to be a lever for the dissemination of values and the implementation of societal approaches, thus influencing the level of commitment from their employees. These leaders have legitimized their leadership through concrete actions for the welfare of their staff.

In addition, the need for a strategy that took care of human resources was evident to local leaders. The human resources director of Epsilon, who took part in the development of their CSR strategy, explained its characteristics: "We have to develop our own specific strategy in accordance with the specificities of Tunisia since the European context is not like the North-African or the Arab contexts." Each company should take care of its staff while considering their cultural differences.

The leadership practices identified have allowed for the development of the "affective commitment." So, the leadership practices and the relationship between leaders and employees can enhance CSR acceptance and its impact on employee commitment over the crisis period.

Also, the antecedents specific to the individual are a source of commitment. Indeed, Protestant ethics (Mathieu and Zajac 1990), intrinsic characteristics, positive attitude in the performance of work, the environment in which the individual grew up, and the individualist versus the collectivist side (Hofstede 1980) are specific to certain respondents and influence their spontaneous involvement. For example, the profile and sensitivity of the country chairman of Gamma greatly influenced the dissemination of the principles and the development of a societal strategy. "I can cite the example of Gamma where there were many actions made because there is an outpouring of solidarity. There were charismatic leaders capable of training their team. Now it has become a request. People keep asking you why are we not doing it?"

This would refer to an "affective commitment" as defined by Lee et al. (2001). The altruistic side of people, with a history of commitment, make them predisposed to integrate societal values in general and those societal

Table 4.2 Summary of results

Employee-related factors	Organization CSR practices	Commitment nature
Congruence of values	Organizational ethics Citizen values	Normative commitment
Work conditions	Fair pay Accountability of staff Richness of tasks Social justice Healthy climate Offer of support	Continuance commitment
Individual differences	Sensitivity to deployed CSR practices	Affective commitment
Leadership and relationship with the manager	Quality of communication Involvement in decision-making Manager personality Confidence in the leader Assimilation of the company to the leader	Affective commitment

values deployed by the company in particular. The individual has a selective retention, where any company's CSR actions would be positively perceived, since it would abound in the direction of the predisposition of the latter.

In the table 4.2, we present the main results by crossing between three elements: employee-related factors, organization CSR practices, and commitment nature, according to Meyer et al.'s (1991) typology.

Conclusion

Stakeholder expectations determine CSR's strategic business decisions through the pressures they exert and the expectations they make. At the same time, the societal strategies chosen by the companies have an impact on these stakeholders.

From the managerial point of view, one of the direct repercussions of CSR within the organization, and indirectly on its economic performance, is the positive attitude of its internal stakeholders. Indeed, the efforts deployed for help employees develop a sense of belonging and pride, a desire to give more and to become more involved in an organization that respects ethical and civic values. Both the quality of working conditions and the social climate make employees support their organization during a revolution crisis period. The CSR behavior adopted over a period of crisis enables companies to cushion financial, economic, and social problems.

Moreover, the manager's sensitivity to CSR practices predisposes and inspires CSR behavior (Greening and Gray 1994). It appears that the managerial interpretation of societal pressures influences strategic decisions in terms of CSR strategies. The more the managers are engaged, the more the CSR practices and decisions are supported and promoted. A company that offers a socially responsible environment will reduce the risks of societal pressures and will have a committed and loyal staff during a crisis.

Also, the company's CEO is a local contributor to a better knowledge of the needs of their environment and thus to an anticipation of societal expectations. This has been confirmed through crisis situations that have been anticipated and overcome through a certain understanding of local cultural specificities.

Furthermore, the employee personality and predisposition to commitment make him more receptive to CSR actions and enhance his commitment to his company.

Appendix 1

Company	Interviewee	Position held	Seniority
Alpha	Alpha 1	General manager	Since 2006 (founder)
	Alpha 2	HRD	Since 2008
	Alpha 3	TQM director	Since 2016
	Alpha 4	Operator 1	Since 2009
	Alpha 5	Operator 2	Since 2008
Beta	Beta 1	Financial director	Since 1992
	Beta 2	HRD	Since 2013
	Beta 3	Workshop foreman	Since 2006
	Beta 4	Female worker 1	Since 2007
	Beta 5	Female worker 2	Since 2009
Gamma	Gamma 1	Sales director	Since 1995
	Gamma 2	HRD	Since 1992
	Gamma 3	Director of communication	Since 2000
	Gamma 4	Logistics manager	Since 1984
	Gamma 5	Senior account manager	Since 1991
Epsilon	Epsilon 1	General director	Since 1977
	Epsilon 2	HRD	Since 2004
	Epsilon 3	Union representative	Since 2012
	Epsilon 4	Communication manager	Since 2010
	Epsilon 5	Worker	Since 2005

Appendix 2

Interview Guide

Introduction

- Thanks, subject explanation and determination of the confidentiality terms
- Organization/company presentation: Denomination, year of creation/activity sector/number of employees
- Interviewee presentation: Missions and personal characteristics (age, training, experience)/academic and professional background/current functions/first responsibility as a general manager/director/HRM of the company

Theme 1 General knowledge of the concept

- What is CSR according to you?
  - Questions of issues:

  Economic dimension of the CSR:
  [Assuring substantial financials benefits—controlling employees' productivity—maximizing benefits—creating value for the stakeholders—establishing long-term financial strategies]

- Have you ever heard about societal initiatives in Tunisia or any responsible company (examples)?
- Is CSR a major concern in Tunisia? Why?

Theme 2 Top management CSR attitude/HRM/director: Identifying practices towards internal and external CSR stakeholders

Theme 2.1. CSR practices towards external stakeholders:

- Do you have any CSR actions towards external stakeholders?
  - Questions of issues:

Ethical-legal dimension for the external stakeholders:
[My company doesn't take part in human rights violation—respects laws—offers a complete and precise information for its costumers—doesn't use corruption (bribes, extortion, etc.)—is faithful—preserves environment].

CSR philanthropic dimension:
[My company sponsors sports or cultural events—cares about reducing its negative impacts on environment—contributes to the development of the local industry—sponsors scientific research activities].

Theme 2.2. CSR practices towards internal stakeholders:

- What about CSR practices towards internal stakeholders?
  - Do you involve them in the determination of organizational objectives?
  - Do you have any charters, values, or conducts shared by the entire company?
  - Do you have specific actions towards employees (social advantages, etc.)?

(Action area 1: Job and employee/top management relationship, Action area 2: Work conditions and social protection, Action area 3: Social dialogue, Action area 4: Health and work security, Action area 5: Human capital development)

- Questions of issues:

Ethical-legal dimension towards internal stakeholders:
[Encouraging employees' diversity (age, gender, race)—condemning unethical attitude of all members—considering chances equality as a principle in the employees' promotion process—respecting rules in the recruiting, firing, and promotion processes—having an equal remuneration policy—offering opportunity for employees to handle between private and professional life—being careful about union demands

Theme 3 Managing over crisis period

- Did you have to face crises in your company?
  - Did you have to face demands and pressures from employees because of the Tunisian revolution?
  - If yes, what was your employees' attitude and reaction?
  - If yes, what was the union's reaction?

- How did you act facing crises? What kind of decisions did you make?
- Did you set new actions dedicated to employees because of the revolution?

  • What was your employees' reaction after those new actions?

Theme 4 Link between CSR practices and employees' organizational commitment

- Do you think that your CSR attitude could enhance employee satisfaction and organizational commitment?
- Did your CSR practices help you to get more commitment from employees over crises?
- If yes, what kind of commitment appears and how?

References

Aguilera, R. V., Rupp, D. E., Williams, C. A., & Ganapathi, J. (2007). Putting the S Back in Corporate Social Responsibility: A Multilevel Theory of Social Change in Organizations. *Academy of Management Review, 32*(3), 836–863.

Aguinis, H., & Glavas, A. (2012). What We Know and Don't Know About Corporate Social Responsibility: A Review and Research Agenda. *Journal of Management, 38*(4), 932–968.

Albinger, H. S., & Freeman, S. J. (2000). Corporate Social Performance and Attractiveness as an Employer to Different Job Seeking Populations. *Journal of Business Ethics, 28*(3), 243–253.

Ali, I., Rehman, K., Ali, S. I., Yousaf, J., & Zia, M. (2010). Corporate Social Responsibility Influences, Employee Commitment and Organizational Performance. *African Journal of Business Management, 4*(12), 2796–2801.

Backhaus, K. B., Stone, B. A., & Heiner, K. (2002). Exploring the Relationship Between Corporate Social Performance And Employer Attractiveness. *Business and Society, 41*(3), 292–318.

Barabel, M. (2012). Regard croisés sur l'engagement: "Comment obtenir l'engagement des salariés en 2013?". *Question(s) de management, 1*(2), 123.

Basu, K., & Palazzo, G. (2008). Corporate Social Responsibility: A Process Model of Sensemaking. *Academy of Management Review, 33*(1), 122–136.

Beltaifa, N., & Ben Ammar Mamlouk, Z. (2009). Multidimensionnalité et déterminants de la justice organisationnelle: étude empirique dans le contexte tunisien. *18ème Conférence de l'AIMS*, Grenoble.

Ben Rhouma, A. (2008). *Étude des déterminants de la divulgation environnementale et sociale des entreprises françaises*. Thèse en science de gestion, Université de Nice Sophia-Antipolis.

Blau, G. J., & Boal, K. B. (1989). Using Job Involvement and Organizational Commitment Interactively to Predict Turnover. *Journal of Management, 15*(1), 115–127.

Boutiba, R., Boussoura, E., & Zeribi, O. (2016). La représentation de la responsabilité sociale des entreprises à travers le discours des responsables d'entreprise en Tunisie. *Revue Interdisciplinaire Management, Homme & Entreprise, 20*(1), 25–44.

Bouyoud, F. (2010). *Le management stratégique de la responsabilité sociale des entreprises, thèse de doctorat*. Thèse de doctorat, Conservatoire National des Arts et Métiers.

Bowen, H. R. (1953). *Social Responsibilities of the Businessman*. New York: Harper & Row.

Brammer, S., Millington, A., & Rayton, B. (2007). The Contribution of Corporation Social Responsibility to Organizational Commitment. *International Journal of Human Resource Management, 18*(10), 1701–1719.

Buchanan, B. (1974). Building Organizational Commitment: The Socialization of Managers in Work Organizations. *Administrative Science Quarterly, 19*(4), 533–546.

Caldwell, D. F., Chatman, J. A., & O'Reilly, C. A. (1990). Building Organizational Commitment: A Multi-Form Study. *Journal of Occupational Psychology, 63*(3), 245–261.

Carroll, A. B. (1979). A Three-Dimensional Conceptual Model of Corporate Social Performance. *Academy of Management Review, 4*, 497–505.

Chaabouni, J., & Véry, P. (2015). *Crise, transition. Comment les firmes tunisiennes s'en sortent-elles?* Tunis: Edition C.L.E.

Chouaib, A., & Zaddem, F. (2013). The Ethical Climate at Work. Promoting Trust in Organizations. *RIMHE: Revue Interdisciplinaire Management, Homme & Entreprise, 5*(9), 15–30.

Colquitt, J. A., Conlon, D. E., Wesson, M. J., Porter, C., & Ng, K. Y. (2001). Justice at the Millennium: A Meta- Analytic Review of 25 Years of Organizational Justice Research. *Journal of Applied Psychology, 86*(3), 425–445.

Dawkins, J. (2004). Corporate Responsibility: The Communication Challenge. *Journal of Communication Management, 9*(2), 108–119.

Delallieux, G. (2007). *Responsabilité Sociale des Entreprises et ONG: une approche critique des dimensions politiques de la gestion des ONG*. Thèse de doctorat, Université de Lille I, IAE de Lille.

Eisenhardt, K. M. (1989). Building Theories from Case Study Research. *Academy of Management Review, 14*(4), 532–550.

Freeman, E. (1984). *Strategic Management: A Stakeholder Approach*. Boston: Pitman.

Frimousse, S., & Peretti, J.-M. (2015). Regards croisés sur Engagement RSE & performance. *Question(s) de management, 1*(9), 65–89.

Golli, A., Swalhi A., & Yahyaoui, D. (2011). *Climat éthique et implication organisationnelle: quels liens dans le cadre des entreprises tunisiennes?* AGRH. Available from https://www.agrh.fr/assets/actes/2011golli-swalhi-yahiaoui.pdf. Accessed 15 Feb 2018.

Greening, D. W., & Gray, B. (1994). Testing Model of Organizational Response to Social and Political Issues. *Academy of Management Journal, 37*(3), 467–498.

Greening, D. W., & Turban, D. B. (2000). Corporate Social Performance as a Competitive Advantage in Attracting a Quality Workforce. *Business and Society, 39*(3), 254–280.

Hofman, P. S., & Newman, A. (2013). The Impact of Perceived Corporate Social Responsibility on Organizational Commitment and the Moderating Role of Collectivism and Masculinity: Evidence from China. *The International Journal of Human Resource Management, 25*(5), 1–22.

Hofstede, G. (1980). *Culture's Consequences: International Differences in Work-Related Values*. Newbury Park: SAGE Publications.

Hofstede, G. (2001). *Culture's Consequences: Comparing Values, Behaviors, Institutions and Organizations Across Nations* (2nd ed.). Thousand Oaks: SAGE Publications.

Kalliath, T. J., Bluedorn, A. C., & Strube, M. J. (1999). A Test of Value Congruence Effects. *Journal of Organizational Behavior, 20*(7), 1175–1198.

Kanter, R. (1968). Commitment and Social Organization: A Study of Commitment Mechanisms in Utopian Communities. *American Sociological Review, 33*(4), 499–517.

Kiesler, C. A. (1971). *The Psychology of Commitment*. New York: Academic Press.

Lee, K., Allen, N. J., Meyer, J. P., & Rhee, K.-Y. (2001). The Three-Component Model of Organisational Commitment: An Application to South Korea. *Applied Psychology: An International Review, 50*(4), 596–614.

Martin, T. N., & Hafer, J. C. (1995). The Multiplicative Interaction Effects of Job Involvement and Organizational Commitment on Turnover Intentions of Full- and- Part Time Employees. *Journal of Vocational Behavior, 44*, 310–331.

Mathieu, J. E., & Zajac, D. M. (1990). A Review and Meta-analysis of the Antecedents, Correlates and Consequences of Organizational Commitment. *Psychological Bulletin, 108*(2), 171–194.

Meyer, J. P., & Allen, N. (1991). A Three-Component Model Conceptualization of Organizational Commitment. *Human Resource Management Review, 1*(1), 61–89.

Meyer, J. P., & Herscovitch, L. (2001). Commitment in the Workplace: Toward a General Model. *Human Resource Management Review, 11*(3), 299–326.

Meyer, J. P., & Smith, C. A. (2000). HRM Practices and Organizational Commitment: Test of a Mediation Model. *Canadian Journal of Administrative Science, 17*(4), 319–331.

Meyer, J. P., Stanley, D. D., Herscovitch, L., & Topolnytsky, L. (2002). Affective, Continuance and Normative Commitment to the Organization: A Meta-Analysis of Antecedents, Correlates, and Consequences. *Journal of Vocational Behavior, 61*(1), 20–52.

Miles, M. B., & Huberman, A. M. (2003). *Analyse des données qualitatives* (2nd ed.). Paris: Edition de Boeck Université.

Morrow, P. C. (1983). Concept Redundancy in Organizational Research: The Case of Work Commitment. *Academy of Management Review, 8*(3), 486–500.

Moskowitz, M. (1972). Choosing Socially Responsible Stocks. *Business & Society Review, 1*, 71–75.

Mowday, R. T., Porter, L. W., & Steers, R. (1982). *Employee- Organization Linkages: The Psychology of Commitment, Absenteeism, and Turnover*. New York: Academic Press.

O'Reilly, C. A., & Chatman, J. (1986). Organizational Commitment and Psychological Attachment: The Effects of Compliance, Identification, and Internalization on Prosocial Behavior. *Journal of Applied Psychology, 71*(3), 492–499.

Paillé, P. (2002). L'engagement normatif: essai de reconstruction. *Psychologie du travail et des organisations, 8*(3), 69–96.

Paillé, P. (2005). Engagement organisationnel et modes d'identification. Dimensions conceptuelle et empirique. *Bulletin de psychologie, 6*(480), 705–711.

Pasquero, J. (2006). Introduction: La responsabilité sociale comme nouvelle forme de régulation socioéconomique. *Revue Gestion, 31*(2), 51–54.

Paullay, I. M., Alliger, G. M., & Stone-Romero, E. F. (1994). Construct Validation of Two Instruments Designed to Measure Job Involvement and Work Centrality. *Journal of Applied Psychology, 79*(2), 224–228.

Peretti, J.-M. (2012). Comment obtenir l'engagement des salariés en 2013? *Question(s) de management, 1*(2), 119–137.

Peterson, D. K. (2004). The Relationship Between Perceptions of Corporate Citizenship and Organizational Commitment. *Business & Society, 43*, 296–319.

Porter, L. W., Steers, R. M., Mowday, R. T., & Boulian, P. V. (1974). Organizational Commitment. Job Satisfaction, and Turnover Among Psychiatric Technicians. *Journal of Applied Psychology, 59*(5), 603–609.

Rapport de la Banque Centrale de Tunisie. (2013). États Financiers et Rapport Des Commissaires Aux Comptes Exercice Clos Le 31 Decembre 2012. Available from https://www.bct.gov.tn/bct/siteprod/documents/etat2012.pdf

Reichers, A. E., & Schneider, B. (1990). Climate and Culture: An Evolution of Constructs. In B. Schneider (Ed.), *Organizational Climate and Culture* (pp. 5–39). San Francisco: Jossey-Bass.

Reynaud, S., Leclercq, N., Romaine-Lioud, S., Ferrier-Pagés, C., Jaubert, J., & Gattuso, J.-P. (2003). Interacting Effects of CO_2 Partial Pressure and Temperature on Photosynthesis and Calcification in a Scleractinian Coral. *Global Change Biology, 9*(11), 1660–1668.

Rojot, J., Roussel, P., & Vandenberghe, C. (2014). *Comportement organisationnel: Théories des organisations, motivation au travail, engagement organisationnel*. Paris: De Boeck Education.

Rupp, D. E., Ganapathi, J., Aguilera, R. V., & Williams, C. A. (2006). Employee Reactions to Corporate Social Responsibility: An Organizational Justice Framework. *Journal of Organizational Behavior, 27*(4), 537–543.

Savall, H., & Zardet, V. (2004). *Recherche en sciences de gestion: approche qualimétrique*. Paris: Edition Economica.

Smith, C., Organ, A., Dennis, W., & Near, J. (1983). Organizational Citizenship Behavior: Its Nature and Antecedents. *Journal of Applied Psychology, 68*(4), 653–663.

Story, J., & Neves, P. (2015). When Corporate Social Responsibility (CSR) Increases Performance: Exploring the Role of Intrinsic and Extrinsic CSR Attribution. *Business Ethics: A European Review, 24*(2), 111–124.

Suchman, M. C. (1995). Managing Legitimacy: Strategic and Institutional Approaches. *Academy of Management Review, 20*(3), 571–610.

Thiétart, R.-A. (2014). *Méthodes de recherche en management*. Paris: Edition Dunod.

Trevino, L. K., Hartman, L. P., & Brown, M. (2000). Moral Person and Moral Manager: How Executives Develop a Reputation for Ethical Leadership. *California Management Review, 42*(4), 128–142.

Turki, A. (2015). La PME et le développement durable: une analyse selon la perspective néo-institutionnelle. In J. Chaabouni & P. Véry (Eds.), *Crise, transition: Comment les firmes tunisiennes s'en sortent-elles?* (pp. 173–196). Tunis: Edition C.L.E.

Vazirani, N. (2005). *Employee Engagement. SIES College of Management Studies*, Working Paper Series. Accessed 26 Apr 2011.

Visser, W. (2010). The Age of Responsibility: CSR 2.0 and the New DNA of Business. *Journal of Business Systems, 5*(2), 7–22.

Wood, D. J., & Jones, R. E. (1995). Stakeholder Mismatching: A Theoretical Problem in Empirical Research in Corporate Social Performance. *International Journal of Organizational Analysis, 3*(3), 229–267.

Zayani, N. (2016). *Amélioration de l'engagement organisationnel dans les services nettoiement des collectivités territoriales en Tunisie*. Thèse de Doctorat, Sociologie, Université Paul-Valéry-Montpellier.

Webography

http://www.gallup.com/poll/165269/worldwide-employees-engaged-work.aspx. Accessed 8 Apr. 2017.

http://www.gallup.com/services/176300/state-global-workplace.aspx. Accessed 8 Apr. 2017.

Part II

Communication and Reputation Related to Social Responsibility

5

Classifying Ethics Codes Using Natural Language Processing

Zachary Glass and E. Susanna Cahn

Codes of ethics are written documents whose language is meant to influence both internal and external stakeholders and to convey various understandings of what is right and wrong (Winkler 2011, p. 654). Businesses' codes of ethics have become commonplace, especially following the introduction of the Sarbanes-Oxley Act of 2002, Section 406, which requires an ethics code for senior officers. Most corporations have codes, either of conduct or of ethics, for all employees, directors, and officers. Harris (2004) suggests that codes of conduct and codes of ethics are different in their natures. He maintains that there is a tendency to link conduct and practice with objective outputs, while principles and ethics may be more easily associated with questions of justice and character. In this chapter, we do not distinguish between codes of conduct and codes of ethics, treating both as "written, distinct, formal document[s] which consist of moral standards which help guide employee or corporate behavior" (Schwartz 2002, p. 28).

Many scholars as well as practitioners assert that ethics codes create an organizational environment that is conducive to including ethical values as part of the decision-making process. Critics, however, claim that ethics codes

---

Z. Glass (✉)
Princeton University, Princeton, NJ, USA

E. S. Cahn
Pace University, New York, NY, USA
e-mail: ecahn@pace.edu

© The Author(s) 2019
A. Bartoli et al. (eds.), *Responsible Organizations in the Global Context*,
https://doi.org/10.1007/978-3-030-11458-9_5

proliferate in the wake of corporate scandals, their primary intent being to protect the company from litigation or to control compliance with company policies.

Scholars have found it difficult to distinguish between these opposing claims of decision-making using ethical values versus compliance, as language in ethics codes is not easily quantified or classified. Much corporate social responsibility (CSR) research involving ethics codes simply measures whether a code is present or absent (Kaptein and Schwartz 2008). Our paper is unique in that it uses a model to classify ethics codes rather than human intuition. Computational models generally have the benefits of being measurable and repeatable; models have known and explicit assumptions and in that sense are less subjective than classification based on intuition. They also have the shortcoming of being less nuanced than subjective judgment and may leave out information that is difficult to measure. Ongoing work in NLP aims to develop more sophisticated models that can capture sentiment as well as naïve language (Peldszus and Stede 2016; Stede 2016). Nevertheless, an unbiased objective model adds value by supporting intuition or by challenging intuitive assumptions.

Normative Approach to Ethics Codes

Theoretical prescriptions for developing a good ethics code start with the basic assumption that ethics is about right values and right behavior, as opposed to wrong ones. "Codes of ethics are intended to capture the key values of a firm and to convey those values to both internal and external stakeholders" (Coughlan 2005, p. 45).

Reynolds and Bowie recommend that ethics codes be grounded in the primary motive of doing what is right. They rely on Kant's moral principles as "an externally-established conception of what is right" because Kant's moral principles deal with what is ethically right regardless of the situation. Following the Kantian framework, Reynolds and Bowie argue that an ethics code should have the primary motive of doing what is right; that the code should respect the free will of individual employees, and therefore avoid retaliatory language; and that the organization should provide opportunities for individual contributions to the code so that it is constructed in a way that is agreeable to all. "Employees need discretion in applying the policy, but they also need to be able to suggest changes and improvements in the policy. In so doing, the employees are exercising their rational and moral capacities. By actively participating in this way, their own ability to make better moral decisions is increased." Reynolds and Bowie argue that if, in contrast, measurable outcomes are emphasized rather than values, then the code tends "to legitimize the legalistic and symbolic benefits of an ethics program at the expense of the inherent value of moral behavior." They expect that "an ethics program that is adopted simply to support the bottom line will not have the best consequences" (2004, pp. 276–283).

The constraining effects of ethics codes are emphasized by Weaver (1993, p. 45). He defines ethics codes as "distinct, formal documents specifying self-consciously ethical constraints on the conduct of organizational life."

Harris (2004) emphasizes that ethics codes should be focused on the future to encourage developing good habits, building trust, and acting on principles. He also advocates participation of stakeholders in the process of developing as well as implementing the code. Harris stresses the importance of language giving importance to both objective, quantitative measures and to narrative about principles and values.

Considering that the future is uncertain, ethics codes that highlight values and principles, rather than attempting to address a laundry list of possible scenarios, are useful because they provide employees with justifications for the choices they make when faced with ethical dilemmas. Therefore, "If a code is meant to provide justifications for employees, it must specifically address important values" (Coughlan 2005, p. 48). A particularly important value is procedural justice.

Descriptive Approach to Ethics Codes: *Values Versus Compliance*

The language in actual corporate ethics codes may or may not be in sync with the ideals described above. Researchers have examined various corporate ethics codes with the objective of describing common practices.

Codes of ethics are described by Farrell and Farrell (1998, p. 588) as falling into two categories: inspirational and prescriptive. Inspirational codes are those "in which code writers provide corporate values/principles only," thereby leaving discretion in the application of those values to employees addressed by the code. Prescriptive codes develop expectations of employees for compliance with prescriptions. "Prescriptive codes arise when code writers apply ... corporate values and principles to perceived moral hazards that might occur ... No discretion in the matter is expected." They analyzed the language in a small sample of Australian corporate codes of ethics examining linguistic structures of relational clauses, the passive voice, nominalization, grammatical metaphor, and modality. They concluded that the codes in their study primarily impose conformity to rules; the codes used language to maintain a hierarchical power relationship within the organization and did not empower employees to make ethical decisions.

Winkler (2011) analyzed the ethics codes of the Dax 30 companies—the German blue chips listed at the Frankfurt Stock Exchange—excluding ethical codes for senior financial officers. He identified three parts of ethics codes, namely the introduction, the rules and regulations, and the code enforcement. Next, he examined the role given to the actors and whether the documents ascribe any agency, or if the codes render them as being rather passive. The introductions downplayed the existence of hierarchy and asymmetries; the texts literally elevated ordinary employees in terms of social status and corporate responsibility. Considering the other parts of the documents, however, this initial attribution of agency quickly disappears. The rules and regulation section places employees as the passive receivers of code instructions. "Compliance with the codes of ethics is usually enforced by creating a feeling of fear… the enforcement part of the codes of ethics once again fabricates employees as rather passive actors who are in need of guidance, assistance and control" (Winkler 2011, p. 659). The documents studied by Winkler create a sense of ambiguity by placing a great deal of responsibility on the employees though denying them agency and competence.

The espoused reasons for introducing an ethics code may be different from the operational reason for the code's introduction. Weaver (1993) suggests that social desirability biases may lead to ambiguity in identifying which corporate documents are to be considered ethics codes, and that at times the distinction between company policies and ethics codes may be arbitrary. It is even possible that managers and employees perceive the company's ethics code differently. There may be multiple rationales resulting from organization members' multiple roles.

In practice, the literature suggests that ethics codes follow one of two patterns. One pattern emphasizes values and leaves employees to make their own decisions about the ethical course of action when faced with a dilemma. The other one emphasizes compliance with specific guidelines directing employees to seek the guidance of a supervisor. Sometimes these codes also offer scenarios of potential ethical dilemmas. As described above, research appears to indicate that more codes fall into the compliance category.

Code Impact Literature

There is a body of literature researching the relationship between ethics codes and corporate performance. Kaptein and Schwartz (2008) reviewed studies of the impact of codes on corporate social responsibility (CSR) performance and found mixed results. This is not surprising considering that the internal reasons for adopting a code of ethics may differ from one company to another company. The language used varies considerably among different companies' ethics codes, potentially contributing to different perceptions and behavior among affected employees. Different ways of measuring code content noted above may contribute as well.

Erwin (2011) studied the effect of code quality essentially based on expert opinion, as noted earlier. He found a general relationship between code quality and effectiveness on CSR performance. He contrasts his results to the typical treatment by researchers that compare companies with codes of conduct to those without. Such with or without studies have yielded mixed results as to whether having a code makes a significant difference in CSR performance.

Kaptein (2011) studied the presence of a code along with a number of issues that are addressed by the code. Content was found to be one of the issues without which having a code could be counterproductive. It follows from the importance of quality and content that the intent of a code may be more important than the simple existence of a corporate code of ethics, although it is difficult to measure "intent."

Coughlin's definition of impact is somewhat unusual, but follows from his view of an ethics code as a source of justifications for choice rather than as dictating choice. "A code's usefulness then is not gauged only by its effect on choice, but also by its effect on a decision-maker's justification" (Coughlan 2005, p. 46). He suggests that heavily legalistic codes are not effective guides for decision-makers where laws are inconsistent.

Importance of Language

Farrell and Farrell (1998) studied the language in ethics codes and inferred that language could reinforce a hierarchical power relationship or free employees to be moral decision-makers. They even found that there were conflicting messages as employees are addressed as decision-makers but then asked to conform to the hierarchy. Thus, language can be the means for either empowering or constraining.

Choice of language can influence how effective a code is. Rodrigues and Stegemoller (2010, p. 36) discuss how watered-down language and "weasel wording" were used in some companies' ethics codes to the extent that those codes did not preclude unethical behavior. Existence of codes in those cases could lull investors into a false sense of security, providing the assurance of ethical behavior without actually needing to substantiate the claim. Clearly code language matters.

Measurement

Because of the nature of ethics codes as written documents, measurement of code content or quality is an issue without a consistent solution. Comparative analyses or impact studies are especially problematic. Most often, ethics codes are identified as being either present or absent (Kaptein and Schwartz 2008).

A few researchers go beyond simply the presence of an ethics code. Gaumnitz and Lere (2004) measured code content by dimensions of length, focus, level of detail, thematic content (topic or topics), shape (breadth of theme coverage), and tone (positive vs. negative). He concedes that some professional judgment is involved in making these determinations. Farrell and Farrell (1998) examined the linguistic structures of relational clauses, passive voice, nominalization, grammatical metaphor, and modality to distinguish between inspirational and prescriptive code intent.

Erwin (2011) measured code quality based on benchmarking analyses by the Ethisphere Institute. This method is essentially an expert panel opinion-based grading system that considers various categories of ethical values. Kaptein (2011) measured content by the number of issues that are addressed by a code. Respondents were asked whether or not an issue was addressed in their own organization's code. Wording and tone were not addressed, and appropriateness was addressed only indirectly; thus, the measure could be influenced by respondent perception.

All of these measurement approaches share the variability of human perceptions; people are reading the ethics codes and coming to subjective conclusions. Weaver (1993) observed that subjective measures, such as intentions, may be distorted by social desirability biases. Even some objective measures (e.g. hot-line complaints) may miss the actual level of ethical behavior in an organization. In fact, Kaptein and Schwartz (2008) reviewed studies of the impact of codes on corporate social responsibility (CSR) performance and found mixed results.

Harris discusses the pros and cons of explicitness in codes. "Objective and quantifiable measures are widely seen as essential if voluntary codes are to achieve community acceptance, fairness, and compliance. For those outside the organization, such measures may assist in the building of trust in the intention of the organization to implement the code and in its capacity to do so" (Harris 2004). There is, however, a potential danger that such measures will create false confidence in external stakeholders. Internally, overreliance on quantifiable measures avoids responsibility for consideration of values. Paradoxically, rigid rules may free employees to behave unscrupulously in the gray areas.

Model

In order to develop an objective and quantifiable measure consistent with Harris' (2004) goals, we apply natural language processing (NLP) and machine learning to the problem of distinguishing "intent," or content of ethics codes. The first step of the process is to create a model that is representative of the English language and more specifically of ethics codes as documents. The model used here builds documents from words, scores the documents, and then classifies the documents. All models simplify reality to facilitate some kind of analysis. The model in this chapter, while not all-encompassing, has yielded good results in a variety of cutting-edge applications where a more fully featured description of language would be too complex. One such instance is spam detection, where state-of-the-art systems rival humans in accuracy.

What Is a Word?

This question is trivial from a human standpoint, but to a computer, every text is just a string of characters. A program needs rules for parsing those characters into words. The most fundamental rule is that word boundaries are marked by spaces. However, this chapter will go a step further. Since a main method used here will be automated word counting, once the words are split by whitespace, word variations will be collapsed together by transforming all text into lowercase and *stemming* them. In NLP, stemming is a process that uses rules to remove inflections from a word to reach an approximate base form. The stemming process used here is the one defined by Porter (1980).

For example: ethics, ethical, and ethically all have the *stem*—ethic. Thus they are all considered the same word by this model.

How Do Words Form a Document?

The next step in constructing the model is to define larger structures. This chapter will utilize the "bag of words" model, one of the most widely used in NLP. It has the advantage of being highly descriptive in practice while also being straightforward. As the name implies, the bag of words model ignores sentence structure, just as if all the words of a document had been placed into a bag and shaken up. An observer could pull individual words out of the bag, but would have no idea how those words once fit together. The downside of this model is obvious—much of the meaning of the original document is lost. However, there is still a tremendous amount of information, especially about the document's topic, hidden in the frequency of words that the author chose. For instance, take the example document in Fig. 5.1. When transformed into a bag of words model, the sentences yield the set of frequencies seen in Table 5.1. Words like "ABC," "ethics," "responsibility," and "dilemma" appear more frequently than most other words. An observer without prior knowledge of the underlying sentences could reasonably conclude that the document relates to ethical decisions concerning the ABC company.

How Is the Content of a Document Measured?

Computer algorithms need to quantify each measurement, unlike humans who make qualitative distinctions intuitively. The previously mentioned frequency count of words is the natural starting point; however, that is not quite precise enough a measure of the content of a document for the purposes of this chapter. For instance, in Fig. 5.1, even though words like "all" and "the" occur often, they give little insight into the document due to their commonness

---

Adhering to high ethical standards is the responsibility of all ABC employees, from the mailroom to the boardroom. We at ABC strive to maintain an environment of shared responsibility and utmost integrity in our relationships with all our stakeholders. It is inevitable that you will face ethical dilemmas in your work for ABC from time to time. Refer to this ABC ethics code for guidance making responsible ethical choices as these ethical dilemmas arise at ABC.

Fig. 5.1 Bag of words example document

within the English language. The solution utilized in this chapter is to score each word based on both the frequency with which the word appears within the document at hand and also the frequency with which it appears in any of the documents. It should be noted that in NLP, the full collection of documents under consideration is called a *corpus*. In this case, the corpus is a set of corporate ethics codes.

The weighting scheme described above is called term frequency-inverse document frequency (TF-IDF) (Manning et al. 2008). Mathematically, this is expressed as by Eq. 5.1. The intuition is that the TF-IDF score rewards words that occur often in the current document, but penalizes those that occur in many documents.

$$TF-IDF(w) = F(w) * \log\left(\frac{1}{DF(w)}\right) \tag{5.1}$$

Where:

w = a given word

$F(w)$ = the frequency of word w within a given document

$DF(w)$ = the fraction of all documents in the corpus in which word w occurs

Returning to the example in Fig. 5.1, the words "ABC" and "ethics" occur in very few documents in the corpus, while "the" and "all" occur in nearly all documents in the corpus. See the DF column in Table 5.1 for the document frequencies. Reading from Table 5.1, results for the word "ethic" from the sample document show that 6.579% (TF) of the words in the sample

Table 5.1 Word frequency scores for example document

Word	TF (Term frequency)	DF (Document frequency)	TF-IDF
Abc	0.06579	0.004	0.15776
Ethic	0.06579	0.05	0.08559
To	0.06579	1.0	0.0
Response	0.03947	0.32	0.01953
The	0.03947	1.0	0.0
All	0.02632	0.982	0.00021
At	0.02632	1.0	0.0
For	0.02632	1.0	0.0
From	0.02632	1.0	0.0
Dilemma	0.02632	0.036	0.03799
Utmost	0.01316	0.014	0.02439
Code	0.01316	0.056	0.01647
...			

paragraph have the "ethic" stem. By comparison, 5% (DF) of the documents in the Brown corpus (described in Data section) contain at least one mention of the word "ethic." Reweighting under TF-IDF (see the TF-IDF column of Table 5.1), the scores of "ABC" and "ethics" become much larger relative to "the" and "all." This outcome is in keeping with the descriptiveness of the individual words.

From Comparisons to Classifications

The model of English developed thus far creates a method of quantifying and comparing documents. Comparison depends on the TF-IDF weighting scheme as it measures the frequency content of a document *as compared to other documents*. This chapter goes one step further in developing a methodology for making predictions based on those comparisons. Up until now, this model has assumed all documents (i.e. ethics codes) come from a similar source, or *class*. Consistent with the argument made by Farrell and Farrell (1998) above, the authors hypothesize that there are multiple classes of ethics codes based on corporate intent. Our data was used to investigate differences between two classes of codes: a class we call "Ethical" and a more aggregated group we call "Standard."

How Does an Algorithm Classify?

In order to demonstrate objectively which class an ethics code falls into, ideally a computer algorithm should be able to predict whether a code will fall into one category or the other. Judging whether the predictions are correct is a task which requires knowing the answer ahead of time. This chapter uses published rankings of companies as proxies for the classes to which each examined company belongs. The choice of rankings, and their justification, is described in the data section below.

Building a Classifier

The problem of classification is a mainstay of machine learning. Classification is the problem of assigning a category to a new observation given previously observed data (and their categories), known as the training set. An individual observation in this problem is the content of a given ethics code, as measured using the model set forth earlier in this chapter. The categories in our analysis are "Ethical" and "Standard," which are known for each document based on the published rankings as explained below in the data section. Some of the published data is held back from the training set to be used in later testing of the algorithm's predictions. The reason for holding back data (and potentially losing valuable training material) is that training and testing an algorithmic classifier on the same observations skews the results. This is analogous to showing the answers to a test before administering the exam—students pass easily without knowledge of the subject.

Support Vector Machines

The particular classifier used in this chapter is called a *support vector machine*. As stated previously, the goal of the model is to assign a newly observed document to one of two categories, "Ethical" or "Standard." To accomplish this, the support vector machine presents each document as an n-dimensional vector of its TF-IDF word scores, where n is the number of unique words in the corpus. As a result, all observations exist in an n-dimensional space. To illustrate, for a corpus with only two unique words (see Fig. 5.2 for example), the

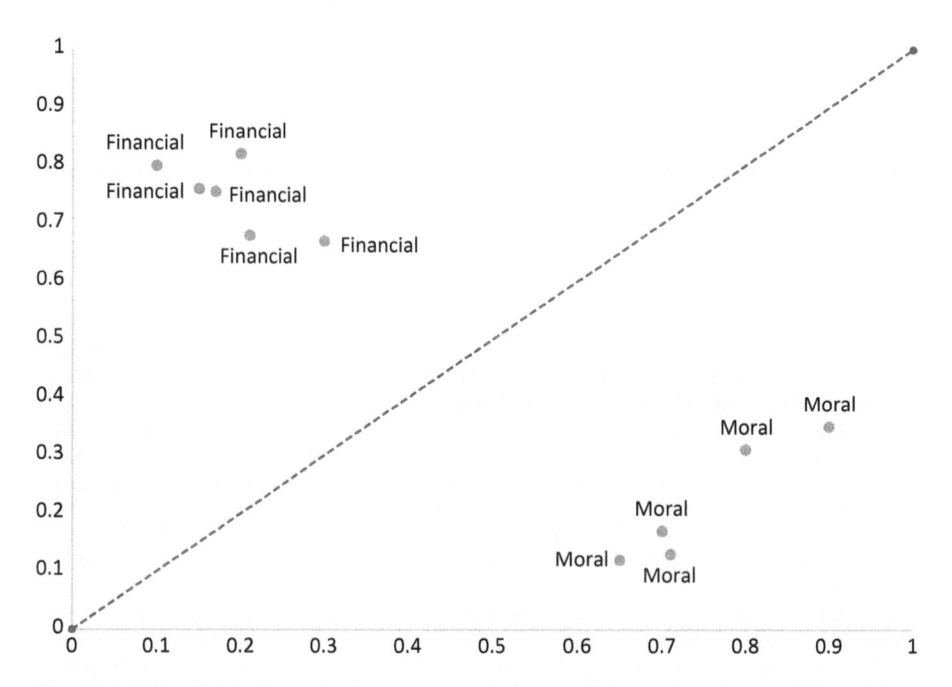

Fig. 5.2 Hypothetical graph of a support vector machine, with observed documents containing only the words "financial" and "moral"

observations would lie in a two-dimensional plane. The support vector machine then creates an (n-1)-dimensional boundary that divides the space into two, with one side corresponding to the "Ethical" section of the space and the other side corresponding to the "Standard" section. In the case of the two-word vocabulary of Fig. 5.2, this boundary would be a line. To maximize the distinction between "Ethical" and "Standard" classifications, the support vector machine chooses the boundary that maximizes the distance between the observations and the boundary (see Fig. 5.2). For further details of the algorithm (including variations to accommodate nonlinear boundaries), see Russell and Norvig (2002), p. 744. Please note that our data have many more than the two unique words in Fig. 5.2, so our results will actually occur in a much higher number of dimensions.

Data

Ethics codes from a sample of the Fortune 500 companies were used as the baseline for "Standard" ethics codes. Four alternative data sources were used for ethics codes of notably "Ethical" companies: Ethisphere's list of most ethical companies,[1] Corporate Responsibility Magazine's 100 Best Corporate Citizens,[2] Fortune's list of Most Admired Companies,[3] and the Fortune 100 Best Companies to Work For.[4] The lists were chosen under the hypothesis

---

[1] Ethisphere's Most Ethical Companies program honors companies that excel in three areas—promoting ethical business standards and practices internally, enabling managers and employees to make good choices, and shaping future industry standards by introducing tomorrow's best practices today. (Retrieved from http://worldsmostethicalcompanies.ethisphere.com/ on May 1, 2017.)

[2] *Corporate Responsibility Magazine* year's 100 Best List began with their research team documenting 260 data points of disclosure and performance measurements for the entire Russell 1000. The data was gleaned from publicly available information and each company was ranked in seven categories: environment, climate change, employee relations, human rights, corporate governance, financial performance, and philanthropy and community support. (Retrieved from http://www.thecro.com/100-best/100-best-methodology-how-we-determine-the-winners/ on January 1, 2017.)

[3] The Most Admired list is a report card on corporate reputations compiled by Fortune in partnership with Korn Ferry Hay Group. Executives, directors, and analysts were asked to rate companies in their own industry on nine criteria, from investment value to social responsibility. A company's score must rank in the top half of its industry survey to be listed (retrieved from http://fortune.com/worlds-most-admired-companies/ on October 5, 2016). The Fortune rankings have been used empirically by Spencer and Taylor (1987) and by McGuire et al. (1988) and by Wartick (1992) as a measure of corporate social responsibility.

[4] To identify the 100 Best Companies to Work For, each year Fortune partners with Great Place to Work to conduct an extensive employee survey. Two-thirds of a company's survey score is based on the results of the Trust Index Employee Survey, which is sent to a random sample of employees from each company. This survey asks questions related to employees' attitudes about management's credibility, overall job satisfaction, and camaraderie. The other third is based on responses to the Culture Audit, which includes

that inclusion in the list is a reasonable proxy for more ethical corporate behavior as compared to other large companies, which typified more generic corporate behavior. Inclusion in a named list is a way to create a convenient one-dimensional composite measure for the inherently multi-criteria nature of ethical decision-making (Cahn 2014). These published data were used as a proxy for determining whether an ethics code was in the "Ethical" or "Standard" class. All are measures with a long history and a stable definition.

The ethics codes were accessed from company websites and were the most current available at the time of this study, ranging from 2013 to 2016. Each data set of "Ethical" codes was compared to a comparable number of codes from the set of "Standard" codes taken from the Fortune 500 companies, excluding those from the companies in the corresponding "Ethical" set.

Of Ethisphere's Most Ethical Companies, 89 were US companies with available ethics codes. Corporate Responsibility Magazine's Best Corporate Citizens had 71 US companies with available ethics codes. Fortune's list of Most Admired Companies had 47 with available ethics codes. Of the Fortune 100 Best Companies to Work For, 79 had ethics codes available.

Our data set included 184 of the largest of the Fortune 500.

The classifier described in this chapter uses a model that quantifies documents in relation to a corpus (see section: *How is the content of a document measured*). In this case, that corpus is the set of ethics codes taken from the lists described above. The authors chose the Brown corpus as a proxy for general English as it is a well-known, topically balanced, corpus.[5] The purpose of the comparisons is to demonstrate the difference between the language that distinguishes ethics codes from other texts (e.g. a novel or newspaper article) and the language that distinguishes ethics codes from each other.

Tools

The authors developed the classifier described in this chapter in Python. In coding the model and classifier, the authors used several freely available software packages, chiefly the natural language toolkit (Bird et al. 2009) and SciKit-Learn (Pedregosa et al. 2011).

---

detailed questions about pay and benefit programs and a series of open-ended questions about hiring practices, methods of internal communication, training, recognition programs, and diversity efforts (retrieved from http://fortune.com/best-companies/ on October 5, 2016). Some of these metrics reflect ethical management, but as an aggregate measure it is not exclusively about ethics. As the respondents are from each company, the data may be subject to self-reporting bias.

[5] A Standard Corpus of Present-Day Edited American English, for use with Digital Computers (Brown). 1964, 1971, 1979. Compiled by W. N. Francis and H. Kučera. Brown University. Providence, Rhode Island.

Results

Model Measurements

In the first step toward building, or *training*, a classifier, the authors measured each ethics code sampled from each of the "Ethical" listings (see Data section) as compared to Fortune 500 ethics codes using the TF-IDF measurement described previously. Note that the comparative portion of the TF-IDF measurement is in the IDF, the document frequency of a particular word being how many ethics codes in total contain that particular word. The word "ethics" does not rank highly in this measurement precisely due to this comparison. Simply put, most ethics codes use the word "ethics." As such, "ethics" is a poor feature for distinguishing one class of ethics codes from another. In contrast, "ethics" is a strong distinguishing feature of ethics codes relative to English in general. Words like "ethics" rank highly relative to the Brown corpus, which is representative of general English texts by virtue of including a variety of sources. Intuitively, "ethics" seems reasonably likely to derive from a common set of vocabulary shared among all ethics codes. As such, it is a useful feature in identifying that a document is in fact an ethics code, but not useful for distinguishing *between* ethics codes.

Training and Testing

In training the classifier, each ethics code's measurements were taken to be the features of each observed document and the training label of *Ethical/Standard* was taken from whether the ethics code was drawn from an "Ethical" list or the "Standard" Fortune 500.

As described previously, the dataset of ethics codes is split into two groups, one (larger) set for training the classifier and the other for testing it. In the training step, the model is fed a set of observed class labels (*Ethical/Standard*) to learn from along with the measured features of the sample documents. In the testing steps, the class labels are withheld and the now-trained classifier predicts the class of each document in the testing set. How frequently the classifier correctly predicts each document's class (which is known) is an indication of the overall accuracy of the classifier.

The number of ethics codes used here would be considered a small sample size in machine learning methodology. One drawback of a small sample size is that removing any piece of the dataset from training can significantly affect the resulting classifier. Another is that the model may not have observed enough data to accurately predict classifications. As such, our analysis resorts to a technique called *cross-validation* in order to maximize the amount of training data available and find a smoothed estimate of the model's accuracy. In cross-validation, the data set is divided into N equal groups. The classifier is then trained N times using all but one of the groups, with a different group being left out each time. The average accuracy of the N iterations is taken to be the overall model accuracy.

Classification

Once the ethics codes were divided into the two groups, they were input into the learning model previously described. Results suggest that the computational classifier used in this research was able to sort companies based on measures of their ethics codes for some, but not all, of the data sets studied. Corporate Responsibility Magazine's 100 Best Corporate Citizens as well as Ethisphere's Most Ethical Companies had ethics codes that were distinguishable by the model from those of the "Standard" Fortune 500 companies. The "Ethical" accuracy in Table 5.2 reflects the percentage of codes that the model identified as "Ethical" that did indeed come from the corresponding set of "Ethical" companies; the "Standard" accuracy correspondingly represents the percentage of ethics codes that the model identified as "Standard" that really came from the Fortune 500 list. For the two Fortune lists, neither was distinguishable from "Standard" companies' ethics codes by the model. While each of the data sources is a list of companies that have distinguished themselves in some way, Corporate Responsibility Magazine's list and Ethisphere's list are distinguishable by measuring their ethics codes. The two Fortune lists were not.

Table 5.2 Classification accuracy

	Accuracy "Ethical"[a]	Fortune 500 ("Standard")	Average
Ethisphere's Most Ethical Companies ("Ethical")	0.61	0.56	0.588
Corporate Responsibility Magazine's 100 Best Corporate Citizens ("Ethical")	0.55	0.53	0.54
Fortune's Most Admired Companies ("Ethical")	0.50	0.49	0.496
Fortune 100 Best Companies to Work For ("Ethical")	0.47	0.53	0.50

[a]See rows for hypothesized "Ethical" data set

Discussion

Ethics codes may in fact be distinguished from each other based on their terminology. NLP models can be a tool to help identify which companies' ethics codes are distinguishable. The implication that the objectively measured content of ethics codes can be distinguishable from one company to another, lends support to the idea that code content and quality can make a difference in organizational behavior and performance.

Ethics codes from some of the lists of companies recognized as "Ethical" are different from those companies measured to be large corporations. This measurable difference doesn't prove causality; we cannot say whether companies that are already more ethical write better codes or whether careful attention to code language improves those companies. But taking the demonstration that the codes are different together with suggestions of earlier researchers about ethics code tone and intent, we can say that the codes of these "Ethical" companies can serve as models on which to base writing of an ethics code.

Extensions

Future research might refine the application of NLP to ethics codes by studying variations in the a priori assumption that all the "Ethical" companies listed represent a unified set identified by ethical intent. Alternate sets of ethics codes might be studied, or alternate ways of dividing companies into categories.

Using a computational classifier of ethics codes as a measure of intent together with financial data could advance research on the connection between corporate social responsibility and financial performance.

This chapter uses NLP to develop a quantitative classifier to identify ethics code "intent." Extending this research, this measure could be used to study how ethics code intent impacts financial performance or other CSR measures.

Acknowledgement The authors wish to thank Adam Meyers of New York University for his invaluable advice on this project.

References

Bird, S., Loper, E., & Klein, E. (2009). *Natural Language Processing with Python.* Beijing: O'Reilly Media Inc.

Cahn, E. S. (2014). Measures of Corporate Social Business Performance and Ethical Decisions: A Review and Critique. *Southern Journal of Business and Ethics, 6,* 142–152.

Coughlan, R. (2005). Codes, Values and Justifications in the Ethical Decision-Making Process. *Journal of Business Ethics, 59*(1–2), 45–53.
Erwin, P. M. (2011). Corporate Codes of Conduct: The Effects of Code Content and Quality on Ethical Performance. *Journal of Business Ethics, 99*(4), 535–548.
Farrell, H., & Farrell, B. J. (1998). The Language of Business Codes of Ethics: Implications of Knowledge and Power. *Journal of Business Ethics, 17*(6), 587.
Gaumnitz, B. R., & Lere, J. C. (2004). A Classification Scheme for Codes of Business Ethics. *Journal of Business Ethics, 49*(4), 329–335.
Harris, H. (2004). Performance Measurement for Voluntary Codes: An Opportunity and a Challenge. *Business and Society Review, 109*(4), 549–566.
Kaptein, M. (2011). Toward Effective Codes: Testing the Relationship with Unethical Behavior. *Journal of Business Ethics, 99*(2), 233–251.
Kaptein, M., & Schwartz, M. (2008). The Effectiveness of Business Codes: A Critical Examination of Existing Studies and the Development of an Integrated Research Model. *Journal of Business Ethics, 77*(2), 111–127.
Manning, C. D., Raghavan, P., & Schütze, H. (2008). Scoring, Term Weighting, and the Vector Space Model. In *Introduction to Information Retrieval* (p. 100). Delhi: Cambridge University Press.
McGuire, J. B., Sundgren, A., & Schneeweis, T. (1988). Corporate Social Responsibility and Firm Performance. *Academy of Management Journal, 31*(4), 854–872.
Pedregosa, F., Varoquaux, G., Gramfort, A., Michel, V., Thirion, B., Grisel, O., Blondel, M., Prettenhofer, P., Weiss, R., Dubourg, V., Vanderplas, J., Passos, A., Cournapeau, D., Brucher, M., Perrot, M., & Duchesnay, É. (2011). Scikit-Learn: Machine Learning in Python. *Journal of Machine Learning Research, 12*, 2825–2830.
Peldszus, A., & Stede, M. (2016). Rhetorical Structure and Argumentation Structure in Monologue Text. *ACL*, 103.
Porter, M. F. (1980). An Algorithm for Suffix Stripping. *Program, 14*(3), 130–137.
Reynolds, S. J., & Bowie, N. E. (2004). A Kantian Perspective on the Characteristics of Ethics Programs. *Business Ethics Quarterly, 14*, 275–292.
Rodrigues, U., & Stegemoller, M. (2010). Placebo Ethics. *Virginia Law Review, 96*(1), 1–68.
Russell, S., & Norvig, P. (2002). *Artificial Intelligence: A Modern Approach* (2nd ed.). Upper Saddle River: Prentice Hall.
Schwartz, M. S. (2002). A Code of Ethics for Corporate Code of Ethics. *Journal of Business Ethics, 41*(1–2), 27–43.
Spencer, B. A., & Taylor, G. S. (1987). A Within and Between Analysis of the Relationship Between Corporate Social Responsibility and Financial Performance. *Akron Business and Economic Review, 18*(3), 7–18.
Stede, M. (2016, October 7). *Argumentation and Discourse Structure: Some Relationships*. NLP Talk Presented at Columbia University.

Wartick, S. L. (1992). The Relationship Between Intense Media Exposure and Change in Corporate Reputation. *Business & Society, 31*(1), 33–42.

Weaver, G. R. (1993). Corporate Codes of Ethics: Purpose, Process and Content Issues. *Business & Society, 32*(1), 44–58.

Winkler, I. (2011). The Representation of Social Actors in Corporate Codes of Ethics: How Language Positions Internal Actors. *Journal of Business Ethics, 101*(4), 653–665.

6

Because It's Worth It? A Critical Discourse Analysis of Diversity: The Case of L'Oréal

François Goxe and Michaël Viegas Pires

Introduction

For decades, a large number of international and US-based corporations in particular have vaunted the merits of diversity in the workplace. Diversity and its multiple forms have been suggested to enhance various capabilities of firms, to provide better service to a diverse customer base, to boost organizational creativity, to foster attractiveness towards talented and multicultural managers, and so on. To harness these positive effects, organizations engage in "diversity management," organizational programs that increasingly appear as necessary to simply remain competitive (Gilbert et al. 1999).

Following practitioners' interest in how to "manage" diversity in organizations, diversity also emerged as a research domain. A substantive body of literature has investigated the effects of diversity on organizations. Such literature generally assumes that differences among organization members are a major asset, and diversity is likely to provide a competitive advantage. The impact of various differences (in terms of age, disability, values, etc.) on collective cognitive processes, group dynamics, groups' work outcomes, and performance has thus been thoroughly studied (see Zanoni et al. 2010 for a review).

While this "mainstream" literature improved our understanding of the effects of diversity in the workplace, a growing number of critical scholars also pointed to some shortcomings. It is argued that literature as well as practitioners never

F. Goxe (✉) • M. Viegas Pires
University of Versailles, Versailles, France
e-mail: francois.goxe@uvsq.fr; michael.viegas-pires@uvsq.fr

© The Author(s) 2019
A. Bartoli et al. (eds.), *Responsible Organizations in the Global Context*,
https://doi.org/10.1007/978-3-030-11458-9_6

questions who is constructed as different, for what purposes and consequences. It is also argued that the social and organizational contexts as well as power dynamics are neglected. The mainstream literature thus forgets that diversity can be manipulated, or at least controlled, in order to achieve organizational goals (Blommaert and Verschueren 1998; Vince and Booth 1996).

Diversity is socially constructed, and language plays a central role in such process. Some studies explored the microdiscursive practices of managers, employees, and other individuals in their discourses on diversity (Zanoni et al. 2010; Zanoni and Janssens 2004, 2015). We now know more about the nature of discourse on diversity, its definitions and construction at microlevel. However, still little is known about diversity discourses at a broader level, and especially about the discourse of organizations as a whole. Additionally, very little has been done to explain how and for what purpose such discourse can be utilized. In particular, although multinational corporations (MNCs) are among the main actors of diversity management, we do not know how they discursively handle diversity and related issues, notably to legitimize their existence and activities.

This study aims to bridge this gap, and intends to contribute to the critical turn in the study of diversity management (Lorbiecki and Jack 2000). It builds on previous works on discursive legitimation (Erkama and Vaara 2010; Vaara 2006; Vaara and Monin 2010; Vaara and Tienari 2002, 2008, 2010) to explore how MNCs can craft and mobilize certain forms of discourse on diversity and diversity management for strategic purposes. This study dwells on the case of French cosmetic multinational L'Oréal, well known for its promotion of diversity and its diversity management policies. Based on the critical analysis of diversity reports, corporate communication and public statements made by the firm's decision-makers, we address two research questions: (1) What is the underlying definition of diversity in a multinational company like L'Oréal? (2) How does the firm mobilize this concept to try to gain legitimacy in the eyes of the stakeholders?

Our contribution is twofold. First, we identify L'Oréal's definitions of diversity. By doing so, we empirically illustrate how a few sociodemographic traits are used to build broad, homogeneous, categories of people. More precisely, we analyze the language mechanisms behind the process. Second, our analysis also resulted in the identification of different types of discourse, discursive frameworks through which diversity issues are addressed in L'Oréal's corporate communication: (1) rationalistic, (2) societal, and (3) appropriative discourse. The three types of discourse are interlocked and, considered globally, picture diversity as a very plastic concept that can as such be mobilized differently in order to create various forms of legitimacy for various stakeholders.

This chapter is structured as follows. First, we briefly review existing research in the domain of diversity and in the field of discursive legitimation as well. Second, we introduce the case of L'Oréal and describe our methods. Then we present our main findings and subsequently discuss our contributions.

Literature Review

"For many reasons, the organizational literature on diversity is confusing – difficult to understand and difficult to synthesize" (Harrison and Klein 2007, p. 1200). Some of the key reasons why the literature is confusing are certainly the proliferation of definitions and variables, probable consequences of the various turns that the field has known for the past decades, among which a critical turn (Lorbiecki and Jack 2000).

Diversity Management: Turning Critical

Research on diversity is not new and scholars and practitioners alike frequently use the term "diversity" to designate various phenomena and practices. Simply put, "diversity" is the state of being diverse, showing a great deal of variety or differences but the nature of the differences considered, the factors under study differ significantly. Diversity can be conceptualized as separation, variety, or disparity (Harrison and Klein 2007) with regard to many factors or variables, depending on the focus of attention.

Diversity emerged as a research field in the USA in the late 1980s when many business people and academics took note of the Workforce 2000 report (Johnston and Packer 1987) forecasting that, in the final years of the twentieth century, the US workforce would become *"older, more female, and more disadvantaged."* The initial focus was therefore the changing demographic situation and its effects (Lorbiecki and Jack 2000). US politicians progressively gained interest in the notion of diversity as an alternative to "affirmative action" policies. Meanwhile, *"corporate executives found diversity a lot easier to swallow than affirmative action, and much easier to sell to a predominantly white workforce"* (Lowery 1995, p. 150). Politicians, academics, and practitioners also emphasized the economic and strategic benefits of a diverse workforce for organizations, turning diversity management into an economic concern, a "business case" (Lorbiecki and Jack 2000, p. S21).

As more and more diversity management policies proved unsuccessful or counterproductive (male backlash, white rage, frustration and disappointment regarding workforce equality and so on), the literature on diversity management started to turn more critical (Lorbiecki and Jack 2000). Some began to question the do-ability of diversity management as promoted by its celebratory rhetoric and lamented the *"absence of serious scholarship on the process of managing diversity itself"* (Prasad and Mills 1997, p. 5). Some of the questions and issues raised by that emerging literature include (Lorbiecki and Jack 2000) the meaning of "differences," "diversity," and "diversity management," the latter's claims to enhance performance and productivity or its underlying paradigms and assumptions.

Critical diversity scholars spotted three major issues regarding the mainstream literature (Zanoni et al. 2010). First, mainstream studies suffer from a positivistic ontology according to which identities are *"ready-made, fixed, clear-cut, easily measurable categories"* (Zanoni et al. 2010). Such approach denies individuals' singularity and narrows one's identity to one—usually sociodemographic trait. Individuals are thus mere representatives of a single, homogeneous group (e.g. men/women, abled/disabled, white/black). Besides, diversity is not considered in itself but as a deviation from a norm, a marginal position from the vantage point of a dominant, white middle-aged western abled man (Calas 1992). Second, mainstream studies often consider that diversity takes place in a social and organizational vacuum. Diversity is frequently predefined, regardless of contextual elements that may significantly affect its meaning and the meaning of underlying identities, as well as its outcomes. Third, mainstream diversity studies neglect or downplay power dynamics certainly structuring all contexts or fields (Bourdieu and Nice 1977) and fail to consider that definitions and approaches on diversity can certainly be manipulated. Zanoni and Janssens (2004) even argue that diversity literature frequently adopts the instrumental perspective of the dominant according to which workforce and consumers' differences are seen as a potential source of value that should be managed or manipulated to attain a better performance.

Discourse and Discursive Legitimation

Management scholars recently took interest in the question of discursive legitimation. Vaara and a few European colleagues have been so far the main contributors to this area of study (Erkama and Vaara 2010; Vaara 2006; Vaara and Monin 2010; Vaara and Tienari 2002, 2008, 2010). Most of these works are set in the critical discourse analysis (CDA) stream, which considers that discourse does not objectively account for reality but rather reflects and contributes to its social construction (Fairclough 2005).

CDA strives to examine the textual construction of phenomena in a broader social context (Leitch and Palmer 2010). It reveals the role played by language in the construction of power relationships and reproduction of ideas, ideologies, and structures of domination, power relationships, and structures of inequality (van Dijk 1993, 1995; Fairclough 1997; Fairclough and Wodak 1997). In other words, CDA focuses on revealing the (discursive) strategies used by various actors to rally others to their cause or interests and to maintain or improve their respective positions in the field (Fairclough 1997).

Discourse includes texts and other forms of communication but also the broader social and cultural structure surrounding them (Fairclough 1997; Phillips and Hardy 1997). Discourse as texts and other forms of communication (e.g. speeches, videos, images) has at least three functions (Answorth and Hardy 2004, p. 236). It has an ideational function as it constitutes forms of knowledge and beliefs: *"[Discourse is] a group of statements which provide a language for talking about a topic and a way of producing a particular kind of knowledge about a topic. Thus, the term refers both to the production of knowledge through language and representations and the way that knowledge is institutionalized, shaping social practices and setting new practices into play"* (du Gay 1996, p. 43). It has an interpersonal function as it contributes to define and represent self or social identities and a relational function as it influences social relations: *"[Discourse] establishes, sustains and changes power relations, and the collective entities (classes, blocs, communities, groups) between which power relations obtain. [It also] constitutes, naturalizes, sustains and changes significations of the world from diverse positions in power relations"* (Fairclough 1992, p. 67). Through these functions, discourse is a form of social practice and action (Fairclough 1997) that contributes to shaping the identity and behaviors of individuals and groups (and organizations) (Fairclough 2005; Gergen 2001).

Diversity Management and Discursive Legitimation

A number of recent researches (Basu and Palazzo 2008; Joutsenvirta and Vaara 2015; Palazzo and Scherer 2006; Scherer and Palazzo 2011; Siltaoja and Onkila 2013) started to study corporate social responsibility (CSR) discourse in particular as a mechanism for corporate legitimization. This new focus on the political actions and responsibilities of corporations (Matten and Crane 2005; Scherer and Palazzo 2011), in particular through discourse, has sometimes been considered as part of a "political turn" in the study of CSR. This new approach to CSR emphasizes the role of legitimacy and questions how companies build, maintain, or repair legitimacy through rhetoric and various forms of discourse (Castelló and Lozano 2011; Elsbach 1994; Patriotta et al. 2011; Phillips and Hardy 1997; Phillips et al. 2004). As underscored by Palazzo and Scherer (Palazzo and Scherer 2006; Scherer and Palazzo 2011) and Joutsenvirta and Vaara (2015), with this turn, we move *"from an output and power oriented approach to an input related and discursive concept of legitimacy"* (Palazzo and Scherer 2006, p. 71) where legitimacy is *"socially and argumentatively constructed by means of considering reasons to justify certain actions, practices, or institutions and is thus present in discourses between the corporation and its relevant publics"* (Scherer and Palazzo 2011, p. 916). As noted by Patriotta et al. (2011, p. 1805), some (Zilber 2002, 2006) *"have highlighted the symbolic work by which social actors construct legitimating accounts linking contentious issues to broader cultural views and competing logics [...] but little attention has been paid to the fact that [...] legitimacy may require social actors to justify their positions vis-à-vis a public audience."*

Despite this rising interest in the discursive legitimation of CSR at a general level, studies with a specific focus on diversity remain scarce. Among the few examples of such studies, Garnsey and Rees (1996) demonstrated how the persistence of gender inequalities may, without apparent intention, be encoded in language. Indeed, their analysis of a major UK initiative to increase women's participation in the workforce shows that the related texts are actually built on essentialist norms and assumptions about their lifestyles and behaviors and thus only perpetuate stereotypes and domination structures. In a similar way, Trethewey (1999) showed how organizational and gendered discourses often constrain women's professional identities. Another piece (Riach 2007) showed how the social construction of the "older worker" may in itself serve to marginalize and contribute towards age inequalities through discursive strategies. Some very few empirical studies thus examined how discourse could contribute to mask some negative aspects, consequences, side effects, or not-so-glorious objectives of diversity management policies or firms vaunting the merits of a diverse workforce or market.

Despite some advances, studies on the discursive legitimation of diversity is still in its infancy and needs more empirical investigations as *"organizational actors do not simply take over existing grand, hegemonic discourses of diversity but rather selectively appropriate them, and re-combine them with other available discourses to make sense of diversity, their organization, and of their work"* (Zanoni et al. 2010, p. 17). For instance, Zanoni and Janssens (2004) demonstrated how Human Resource managers constructed the concept of diversity and how this construction reflected existing power relations. In a similar vein, the same authors showed the interlocking nature of occupational identities and discourses on diversity (Zanoni and Janssens 2015).

To this day, if calls for research are plentiful and conceptual contributions rapidly increasing, empirical evidence is still scarce. The purpose of this research is to bridge this gap.

Case and Methods

This research is based on the case of L'Oréal. The world's largest cosmetics company has spearheaded the interest and involvement of French multinationals in diversity management. It is a good example for the recent and quite sudden corporate preoccupation with diversity issues in continental Europe.[1] Since the turn of the century, diversity is at the heart of L'Oréal's global development. This company is well known for its diversity policy and often considered as a typical example of successful diversity management. Additionally, L'Oréal massively communicates about its diversity policy, its initiatives, and fulfilments. Thus, the case of L'Oréal appears to be very relevant for studying the discursive production about diversity of a multinational corporation.

We studied L'Oréal's corporate communication, in order to analyze how this communication conveys a particular view of diversity. To do so, we collected a wide range of empirical material including texts and videos as well. This material was collected from three different sources, namely L'Oréal's corporate website, its diversity dedicated website, and finally its careers website. These sources cover many different topics, such as the group's governance, its strategy, or even its brands. We did not focus on particular topics, and collected all the diversity-related content. Several clues helped us in deciding whether a piece of empirical material should be included in our data sample or not. For instance, the presence of the word "diversity", or references to multiethnicity were used as discriminating criteria. This approach provided

---

[1] Contrary to the US, where diversity management emerged as early as the 1980s, after the enactment of antidiscrimination laws, and is now common practice, in France, diversity and discrimination emerged much more recently and spread simultaneously and as related concerns and practices (Klarsfeld 2009, p. 366).

Table 6.1 Summary of empirical material

	Documents[a]	Videos	Total
Careers Website	3		3
Corporate Website	18		18
Diversity Website	36	29	65
Total	57	29	86

[a]Including web pages

us with a comprehensive view of L'Oréal's vision of diversity. Table 6.1 provides a summary of our empirical material.

A critical discourse analysis (CDA) was carried out on this dataset. CDA is more than just a semantic analysis. It also involves paying attention to linguistic details, such as the use of particular lexical fields. Accordingly, our empirical material was analyzed at both a thematic and a lexical level. In other words, we paid attention to what is expressed (thematic analysis) and the way it is expressed as well (lexical analysis), considering that both aspects participate in the construction of meaning. We endeavored to identify both the large groups of ideas in our corpus (themes) and large groups of words used to formulate these ideas (universe or lexical fields).

This analysis was carried out with Nvivo software. Concretely, our empirical material was coded in terms of content. Big portions of text were spread between different categories according to the dimensions of diversity they were referring to. We also coded the material in terms of the actors concerned by these dimensions. We finally identified recurring themes within the texts. As far as lexical analysis is concerned, by using Nvivo text queries, we strove to identify recurring words and expressions, especially those referring to actors and definitions of diversity. This approach means that lexical and thematic analyses are interlocked. A single portion of text can be coded in different categories. This allows using the matrix coding queries of Nvivo in order to identify how the different types of diversity, actors, the themes, and the vocabularies are recurrently associated.

In this approach, the various types of discourse or discursive frameworks can be identified with the help of a number of "traces" such as particular lexical fields or themes (Vaara and Tienari 2002). This implies that the results thus generated have a subjective dimension and must subsequently be discussed and criticized. Such results do not pretend to be exhaustive or to represent the truth. They merely offer plausible and consistent explanations of discourses and their use (Tienari et al. 2003).

Results

The Discursive Construction of Diversity in L'Oréal's Communication

Adopting a critical perspective on diversity implies considering that the definition of the concept itself is not given per se, but results from a social construction process. Our empirical study illustrates how L'Oréal does handle this concept by producing discourse about its diversity management policy, thus participating in the social construction of diversity.

> For L'Oréal, diversities include all the visible or invisible differences among its employees which influence the attitudes, behavior, values and ways of working adopted by men and women. (Diversities Overview Report)

At first reading, as the quotation above illustrates, L'Oréal's definition of diversity seems to be both very clear and comprehensive. However, our analysis of diversity dimensions involved in L'Oréal's corporate communication shows that the vision behind this formal definition is much more nuanced (Table 6.2). Two approaches seem to coexist in the group's corporate communication. On the one hand, diversity is often referred to in very general terms. On the other hand, diversity is also defined much more explicitly with reference to sociodemographic characteristics.

L'Oréal's corporate communication most frequently mentions "diversity" without any reference to the dimensions involved (Table 6.2, Line 1). This suggests that the concept is a standalone one, and its content is implicit (see excerpts below).

> L'Oréal is a one-of-a-kind community that offers a wealth of diversity—not to mention a certain organized chaos! (Our culture, Careers website)

> L'Oréal integrates the concept of diversity at all levels of the company to carry out its mission: beauty for all. (Diversity and inclusion, Corporate website)

As far as sociodemographic traits are concerned, one can observe that L'Oréal's vision does not actually include *all forms of difference* as the definition we initially quoted could suggest. It is rather defined through a limited number of characteristics (Table 6.2, Line 2 and following). Among these characteristics, disability (Line 3), gender (Line 4), and origins (Line 2), the latter including three subdimensions (nationality, ethnicity, and social origins), appear to be the most frequently mentioned. They represent the pillars of L'Oréal's diversity policy.

Table 6.2 Dimensions of diversity

No.	Node	S	R	Node description
1	General	44	127	References to diversity without any details about the dimension at stake
2	Origins	38	98	References to diversity defined in terms of origins
2a	National culture	19	28	References to diversity defined in terms of nationality and national culture
2b	Ethnicity	18	30	References to diversity defined in terms of ethnicity
2c	Social	16	36	References to diversity defined in terms of social origin
2d	Origin	4	4	References to diversity defined in terms of origin (without any details about the dimensions of "origin" at stake)
3	Disability	36	85	References to diversity defined in terms of disability
4	Gender	36	73	References to diversity defined in terms of gender
5	Age	13	19	References to diversity defined in terms of generations
6	Culture	10	12	References to diversity defined in terms of culture (without any details about the cultural level at stake)
7	Religion	6	6	References to diversity defined in terms of religion
8	Parenthood	5	5	References to diversity defined in terms of parenthood
9	Skills	4	9	References to diversity defined in terms of skills
10	Orientation	3	4	References to diversity defined in terms of sexual orientation

The various sociodemographic characteristics that are used to define diversity are also often associated with groups of people in the multinational's corporate communication. This phenomenon is particularly salient at the lexical level. One can observe that individuals are often subsumed under broad labels. For instance, as far as disability is concerned, individuals are most often referred to as "people with disabilities" or "disabled people" (Table 6.3 and excerpt below). Other aspects of their social status are rarely mentioned, which means that individuals suffering from disability are reduced to this single dimension. Such labelling thus involves categorization, that is, assigning broad and simple categories to people. This downplays other aspects of their identity that might be important as well.

> We try to focus on really getting people with disabilities, which was not something that was natural. (Interview with Alexandre Popoff, executive vice-president eastern Europe zone Diversity Website)

Table 6.3 Labels for individuals suffering from disability

Label[a]	Sources	References
People with disability(ies)	27	85
Disabled people	16	23
The disabled	4	4
Disabled person(s)	3	3

[a]The words and expressions included in the table are issued from a word frequency query (no list of words was defined a priori)

Table 6.4 Frequency of disability-related words and expressions (general vs specific)

Category	Words and expressions [number of sources (total frequency)]	Example
General	Diversity [28(126)]	L'Oréal Italy has taken very pragmatic approach towards **the question of disability**. (Diversity in Italy, Diversity Website)
Specific	Hearing impair[a] [5(6)], deaf [5(5)], autism [2(5)], physical [2(3)], intellectual [2(3)], blind [1(1)], visually impair [1(1)], albinism [1(3)]	To date, nine employees with autism have completed internships in our offices and production facilities. (Diversity in Italy, Diversity Website)

[a]The words and expressions included in the table are issued from a word frequency query and indicate truncated forms (e.g. "Impair" stands for both "Impairment" and "Impaired")

This categorization also involves homogenization. Still with regard to disability, one can for instance observe that the concept is most frequently referred to in very general terms, without any details about the sort of disability in question (Table 6.4).

Sometimes examples of individuals suffering from disability are given, but such examples remain scarce in the texts we studied (only five in total), and the portraits of these individuals are always very short. Additionally, in these portraits, individuals are not considered for themselves but as representatives of the broad category of "the disabled" (see excerpt below). This only helps illustrating how L'Oréal addresses the broad issue of disability.

> Nicole is the first **disabled person** recruited by L'Oréal in Chile as a beauty advisor. When her co-workers were asked how she was doing in her new job, their answers were unanimous: "Nicole is doing very well and is fully integrated." (Diversity in Chile, Diversity Website)

Such depersonalization, and other aforementioned lexical aspects, tends to hide the various situations of people suffering from disability, suggesting that "people with disabilities" can be considered as a single and objective reality.

Discourse Types About Diversity Issues

Beyond the sole discursive construction of the concept of diversity, our analysis also resulted in the identification of three different discourse types. Such types represent distinctive discursive frameworks through which diversity issues are addressed in L'Oréal's corporate communication. Two out of the three discourses we identified present strong similarities with other discursive frameworks identified by Vaara and his colleagues about restructuring issues (2002, 2003). We labelled these discourses "rationalistic" and "societal" with reference to these previous studies. The last discourse was labelled "appropriative." It appears to be more specifically related to diversity issues.

Rationalistic Discourse

Such discourse focuses on the company level and refers to an economic and strategic rationale. Interestingly, in the context of diversity management, this discourse appears to be a two-sided one (Fig. 6.1).

On its external side, the rationalistic discourse refers to diversity as a part of the global business environment in which MNCs operate. Diversity is thus viewed as an inescapable phenomenon that a company "faces" and has to adapt to. L'Oréal's corporate communication frequently mentions diversity as a major trend affecting the group's business environment, whether at a global, regional, or even national level. The following excerpts are examples of this.

> In the US, the number of people aged 85 and over, is projected to grow to 8.9 million in 2030. Baby boomers are the first generation of "high potential" seniors. In 2013, the beauty market for women over 50 in the United States was estimated at 15 billion dollars. (Diversity and Marketing at L'Oréal, Diversity Website)

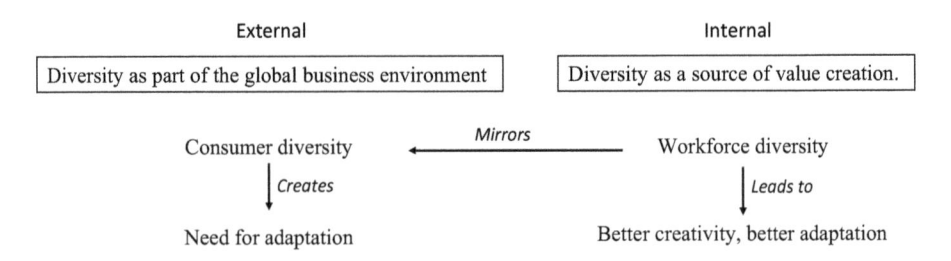

Fig. 6.1 The two sides of rationalistic discourse

Our markets are very diverse. If you take the US for instance, in 2042, you're gonna have in the US more than 50% of consumers non-Caucasian. (Interview with Frédéric Rozé, executive vice-president of the Americas zone, Diversity Website)

L'Oréal clearly claims to adapt to this diversity, and such adaptation is seen as a business imperative. The means by which such adaptation is fulfilled are regularly put forward across the texts. These means notably include the group's strategy, its organization, its marketing policy, its R&D policy, and of course its diversity management policy. L'Oréal's mission statement clearly illustrates this adaptation at the strategic level:

For more than a century, we have devoted our energy and our competencies solely to one business: beauty. We have chosen to offer our expertise in the service of women and men worldwide, meeting the infinite diversity of their beauty desires. We are committed to fulfilling this mission ethically and responsibly. (Who we are, Corporate website)

L'Oréal's mission statement also illustrates another important feature of rationalistic discourse. On its external side, this discourse focuses on consumers, whose diversity is generally defined without any reference to sociodemographic characteristics. More precisely, consumers' diversity is most often defined in marketing terms, and the differences are mainly apprehended in terms of "needs," "expectations," "desires," "aspirations," or even "habits" and "lifestyle."

On its internal side, the rationalistic discourse considers diversity as a source of value creation. It focuses on internal actors (top management and employees) whose diversity is considered to have many positive effects. These effects first include better creativity.

In the Americas Zone, L'Oréal doesn't view diversity as a barrier but rather as an asset that fuels creativity and drives innovation. (The Americas zone, Diversity Website)

A diverse workforce in all functions and at all levels enhances our creativity… (Jean-Paul Agon, President and CEO of L'Oréal, Diversity Website)

Diversity is also expected to enhance marketing performance. The rationale for this effect is that internal diversity allows L'Oréal to "reflect" or "mirror" the society surrounding its activities, which leads to a better understanding of customers' expectations.

I believe that our duty as a company is to mirror the diversity of the society we are serving so this is why it is so important for us to have people from everywhere, from all genders, from all orientations, people with disabilities, people from different backgrounds, in order for us to be more relevant for the consumers we are serving every day, with all the products we design and we craft for them. (Interview with Lubomira Rochet, Chief Digital Officer, Diversity Website)

By placing consumers at the center of our strategy, L'Oréal has to explore and reflect on the infinite diversity of styles, habits and expressions of beauty all over the world in order to develop and market the most suitable products. (Annual report 2016)

Societal Discourse

Societal discourse places MNCs at the heart of broad societal issues. It focuses on the company level, the broad societal context in which diversity management takes place, and the positive consequences of this policy for society. This discourse is, first, empirically reflected in numerous descriptions of sociodemographic trends affecting society.

In Ghana, women constitute 51% of the population but generally due to gender discrimination and deep rooted unfair cultural practices, they have less access to economic activities. (Diversity in Ghana, Diversity Website)

These trends' consequences for L'Oréal's activities are not mentioned (as such was is the case for the rationalistic discourse). Such trends are rather presented as part of a broad societal context in which L'Oréal's diversity management policy takes place, suggesting this policy addresses broad societal challenges. The positive consequences of L'Oréal's initiatives for society are also frequently underlined (and not only the positive consequences of diversity for L'Oréal's business as it is the case with rationalistic discourse).

We make a positive contribution to the countries and communities in which we are present. (Acting Ethically, Corporate website)

The partnerships between L'Oréal and actors in the civil society are frequently mentioned (NGOs, political institutions, international institutions, etc.). This suggests that the firm is not only an economic but also a social actor. This clearly places L'Oréal at the heart of society, and not only markets.

Since 2006, L'Oréal has set up a significant number of partnerships with associations (IMS, Afij, Afip, Tremplin, Nos Quartiers ont des Talents, Mozaïk RH…), recruitment and temporary work agencies in order to diversify its candidate source for internships and jobs. Since 2008, the Group has added a non-discrimination clause to contracts drawn up with its recruitment agencies. (Diversities Overview Report)

L'Oréal's corporate communication also frequently gives voice to external stakeholders who are invited to express their opinion about the group's initiatives and the associated societal challenges. Unsurprisingly, these voices never challenge L'Oréal's vision of diversity and diversity management. Evaluations of the group's policy are most often positive. Stakeholders' discourse always takes place within the framework of diversity dimensions we discussed above, which, in turn, consolidates L'Oréal's vision.

Finally, in the context of societal discourse, one observed that the dimensions of diversity are unambiguously mentioned. This again marks a clear difference from rationalistic discourse according to which consumers' diversity is defined in very general (and mostly marketing oriented) terms.

Appropriative Discourse

Unsurprisingly, an important part of L'Oréal's corporate communication is devoted to the description of the group's initiatives for promoting diversity. Such description is not purely factual and objective. It also suggests that the French group has a certain level of competence in diversity management. Broadly speaking, a crucial, yet implicit, aspect of L'Oréal's corporate communication about diversity is the idea that the group represents a legitimate voice for addressing this issue. This is what we labelled an "appropriative" discourse.

Different arguments give support to this idea in the group's corporate communication. First, the recognition of the firm's fulfilments by international institutions is frequently emphasized. L'Oréal's communication thoroughly enumerates the various prizes awarded to L'Oréal for its diversity policy. Such enumeration is not purely factual, but it also reinforces the group's legitimacy to have a discourse on diversity by providing it an external legitimacy.

In 2016, L'Oréal was recognized by Thomson Reuters as one of the 20 best companies with regard to Diversity and Inclusion out of over 5,000 companies. (Annual report 2016)

In the same vein, L'Oréal's discourse on diversity contains other self-legitimizing arguments. Some of these elements pertain to the group's status. Being a world leader *"comes with an obligation: to be a role model for others"* (Diversity in HR at L'Oréal, Diversity Website). L'Oréal accordingly claims its ambition to become *"the world leader in the management of diversities"* (Diversity and inclusion, Corporate website). Broadly speaking, diversity is often presented as an intrinsic characteristic of the French group. *"Diversity is embedded into L'Oréal Group's DNA"* (Diversity and inclusion, Careers Website). In other words, diversity is seen as a part of L'Oréal's culture: *"Human is at the heart of L'Oréal's corporate culture and we have long been convinced that team diversity is a key to our success"* (Diversity in HR at L'Oréal, Diversity Website). Overall, these arguments converge to legitimate the fact that L'Oréal is well placed to have a discourse about diversity and related issues.

Discussion

The purpose of this study was to critically analyze the discourse on diversity of a multinational company. Our results first show how diversity is defined by corporate communication and some leaders and executives either in general and implicit terms or, more frequently, in social and demographic terms. More specifically, we demonstrated that L'Oréal's definition of diversity is based on three sociodemographic characteristics: gender, disability, and origins.

This clearly illustrates how the discursive construction of diversity operates. By considering a limited number of sociodemographic characteristics, this vision understates, or even excludes, the importance of other commonly discussed dimensions of diversity, such as sexual orientation for instance. This vision of diversity and the associated categories are never questioned nor justified in L'Oréal's discourse, suggesting that they are self-evident.

This naturalization of the definition of diversity also results in an essentialization of identities (Zanoni et al. 2010). Diversity-related categories are considered as homogeneous, and individuals falling in those categories are considered as representatives of specific social groups (even if people in question may not define themselves as members of the social groups). L'Oréal's diversity policy partly consists in addressing the specific needs of those groups. Heterogeneity within those groups is neglected and L'Oréal's discourse provides a monolithic view of their members.

Our results add up to a number of existing—mainly conceptual—studies (Zanoni et al. 2010), by clearly showing the language mechanisms behind this essentialization of identities. We noticed that such essentialization mainly occurred through a process of labelling, that is, naming individuals with broad denominations. This creates a depersonalization, as the terms used tend to homogenize the "diverse" workforce. Such process is very similar to stereotyping, because labels ignore the uniqueness of individuals and tend to paint all members of a group with the same brush.

Our results also show that different discursive frameworks do coexist in the discourse on diversity of a multinational corporation. Such discourse is first rationalistic. Diversity management thus appears as a necessity, both to adapt to the global business environment and to take advantage of the positive effects of a diverse workforce. This shows how global capitalism, as discourse relying on economic and managerial rationale (Fairclough 1999; Tienari et al. 2003), pervades all aspects of MNCs, including the softest aspects. This also converges with the critiques that some scholars made regarding the instrumentality of diversity management. Discourse on diversity is also societal. The focus is on the company and the central position of MNCs at the forefront of broad societal issues such as disabilities, aging, gender equality, and so on. Last but not least, discourse is appropriative and self-legitimating. Not only does the company and its executives' discourse advance specific meanings of diversity, but by doing so they also reconstruct and reaffirm the idea that they represent a legitimate voice for addressing this issue. As already noted by some critical authors, *"diversity is enjoined as a symbolic currency to advance a [...] reality that reaffirms speakers' right to speak"* (Zanoni and Janssens 2015, p. 1478; see also Alvesson and Willmott 2002; Phillips and Hardy 1997).

The three types of discourse are interlocked in corporate communication. Considered globally, these discursive frameworks picture diversity in a very plastic manner, one that is likely to create a sense of legitimacy for the various stakeholders. Diversity discourse depicts a company where human matters, and the specificities of the one and the others are deemed crucial. This is likely to result in positive evaluations from employees. Diversity discourse also reinforces the customer orientation of the organization, and underlines the attention that it pays to a thorough understanding of its customer base. This orientation, as well as other aspects of rationalistic discourse, also contributes to create a sense of legitimacy for shareholders and other stakeholders that might be preoccupied with the economic performance of the firm. Finally, the societal dimension of diversity discourse also helps legitimizing the multinational corporation to the civil society. It clearly positions the firm in the social sphere, at the heart of broad societal challenges, and contributes to make it responsible in the eyes of civic stakeholders.

References

Alvesson, M., & Willmott, H. (2002). Identity Regulation as Organizational Control: Producing the Appropriate Individual. *Journal of Management Studies, 39*(5), 619–644.

Answorth, S., & Hardy, C. (2004). Critical Discourse Analysis and Identity: Why Bother? *Critical Discourse Studies, 1*(2), 22–259.

Basu, K., & Palazzo, G. (2008). Corporate Social Responsibility: A Process Model of Sensemaking. *Academy of Management Review, 33*(1), 122–136.

Blommaert, J., & Verschueren, J. (1998). *Debating Diversity: Analysing the Discourse of Tolerance*. London: Routledge.

Bourdieu, P., & Nice, R. (1977). *Outline of a Theory of Practice*. Cambridge: Cambridge University Press.

Castelló, I., & Lozano, J. M. (2011). Searching for New Forms of Legitimacy Through Corporate Responsibility Rhetoric. *Journal of Business Ethics, 100*(1), 11–19.

du Gay, P. (1996). *Consumption and Identity at Work*. London: SAGE Publications.

Elsbach, K. D. (1994). Managing Organizational Legitimacy in the California Cattle Industry: The Construction and Effectiveness of Verbal Accounts. *Administrative Science Quarterly, 39*(1), 57–88.

Erkama, N., & Vaara, E. (2010). Struggles Over Legitimacy in Global Organizational Restructuring: A Rhetorical Perspective on Legitimation Strategies and Dynamics in a Shutdown Case. *Organization Studies, 31*(7), 813–839.

Fairclough, N. (1992). *Discourse and Social Change* (259 p). Reprinted. Cambridge Polity Press.

Fairclough, N. (1997). *Critical Discourse Analysis: The Critical Study of Language*. London: Longman.

Fairclough, N. (1999). Global Capitalism and Critical Awareness of Language. *Language Awareness, 8*(2), 71–83.

Fairclough, N. (2005). Peripheral Vision Discourse Analysis in Organization Studies: The Case for Critical Realism. *Organization Studies, 26*(6), 915–939.

Fairclough, N., & Wodak, R. (1997). Critical Discourse Analysis. In T. van Dijk (Ed.), *Discourse as Social Interaction* (pp. 258–284). London: SAGE Publications.

Garnsey, E., & Rees, B. (1996). Discourse and Enactment: Gender Inequality in Text and Context. *Human Relations, 49*(8), 1041–1064.

Gergen, K. J. (2001). *Social Construction in Context*. London: SAGE Publications.

Gilbert, J. A., Stead, B. A., & Ivancevich, J. M. (1999). Diversity Management: A New Organizational Paradigm. *Journal of Business Ethics, 21*(1), 61–76.

Harrison, D. A., & Klein, K. J. (2007). What's the Difference? Diversity Constructs as Separation, Variety, or Disparity in Organizations. *Academy of Management Review, 32*(4), 1199–1228.

Johnston, W., & Packer, A. (1987). *Workforce 2000: Work and Workers for the Twenty-First Century*. Indianapolis: Hudson Institute.

Joutsenvirta, M., & Vaara, E. (2015). Legitimacy Struggles and Political Corporate Social Responsibility in International Settings: A Comparative Discursive Analysis of a Contested Investment in Latin America. *Organization Studies, 36*(6), 741–777.

Klarsfeld, A. (2009). The Diffusion of Diversity Management: The Case of France. *Scandinavian Journal of Management, 25*(4), 363–373.

Leitch, S., & Palmer, I. (2010). Analysing Texts in Context: Current Practices and New Protocols for Critical Discourse analysis in Organization Studies. *Journal of Management Studies, 47*(6), 1194–1212.

Lorbiecki, A., & Jack, G. (2000). Critical Turns in the Evolution of Diversity Management. *British Journal of Management, 11*(s1), S17–S31.

Lowery, M. (1995). The War on Equal Opportunity. *Black Enterprise, 27*(7), 148–154.

Matten, D., & Crane, A. (2005). Corporate Citizenship: Toward an Extended Theoretical Conceptualization. *Academy of Management Review, 30*(1), 166179.

Palazzo, G., & Scherer, A. G. (2006). Corporate Legitimacy as Deliberation: A Communicative Framework. *Journal of Business Ethics, 66*(1), 71–88.

Patriotta, G., Gond, J.-P., & Schultz, F. (2011). Maintaining Legitimacy: Controversies, Orders of Worth, and Public Justifications: Maintaining Legitimacy. *Journal of Management Studies, 48*(8), 1804–1836.

Phillips, N., & Hardy, C. (1997). Managing Multiple Identities: Discourse, Legitimacy and Resources in the UK Refugee System. *Organization, 4*(2), 159–185.

Phillips, N., Lawrence, T. B., & Hardy, C. (2004). Discourse and Institutions. *The Academy of Management Review, 29*(4), 635–652.

Prasad, P., & Mills, A. J. (1997). From Showcase to Shadow: Understanding the Dilemmas of Managing Workplace Diversity. In P. Prasad, A. J. Mills, M. B. Elmes, & A. Prasad (Eds.), *Managing the Organizational Melting Pot: Dilemmas of Workplace Diversity* (pp. 3–27). London: SAGE Publications.

Riach, K. (2007). "Othering" Older Worker Identity in Recruitment. *Human Relations, 60*(11), 1701–1726.

Scherer, A. G., & Palazzo, G. (2011). The New Political Role of Business in a Globalized World: A Review of a New Perspective on CSR and Its Implications for the Firm, Governance, and Democracy. *Journal of Management Studies, 48*(4), 899–931.

Siltaoja, M. E., & Onkila, T. J. (2013). Business in Society or Business and Society: The Construction of Business–Society Relations in Responsibility Reports from a Critical Discursive Perspective. *Business Ethics: A European Review, 22*(4), 357–373.

Tienari, J., Vaara, E., & Björkman, I. (2003). Global Capitalism Meets National Spirit Discourses in Media Texts on a Cross-Border Acquisition. *Journal of Management Inquiry, 12*(4), 377–393.

Trethewey, A. (1999). Disciplined Bodies: Women's Embodied Identities at Work. *Organization Studies, 20*(3), 423–450.

Vaara, E. (2006). Pulp and Paper Fiction: On the Discursive Legitimation of Global Industrial Restructuring. *Organization Studies, 27*(6), 789–810.

Vaara, E., & Monin, P. (2010). A Recursive Perspective on Discursive legitimation and Organizational Action in Mergers and Acquisitions. *Organization Science, 21*(1), 3–22.

Vaara, E., & Tienari, J. (2002). Justification, Legitimization and Naturalization of Mergers and Acquisitions: A Critical Discourse Analysis of Media Texts. *Organization, 9*(2), 275–304.

Vaara, E., & Tienari, J. (2008). A Discursive Perspective on Legitimation Strategies in Multinational Corporations. *Academy of Management Review, 33*(4), 985–993.

Vaara, E., & Tienari, J. (2010). On the Narrative Construction of Multinational Corporations: An Antenarrative Analysis of Legitimation and Resistance in a Cross-Border Merger. *Organization Science, 22*(2), 370–390.

van Dijk, T. (1993). *Elite Discourse and Racism.* Newbury Park: SAGE Publications.

van Dijk, T. (1995). Discourse Analysis as Ideology Analysis. *Language and Peace, 10*, 47–142.

Vince, R., & Booth, C. (1996). *Equalities and Organizational Design.* Luton: Local Government Management Board.

Zanoni, P., & Janssens, M. (2004). Deconstructing Difference: The Rhetoric of Human Resource Managers' Diversity Discourses. *Organization Studies, 25*(1), 55–74.

Zanoni, P., & Janssens, M. (2015). The Power of Diversity Discourses at Work: On the Interlocking Nature of Diversities and Occupations. *Organization Studies, 36*(11), 1463–1483.

Zanoni, P., Janssens, M., Benschop, Y., & Nkomo, S. (2010). Guest Editorial: Unpacking Diversity, Grasping Inequality: Rethinking Difference Through Critical Perspectives. *Organization, 17*(1), 9–29.

Zilber, T. B. (2002). Institutionalization as an Interplay Between Actions, Meanings, and Actors: The Case of a Rape Crisis Center in Israel. *Academy of Management Journal, 45*(1), 234–254.

Zilber, T. B. (2006). The Work of the Symbolic in Institutional Processes: Translations of Rational Myths in Israeli High Tech. *Academy of Management Journal, 49*(2), 281–303.

7

Aesthetic CSR Communication: A Global Perspective on Organizational Art Collections

Angela Bargenda

Introduction

While business ethics and corporate social responsibility (CSR) have received growing attention in the twentieth century, organizational aesthetics (OA) has mainly gained momentum in the twenty-first century (Biehl-Missal 2011, pp. 8–9). Largely discussed as a supportive and peripheral function of business activity, aesthetics has only recently emerged as a strategic component of organizational life. Berleant was among the first to consider that art collections, artist-led interventions, and the overall aestheticization of the work environment create an immediate, direct, and unified relationship with an organization (Berleant 1970, 1993, 2010).

Aesthetic artifacts build a positive brand image (Popoli 2011), promote sustainability (Waistell 2016), afford sensory perceptions (Strati 2000a), create values of sensemaking and mindfulness (Barry and Meisiek 2010), and enhance a firm's competitiveness and reputation (Orlitzky et al. 2011).

Barry and Meisiek (2010) show how the concept of *workarts* positively affects managerial practices and organizational identity. Biehl-Missal (2011, 2013) demonstrates how organizational artifacts create an atmosphere conducive to emotional and cognitive responses. While Wu (2002) shows the

A. Bargenda (✉)
ESCE International Business School, Paris, France
e-mail: angela.bargenda@esce.fr

increasing privatization of art, Bargenda's (2014) study on the aesthetics of finance provides insights into the meaning-generating properties of art collections in the banking sector.

Nissley (1999) explores the display of artwork as reflective of changes in management practices. Doherty (2009) discusses organizational arts within a historical perspective and advocates the incorporation of arts and organizational aesthetics into management studies.

This chapter is inspired by Waistell's (2016) study on the promotion of sustainability through environmental aesthetics, as it seeks to connect aesthetics with ethics.

Positioned within the emerging field of organizational aesthetics (OA), the interrelatedness of artistic artifacts with issues of corporate sustainability (CS) is critically examined. In doing so, the chapter seeks to widen the scope of extant sustainability literature by integrating the underrepresented field of OA. The chapter makes the argument that artwork in the organizational environment critically determines the outcome of triple bottom line (TBL) policies. By suggesting the strategic relevance of aesthetics in the sector of CS, the contribution opens up new perspectives for researchers and managers.

It is argued that the role of aesthetics goes beyond ancillary and decorative functions, as art collections support social TBL objectives. The following research question is therefore addressed: "How do aesthetic artifacts and arts-based initiatives promote socially responsible CS in the context of global finance?"

The chapter's theoretical groundings are based on interdisciplinary scholarship. It first features an overview of aesthetic theory, which serves to advance the understanding of the visual arts as a sensemaking vehicle. After a presentation of Berleant's (1970) and Strati's (2000b) conceptualizations of organizational aesthetics, the concept of CS is discussed. Then, aesthetic communication strategies of major global banks are presented and analyzed. Finally, critical thoughts and future perspectives discuss challenges and forward-thinking viewpoints on the aestheticization of the organizational environment.

Organizational Aesthetics (OA)

Aesthetics is concerned with sensory perception, judgment, affect, and feeling of artifacts and natural environments (Strati 2000a). Based on the perception and appreciation of the beautiful in art and nature (Strati 1999), aesthetics is a complex and polysemic concept, with a "complicated, heterogeneous, conflicted and disordered genealogy" (Shusterman 2006, p. 237). Aesthetics is different from art, in that it provides a way to appreciate art through the senses and to facilitate our understanding of reality, offering a perspective and testimony, representation and argumentation (Young 2001).

In the organizational environment, colors, logo design, office layout, decoration, architecture, smells, floor plans, and so on create particular atmospheric conditions that are perceived through the senses and impact engagement, motivation, and "feelings of emotional well-being" (Panagopoulos 2009). The focus of this chapter lies on the aesthetics of artworks in the organizational environment, as this area remains vastly undertheorized in management literature. The transformative power of art, expanding the vision and the way we see the world (Cavell 1995), infuses new thinking and alters perceptions and attitudes (Hepburn 1984).

Objects of art are subjectively experienced by stakeholders such as employees, business partners, local communities, clients, and so on. Given that the imaginative association between the arts and the organization derives from culturized modes of reception, the twofold process of local culture and global reach offers challenging opportunities when incorporating the arts in international organizations.

Corporate Social Responsibility (CSR) and Corporate Sustainability (CS)

Corporate social responsibility (CSR) is defined as "actions that appear to further some social good, beyond the interests of the firm and that which is required by law" (McWilliams and Siegel 2001, p. 117). As a sub-category of CSR, corporate sustainability (CS) has not yet been conceptualized within a common definitional frame (Orlitzky et al. 2011), as it "means different things to different companies and different stakeholders" (Searcy and Buslovich 2014, p. 167).

The concept of corporate sustainability (CS) encompasses social, environmental, and economic aspects of the triple bottom line (TBL) (Bilgin 2009), as a "tridimensional construct that includes environmental, economic, and social dimensions" (Montiel 2008, p. 254). Stipulating that companies take into consideration environmental and social impacts when setting economic objectives (Strand 2014), businesses are seen as social systems that are connected to society at large (Zollo et al. 2013). CS "seeks to balance social concerns with environmental concerns" (Shrivastava and Kennelly 2013, p. 86).

With a "variety of sustainability worldviews" (Stubbs and Cocklin 2008, p. 104), the term lacks a common definition. Thus, "CS-related terms such as sustainable development, sustainable business, or sustainability" are "used differently in the management literature" (Montiel and Delgado-Ceballos 2014, p. 123). There is even an "ambiguity about whether CS should be a tridimensional construct (economic, social, and environmental), a bidimensional one (social and environmental), or a synonym for environmental management," although "a large proportion of scholars agree on the definition that encompasses economic, social, and environmental dimensions" (Montiel and Delgado-Ceballos 2014, p. 123).

Considering that sustainability generally includes social and ecological systems and provides meaning and value (Jennings and Zandbergen 1995), organizations promote sustainability values to alter attitudes, actions, and behaviors (Starik and Rands 1995). In this perspective, sustainability can be strategically used to provide benefits to a firm (Husted and Salazar 2006).

One such strategic tool to achieve organizational sustainability targets consists of the implementation of arts-based methods. We heed the call that "greater progress might be possible if researchers started to focus more on specific dimensions of CSR" (Orlitzky et al. 2011, p. 9). The focus on the arts, aesthetics, and artifacts in the advancement of CSR objectives is central for Shrivastava et al. (2012, p. 23) arguing that "we can get better action and behavioral commitments to sustainability by using the arts, art-based methods, and aesthetics to develop passion and emotional connection for sustainable organizing."

Artwork and artistic philanthropy are considered to be part of integrated CSR policies (Leclair and Gordon 2000). The Business Committee for the Arts, established in 1966 to encourage support for a range of cultural activities by businesses, claims that support for the arts "… can provide a company with extensive publicity and advertising, a bright public reputation, and an improved corporate image. It can build better customer relations; a nimble acceptance of company products […]. Promotion of the arts can improve the morale of employees and help attract qualified personnel" (David Rockefeller quoted in King and Levin 2006, p. 10).

In a CSR perspective, philanthropic engagement with the arts is motivated by reputational and image-related benefits, the increased performance of employees, and workplace attractiveness. Access to foreign markets and public relations opportunities are additional positive outcomes of investment in the arts (Buckley 2005). In a promotional perspective, support for the arts ranks with other advertising expenditures, rather than the community investment budget (Moore 1995, p. 176).

Philanthropic initiatives in the arts are driven by a community-based view, where donations to arts organizations are aligned with a larger stakeholder approach and support for other causes, such as homelessness and educational programs (Scott and Lane 2000). In this sense, Porter and Kramer (2002) encourage more corporate giving to improve the environment in which firms operate.

Therefore, contrary to a museum-like setting, aesthetic artifacts in the organizational environment transcend the gratuitous mode of art for art's sake. Their presence results from a strategic objective to associate the organization with a noble cause. Responsible organizations demonstrate and communicate the social components of TBL standards through art sponsorship and collections, as the aesthetic experience per se generates goodwill and a positive behavioral response. Extending on the scant scholarship that incorporates aesthetics and arts into CS literature (Waistell 2016; Shrivastava 2012; Shrivastava et al. 2012), this chapter analyzes the role of art collections in the CSR practices of global finance sectors.

Aesthetic Communication Strategies of Global Banks

An empirical study was conducted at the headquarters and main branches of global banking institutions from 2011 to 2016. Site-specific data was collected in interviews with practitioners, archival research, and internal documents, such as promotional material, brochures, posters, flyers, advertising images, and art-related giveaways (calendars, postcards, etc.). Personal one-to-one interviews were conducted with professionals such as directors of art collections and corporate museums, artists prominently represented in the collections, branch managers, marketing and communication managers, heads of heritage, and directors of historic archives.

The selection of banks was based on the relevance and scope of their art collections, strategic use of artistic artifacts for managerial and communicational objectives, explicit commitment to CSR, diversity of the acquisition and curatorial policies, as well as artistic variety of works collected (epochs and styles, media, and modes of exhibition). The shortcomings of this selection process concern the fact that the sample is not exhaustive and that data collected might be biased by the semi-structured interview format.

The analysis of the interviews conducted with practitioners is based on a coding process of salient lexical elements following Thietart (1999, pp. 502–503) to crystallize organizational logics, values, and beliefs associated with arts-based CSR practices.

Insights into Financial Aesthetics

Data was collected from the following globally operating banks (Table 7.1):

The selection of banks is based on the fact that they share a common strategic approach to the arts and therefore represent a variety of arts-based practices. This allowed for the inclusion of a representative panel of the type of art collected. The study thus features art collections that range from medieval works to contemporary video installations, encompassing all major periods and artistic expressions throughout art history.

Société Générale

When moving its headquarters from the historic building in the city center of Paris to La Défense business district in 1995, Société Générale started an art collection for practical reasons. Indeed, the initial purpose of the collection was purely decorative, as the postmodern high-rise buildings should be made appealing to employees while their work environment was changing. Gradually, the art collection has received a higher meaning and a symbolic dimension in the transition from the historic building to postmodern aesthetics.

Change represents a moment of destabilization and anxiety for employees and the incarnation of organizational identity through the art project's stability and reference. Artwork serves as a vector to create enthusiasm and adhesion (Frèches 2005, p. 173), while also offering new managerial opportunities for team-building and training in creativity and innovation. The transition from the historic headquarters to the high-rise buildings was facilitated by the emotional value provided by artwork in the new environment. For example, the awkward-looking elephant statue by Barry Flanagan in the lobby of the new headquarters of Société Générale has become a mascot and an affective reference point for many employees. The bronze statue represents an inward-turned elephant in an abnormal position, expressing the artist's questioning of traditional views on sculpture. Flanagan wants to make people

Table 7.1 Studied cases

Institution	Country	City
Société Générale	France	Paris
Banca Monte dei Paschi di Siena	Italy	Siena
UBS	Switzerland	Zurich and Lucerne
Deutsche Bank	Germany	Berlin

laugh, but in an environment driven by financial performance and high-achieving executives, the elephant also articulates the fragility and uncertainties of an animal that refuses to step forward. The researcher observed that employees maintain an affectionate relationship with this statue, caressing it when walking by and meeting with co-workers by the elephant.

A touch of fantasy and imagination pervades the entire office towers of the bank, as artwork is exhibited in all offices, conference rooms, hallways, the cafeteria, and auditoriums in the headquarters at La Défense. The collection features contemporary abstract art, photography, and sculpture from the 1960s onwards.

The art collection also fulfills promotional needs in the various cause-related marketing campaigns launched by the bank to articulate its societal commitment. Advertising campaigns communicate external exhibition venues in French and global museums. Together with arts sponsorship, the art collection serves as a marketing tool, a practice that started in the 1980s (Wu 2002). However, in France, arts-based initiatives have so far been underused for marketing and sales promotions, as it has long been considered taboo to instrumentalize the arts for commercial purposes (Frèches 2005, p. 202).

When interviewed about the relationship between aesthetics and ethics, the manager of the art collection insisted on the importance of a meaning-generating communication and managerial activities that accompany the display of the works, as the artwork alone does not suffice to implement a CSR momentum. For example, the bank provides a bilingual website dedicated to the collection, which makes the work accessible to global audiences (see http://www.collectionsocietegenerale.com/en/). It also features valuable extras, such as virtual guided tours presented by art historians, who provide information about the artists, styles, materials, epoch, and relevance of the art. This educational supplement connects the artwork with CSR parameters, as it furthers knowledge about the arts and promotes social good.

Banca Monte dei Paschi di Siena (MPS)

The beginnings of the art collection of Banca Monte dei Paschi di Siena (MPS) go back to the fifteenth century, concomitant with the bank's foundation in 1472. According to the bank's official communication, "the first art works were created especially to give luster and fame to the institution at the time of its foundation and on the occasion of important dates in its history" (www.mps.it). The collection comprises about 800 works of medieval Sienese art, including sculptures, drawings, furniture, and decorative objects, making it the world's largest private collection of the Sienese school (Green 1991).

Toward the end of the sixteenth century, the bank commissioned a work from Lorenzo Rustici to commemorate the reform conducted by Cosimo de' Medici in 1568, which transformed Monte Pio from a charitable organization into a commercial bank. In 1644, the bank ceased its arts commissioning activity with a last work by Rafaello Vanni. Interestingly, 300 years later, in the year 2000, it resumed its commitment to the arts by commissioning a work from Italian artist Valerio Adami.

The narrative of the piece reveals a renewed emphasis on the values of social sustainability and altruism in the twenty-first century. The piece symbolically articulates the bank's historic foundation as a defender of local farmers against usury and shows the milestones of the organizational development. Thus, artwork projects the bank's corporate identity and societal commitment and has become a strategic tool for internal and external communication. The interviewed communication manager emphasized the values of history and tradition that are communicated by the works of art displayed in offices and reception rooms, but also in a dedicated exhibition space.

These art galleries are supplemented by conference venues and historic archives, which further serve to promote the works and artists of the collection. The collection is instrumentalized as an expressive device to tell the story of the bank, to visualize its heritage, and to signal the bank's function as a cultural player. This meta-discursive referentiality correlates societal values and financial interests in a value-laden network, where works of art interact with each other, the bank, and the cultural life of the city. The collection thus constitutes a strategic, meaning-generating device to connect the bank with its local origins.

The collection's acquisition and curatorial policies are entirely based on local Sienese artists. When opening global subsidiaries, the bank displays works of ancient Sienese art to international audiences. For example, when opening an office on Park Avenue in New York, MPS sponsored an exhibit of fifteenth-century Sienese art at the Metropolitan Museum of Art, including works from its collection. In Paris, the bank displays reproductions from its collection in the windows of its branch in the Opéra district. The identity generated by this global bank is derived from the reputational capital of ancient Sienese art. International elites recognize the outstanding artistic achievements of its local culture of origin, associating the bank with values such as longevity, solidity, and performance at the highest level. This association is further explicitly supported by the slogan *Banking is Art*, frequently used in global advertising campaigns.

UBS

The *UBS Art Collection* comprises about 30,000 works of modern and contemporary artists largely from Europe and North America.

Founded in 2004, it resulted from UBS' merger with the US investment bank PaineWebber, whose CEO Donald Marron had been an avid art collector since the 1970s. Marron believed the dynamics of financial markets and artistic creativity bear similarities. To him, Wall Street is a business where the anticipation of the future is a key success factor, which can be reinforced by the presence of inspiring contemporary art (Marron in Pollack 2005).

With the post-merger expansion to emerging markets, works of art from Asia and Latin America have been increasingly incorporated in the collection to represent the cultural and social scope of the 50 countries in which the bank operates.

UBS claims to pursue a responsible stakeholder approach through its aesthetic CSR strategy, frequently lending works from the collection to museums all over the world, as "owning these outstanding works of art implies the responsibility to show and share them—with our clients, our employees, our shareholders, the communities in which we work and everybody else who is interested and passionate about art" (www.ubs.com). In 2008, masterpieces of the UBS collection were exhibited at the MORI Art Museum in Tokyo in an unusual museography, using real-life working environments, like cubicles, meeting rooms, recreational areas, and computers to "create the feeling of a working office within the space of the museum" (Kataoka 2008, p. 26). Visitors could immerse into the authentic working environment of a UBS employee and bond with the organization on a personal level. This symbiotic relationship, where the office space is museumized and the museum mimics the office environment, is reflective of the long-term objective to firmly establish art in the social, private, and professional context by giving it "a position within life and society" (Mori 2008, p. 43).

Thus, the pluralistic functions of the art collection include managerial purposes, such as group cohesion and organizational culture in the aftermath of a global merger, but also to establish the bank's legitimacy in core business areas. For example, through its sponsorship of international museums and art fairs, such as Art Basel Miami, the bank positions itself as a prime player in the art market, offering services ranging from acquisition advice to authentication and certification of artwork, art education, estimates, and guided tours. The specialists of *UBS Art Banking* note that "as the main sponsor of Art Basel, we can offer *Art Banking* clients exclusive access to the most interesting pieces during that preselection phase. In this regard, we are now in a very advantageous position and other banks envy us for it" (Amberg and Bouvrot 2008, p. 4).

In sum, the *UBS Art Collection* combines various organizational objectives: it enhances reputational capital, generates a socially responsible image, differentiates the bank as a cultural player, makes room for emotions and humanity in a mostly technical business sector, builds quality stakeholder relationships, and legitimizes expertise in the emerging asset class of art investment.

Deutsche Bank

Within the context of globally operating banks, Deutsche Bank has formulated an organizational response to the postmodern quest for creativity, personal expression, and spiritual meaning by positioning itself as the *Kunstbank*—the *Artbank*. The art collection owned by Deutsche Bank is currently the largest corporate art collection in the world. Motivated by the conviction that contemporary art fosters the development of innovation and creative dialogue, forecasts social phenomena, and inspires different models of thought, the collection was started in 1979 as a "spiritual dividend" (Grigoteit 2004, p. 4).

Through the *Art Works* program, bank offices and conference rooms in branches around the world are adorned with works of art from the collection. As determined by curatorial choices, works on paper represent the collection's privileged medium. This is due to the experimental nature of paper, with drafts and ideas reflecting the earliest conceptual stages of the creative process. Furthermore, paper refers to the material support of banknotes, thereby connecting the bank's core activity to its artwork. Pieces from young artists of a culturally and geographically diverse background are regularly commissioned. The bank also grants residence fellowships for artists at the Villa Romana in Florence. Deutsche Bank supports museum projects around the world and donates works from its collection. For example, a donation of 600 works was made to the Städel Museum in Frankfurt.

In 1997, the bank set up a unique joint venture with the Guggenheim Museum, resulting in the dual commercial and creative enterprise of *Deutsche Guggenheim*. The "deutsche" refers to "Deutsche Bank," not the word "German," as the name was chosen on purpose to promote the sponsor. This innovative concept marked the beginning of a new era in the field of arts philanthropy, as new synergies between capitalistic and cultural organizations were created. The choice of the Guggenheim Museum as a prestigious global partner was motivated by multiple reasons: the Guggenheim family's Prussian origins culturally link the family name to the city of Berlin, the shared curatorial emphasis on contemporary art, the museum's global network and international visibility, its openness to partnerships with commercial institutions, as well as the Guggenheim Museum's cultured global audience. Political and historical factors also influenced this particular partnership, as the Americans wanted to "leave something behind" (Cowell 1997, p. 2) when they withdrew their troops from Berlin at the end of the Cold War in 1993.

The collaboration of 15 years between the Guggenheim Museum and Deutsche Bank came to an end in 2013, when Deutsche Bank started to use the exhibition gallery to display art from its own collection of more than 56,000 works. Henceforth called KunstHalle, the new venue has now become an artistic reference within the museumscape of Berlin.

Aesthetic Responsibility in the Global Environment

The arts-inspired CSR practices of global banks show the relevance of aesthetic artifacts as key components in the image-driven postmodern society. Art is the new mode of expression in corporate communication, reflecting ideological values through the synthesis of culture and capital. As aesthetic artifacts fulfill CSR objectives, they transcend decorative purposes and align with business strategy and marketing objectives. Used in internal and corporate communication, much like innovative management techniques, artwork contributes sustainable, socially relevant, and meaning-generating values to organizations. Artwork impacts the working habits of people by stimulating dialogue and new thinking, fostering creativity, and enhancing well-being. Through intuitive perceptions, new patterns of thought emerge through interpretive processes that vary from habitual business processes (Freeman et al. 2015).

Artwork also establishes transversal links with other areas of the humanities, such as history, literature, religion, and politics. Potentially, artwork humanizes the financial sector and therefore facilitates the restoration of trust, credibility, and legitimacy.

All practitioners interviewed have identified image and reputational issues as essential areas of concern. The atmospheric condition, that is, the perceived pleasantness of the working environment, also ranks high in the managerial priorities of the banks, for employees' well-being and the creation of social identity are enhanced by the presence of artworks.

When engaging in and building relationships with the arts world, banks build cultural stewardship in a context-dependent local environment, as much as on a global scale. In fact, through their art initiatives, they acquire global cultural competencies that promote organizational identity. This benefit is especially valuable in the case of mergers as a means to integrate contrasting organizational cultures. Aesthetic responsibility is also achieved through cultural philanthropy, arts-inclusive practices, conferences and workshops, museum visits, and artist-led managerial training. These practices transcend the merely decorative function of art by making a sustainable impact on social identity and interaction between organizations and communities.

Critical Views

Nevertheless, the appropriation of the arts for organizational purposes could create ambiguous outcomes. On the one hand, the social acceptance and recognition of art positively connotes an image of organizations that engage in artistic initiatives. On the other hand, stakeholders expect more than the accumulation of compelling artworks and the publicity-generating promotion of artists. In addition, the suspicion of collecting and showcasing contemporary artists to increase their visibility and price in the global art market could compromise the positive connotation of corporate art collections.

The breach in the social status and public acceptance of art is reinforced by potential misinterpretations due to the polysemic meaning of most contemporary artistic creation. In the banking sector, the acquisition of art used to be governed by conservative policies, placing the aesthetic focus mainly on consensual classicism to express values of stability, strength, security, and speed (Schroeder 2003). While some banks, such as MPS and UBS, still pursue this conventional acquisition policy, others have adopted an overtly provocative strategy.

These unsettling, mostly conceptual works might destabilize habitual mental patterns and organizational processes. They symbolically signal disrupture and radical change (Ullrich 2000, p. 28), thereby intimidating employees and other viewers (Hutter 2010, p. 155). Researchers note that top managers could purposefully select these controversial works, as they break free from tradition, continuity, and routine operations, thereby fostering creativity and change. This could cause a sense of exclusion with some categories of employees who lack the tools to understand and interpret the contemporary artworks in their office environment (Biehl-Missal 2011).

Furthermore, the political dimension of arts initiatives is stressed by Useem (1984), who argues that corporate power-elites have vested interests with cultural organizations. Similarly, DiMaggio and Powell (2000) attribute corporate arts initiatives to the social standing they confer to top executives, while Himmelstein notes that corporate philanthropy "presumes a political vision, a tacit understanding about the nature of [...] society and the role of large corporations within it" (Himmelstein 1997, p. 2). Therefore, the use and function of art in the organizational environment remains a divisive issue. The interviews suggested that employees do not unanimously adhere to arts initiatives. For example, some considered that the money spent on artwork should rather be used for salary increases, as employees could not recognize the value of the art displayed in their place of work.

Concluding Remarks

The postmodern proclivity toward the aestheticization of the environment offers new CSR challenges and opportunities for organizations. When engaging in the arts, new organizational discourses and practices emerge that link the iconographic, decorative function of art to a deeper-seeded societal objective. Especially in the finance sector, the integration of arts-based initiatives, such as art collections, philanthropy, artist-led training programs, conferences, workshop visits, and volunteer programs, have become significant managerial and communicational tools. According to the specific organizational culture and values, these practices either stand for tradition, permanence, and legitimacy or signal change, openness, innovation, and flexibility (Ullrich 2000, p. 28). In the changing consumer environment, expectations for CSR initiatives are likely to increase. Culture and the arts still remain underrepresented areas of in-country and global CSR programs, but they do offer significant internal and external outcomes in forward-thinking business strategies.

Future Perspectives

The motivation behind arts-based CSR initiatives might not be solely driven by organizational outcomes. Further research could explore varying motivational factors, such as executive motivations (Baron 2001; Swanson 1995), behind artistic initiatives. In addition, the present conceptual and exploratory approach could be supplemented by a quantitative study of employees and clients. The empirical data used for this chapter was generated from interviews with practitioners, top executives, and artists who might defend a biased view with regard to the acceptance of artistic CSR policies at their respective organizations. It would therefore be worthwhile exploring in greater detail how arts initiatives are received by stakeholders. Research into the reception side of art collections could therefore contribute valuable additional viewpoints on aesthetic CSR communication.

References

Amberg, P., & Bouvrot, A. (2008). Art Collectors Need a Partner They Can Trust. *UBS Art Banking News, 2*(6), 8.
Bargenda, A. (2014). *Communication visuelle dans le secteur bancaire européen, L'Esthétique de la Finance*. Paris: L'Harmattan.
Baron, D. P. (2001). Private Politics, Corporate Social Responsibility and Integrated Strategy. *Journal of Economics and Management Strategy, 10*(1), 7–45.
Barry, D., & Meisiek, S. (2010). Seeing More and Seeing Differently: Sensemaking, Mindfulness, and the Workarts. *Organization Studies, 31*(11), 1505–1530.
Berleant, A. (1970). *The Aesthetic Field: A Phenomenology of Aesthetic Experience*. Springfield: Charles C. Thomas.
Berleant, A. (1993). *Art and Engagement*. Philadelphia: Temple University Press.
Berleant, A. (2010). *Sensibility and Sense: The Aesthetic Transformation of the Human World*. Exeter: Imprint Academic.
Biehl-Missal, B. (2011). *Wirtschaftsästhetik. Wie Unternehmen die Kunst als Inspiration und Werkzeug nutzen*. Wiesbaden: Gabler.
Biehl-Missal, B. (2013). The Atmosphere of the Image: An Aesthetic Concept for Visual Analysis. *Consumption Markets and Culture, 16*(4), 356–367.
Bilgin, M. (2009). The PEARL Model: Gaining Competitive Advantage Through Sustainable Development. *Journal of Business Ethics, 85*(3), 545–554.
Buckley, G. (2005). *Arts and Business Sponsorship Manual* (5th ed.). London: Arts and Business.
Cavell, M. (1995). Taste and Moral Sense. In D. E. W. Fenner (Ed.), *Ethics and the Arts: An Anthology* (pp. 293–302). London: Garland.
Cowell, A. (1997, November 7). New U.S. Sector in Berlin: Little Guggenheim Branch. *New York Times*, Ntl. Edition.
DiMaggio, P. J., & Powell, W. W. (2000). The Iron Cage Revisited Institutional Isomorphism and Collective Rationality in Organizational Fields. In J. A. C. Baum & F. Dobbin (Eds.), *Economics Meets Sociology in Strategic Management* (pp. 143–166). Bingley: Emerald Group Publishing Limited.
Doherty, E. (2009). Management and Art Views of Depression Era Workers: The Need for an Organizational-Arts Perspective. *Management & Organizational History, 4*(1), 5–36.
Frèches, J. (2005). *Art and Cie: L'art est indispensable à l'entreprise*. Paris: Dunod.
Freeman, R. E., Dunham, L., Fairchild, G., & Parmar, B. (2015). Leveraging the Creative Arts in Business Ethics Teaching. *Journal of Business Ethics, 131*(3), 519–526.

Green, T. (1991). From a Pawnshop to Patron of the Arts in Five Centuries. *Smithsonian, 22*(4), 59–69.

Grigoteit, A. (2004). The Art in Deutsche Bank's New Building in Stuttgart. *db-artmag*, Vol. 7. Available from https://db-artmag.com/archiv/2004/e/7/5/276.html. Accessed 3 Dec 2016.

Hepburn, R. W. (1984). *Wonder and Other Essays*. Edinburgh: Edinburgh University Press.

Himmelstein, J. L. (1997). *Looking Good and Doing Good; Corporate Philanthropy and Corporate Power*. Bloomington: Indiana University Press.

Husted, B. W., & Salazar, J. D. J. (2006). Taking Friedman Seriously: Maximizing Profits and Social Performance. *Journal of Management Studies, 43*(1), 75–91.

Hutter, M. (2010). *Wertwechselstrom. Texte zu Kunst und Wirtschaft*. Hamburg: Philo Fine Arts.

Jennings, P. D., & Zandbergen, P. A. (1995). Ecologically Sustainable Organizations: An Institutional Approach. *Academy of Management Review, 20*(4), 1015–1052.

Kataoka, M. (2008). *Art Is for the Spirit. Works from the UBS Art Collection*. Exhibition Catalog, UBS, Zurich.

King, E. A., & Levin, G. (2006). *Ethics and the Visual Arts*. New York: Allworth Press.

Leclair, M. S., & Gordon, K. (2000). Corporate Support for Artistic and Cultural Activities: What Determines the Distribution of Corporate Giving? *Journal of Cultural Economics, 24*(3), 225–241.

McWilliams, A., & Siegel, D. (2001). Corporate Social Responsibility: A Theory of the Firm Perspective. *Academy of Management Review, 26*(1), 117–127.

Montiel, I. (2008). Corporate Social Responsibility and Corporate Sustainability: Separate Pasts, Common Futures. *Organization & Environment, 21*(3), 245–269.

Montiel, I., & Delgado-Ceballos, J. (2014). Defining and Measuring Corporate Sustainability: Are We There Yet? *Organization and Environment, 27*(2), 113–139.

Moore, G. (1995). Corporate Community Investment in the UK – Investment or Atonement? *Business Ethics: A European Review, 4*(3), 171–178.

Mori, Y. (2008). *Making an Art Collection. Art is for the Spirit. Works from the UBS Art Collection*. Exhibition Catalog, UBS, Zurich.

Nissley, N. (1999). *Viewing Corporate Art Through the Paradigmatic Lens of Organizational Symbolism: An Exploratory Study*. Washington, DC: The George Washington University.

Orlitzky, M., Siegel, D. S., & Waldman, D. A. (2011). Strategic Corporate Social Responsibility and Environmental Sustainability. *Business and Society, 50*(1), 6–27.

Panagopoulos, T. (2009). Linking Forestry, Sustainability and Aesthetics. *Ecological Economics, 68*(1), 2485–2489.

Pollack, B. (2005, December). Corporate Power: Branding, Not Buying, Is Smart Business as Corporations Shift Their Focus from Acquiring Art to Supporting It. *Art & Auction*, pp. 114–118.

Popoli, P. (2011). Linking CSR Strategy and Brand Image. Different Approaches in Local and Global Markets. *Marketing Theory, 11*(4), 419–433.

Porter, M. E., & Kramer, M. R. (2002). The Competitive Advantage of Corporate Philanthropy. *Harvard Business Review, 80*(12), 56–68.

Schroeder, J. E. (2003). Architectural Expression in the Electronic Age. In L. M. Scott & R. Batra (Eds.), *Persuasive Imagery: A Consumer Response Perspective* (pp. 349–382). Mahwah: Lawrence Erlbaum.

Scott, S. G., & Lane, V. R. (2000). A Stakeholder Approach to Organizational Identity. *Academy of Management Review, 25*(1), 43–62.

Searcy, C., & Buslovich, R. (2014). Corporate Perspectives on the Development and Use of Sustainability Reports. *Journal of Business Ethics, 121*(2), 149–169.

Shrivastava, P. (2012). Enterprise Sustainability 2.0: Aesthetics of Sustainability. In P. Bansal & A. J. Hoffman (Eds.), *The Oxford Handbook of Business and the Natural Environment* (pp. 630–638). Oxford: Oxford University Press.

Shrivastava, P., & Kennelly, J. J. (2013). Sustainability and Place-Based Enterprise. *Organization and Environment, 26*(1), 83–101.

Shrivastava, P., Ivanaj, V., & Ivanaj, S. (2012). Sustainable Development and the Arts. *International Journal of Technology Management, 60*(1–2), 23–43.

Shusterman, R. (2006). The Aesthetic. *Theory, Culture and Society, 23*(2–3), 237–243.

Starik, M., & Rands, G. P. (1995). Weaving an Integrated Web: Multilevel and Multisystem Perspectives of Ecologically Sustainable Organizations. *Academy of Management Review, 20*(4), 908–935.

Strand, R. (2014). Strategic Leadership of Corporate Sustainability. *Journal of Business Ethics, 123*(4), 687–706.

Strati, A. (1999). *Organization and Aesthetics*. London: SAGE Publications.

Strati, A. (2000a). Putting People in the Picture: Art and Aesthetics in Photography and in Understanding Organizational Life. *Organization Studies, 21*(1), 53–69.

Strati, A. (2000b). The Aesthetic Approach in Organization Studies. In S. Linstead & H. Höpfl (Eds.), *The Aesthetics of Organizing* (pp. 13–34). London: Sage.

Stubbs, W., & Cocklin, C. (2008). Conceptualizing a "Sustainability Business Model". *Organization & Environment, 21*(2), 103–127.

Swanson, D. L. (1995). Addressing a Theoretical Problem by Reorienting the Corporate Social Performance Model. *Academy of Management Review, 20*(1), 43–64.

Thietart, R. A. (1999). *Méthodes de Recherche en Management*. Paris: Éditions Dunod.

Ullrich, W. (2000). *Mit dem Rücken zur Kunst. Die neuen Statussymbols der Macht*. Berlin: Klaus Wagenbach.

Useem, M. (1984). *The Inner Circle, Corporations and the Rise of Business Political Activity in the US and the UK*. New York: Oxford University Press.

Waistell, J. (2016). Can Environmental Aesthetics Promote Corporate Sustainability? *Organization and Environment, 29*(2), 175–193.

Wu, C.-T. (2002). *Privatising Culture: Corporate Art Intervention Since the 1980s*. London: Verso.

Young, J. O. (2001). *Art and Knowledge*. London: Routledge.

Zollo, M., Cennamo, C., & Neumann, K. (2013). Beyond What and Why: Understanding Organizational Evolution Towards Sustainable Enterprise Models. *Organization & Environment, 26*(3), 241–259.

8

Making Multinational Corporations Aware of Their Social Responsibility: Law Versus Reputation?

Benoît Petit

Designed primarily as a moral responsibility, corporate social responsibility (CSR) is a privileged basis from which to question the reputation of multinational companies and thereby to act on their ability to create economic opportunities. In this movement, Law seems relegated to the background, entangled in its difficulties to take over offshore litigation and to reposition the States in a balanced report of power with multinationals. This chapter argues that Law, and specifically "soft law," can consolidate the approach of CSR in its questioning of companies' reputations. Furthermore, and under the condition that it reforms itself, we think that Law can reappear in the foreground of the levers that are available to our societies in order to ensure that multinational companies satisfy social and public interests.

It is generally accepted that Law constitutes the most efficient way to make somebody aware of his/her responsibilities, especially by means of resorting to judicial punishment. However, if one considers the specific situation of multinational corporations, this statement proves to be debatable (Thibierge 2004; Delmas-Marty and Supiot 2015; Jestaz 2016): not only does Law encounter difficulty in seizing extraterritorial disputes, particularly when dealing with ethical, environmental, and/or human rights matters (Corti-Varela 2013; Martin-Chenut and Nord 2016), but the possible sentences that can be pronounced against these corporations seem to be quite useless in the end, if one takes into account their overall financial power.

B. Petit (✉)
University of Versailles, Versailles, France

Simultaneously, the development of the concept of "corporate social responsibility" (CSR) has allowed other ways of making multinational corporations aware of the impacts of their behavior, which are essentially based on the idea of challenging the corporation's reputation (Leroux 2016; Martin-Chenut and Tricot 2016), and consequently their ability to create economic opportunities throughout trust.

Should we therefore infer that Law is sent off the field by reputation management when multinational corporations' ethics are on the agenda? This question is essential, since reputation management has less to do with what is concretely done than with what one wants others to know about their actions and decisions. Law functions under opposite logic.

This notion of reputation is not easy to identify, particularly for businesses. Although an essential intangible asset (Dowling 2002), reputation lacks a definition recognized by all (Walker 2010). Consensus is nevertheless carried out on the principle that a reputation has no accounting value, is intangible and vulnerable, and affects all structures internal to an organization while integrating external factors (Cigref 2012). It generates various perceptions among employees, customers, competitors, investors, and the public on what a business is, what it does and says, and what it represents (Cailleba 2009). Some authors define reputation as the sum of all of the stakeholders' representations of the organization (Fombrun 1996) and, in doing so, describe its ability to produce valued results to them.

In any case, reputation is a perception that concludes with an opinion, which may be positive or negative, and leads to the possibility of establishing a ranking of businesses (Walker 2010). This opinion is built upon the result of all the experiences, beliefs, feelings, knowledge, and impressions from stakeholders, which then constitute an overall perception built from a set of items carried by the company (Boistel 2014). Therefore, reputation is never a neutral signal. It is a continuous and evolving phenomenon that is apprehended differently, based on subjective parameters. Thus, for companies that know their stakeholders well, reputation becomes a strategic issue, a risk that is managed in order to increase trust and economic opportunities.

While not going as far in its understanding of the term—reputation is most often (too) quickly assimilated to that of image—Law apprehends it as the subject of a particularly important protection. It is indeed, in the corporate world, a vital source of creation or destruction of value affecting the attractiveness of brands, and more generally the envy of economic links with the organization. However, legal protections primarily tend only to combat manifestly excessive reputation attacks, especially because Law tries to establish balances with freedom of speech and expression.

We then find ourselves in this odd situation where, except in the case of a manifestly excessive breach, Law seems a priori excluded from this dangerous game consisting, on the one hand, of the company to strategically "shape" its reputation to achieve economic objectives and, on the other hand, of some stakeholders to attack the validity of this representation, from their own subjective approach to the realities.

In other words, we are facing a "war of subjective representations" which largely escapes Law's control, and therefore the social body's control, even though its consequences on our societies are significant and serious. This war is more so fierce that it indulges generally in the field of ethics, that is, on issues that, by nature, import a great deal of subjectivity in them.

Is Law able to mitigate the harmful effects of this "war," particularly by avoiding that the social body that gets manipulated either by the company or its detractors? Throughout its links with the concept of social responsibility, is Law able to impose a little more "social objectivity" in this game of affirmation and cause companies to set responsibilities? To say it more clearly: can Law impose the social body in the role of arbitrator and ensure the respect of a few rules when actors use reputation to try to influence the behavior of companies?

We believe the answer is positive, under certain conditions, particularly if we are defending a broad view of Law, as also constituted by "soft law" (I). We also believe Law can, for the future, develop new levers on this issue (II). These questions will be discussed in this chapter under a conceptual level, more suited to the systemic thinking that arises in Law.

CSR "Soft Law": Using Functional Legitimacies to Affirm or Challenge Reputations

CSR falls completely under what is called "soft law," through the charters, codes of conduct, and other internal standards that a company takes on regarding the subject of ethics, and also by the countless recommendations, repositories, and comments which are edited by external actors on topics of companies' ethics (Mayer 2009; Martin-Chenut and de Quenaudon 2016; Cominetti and Seele 2016; Mazuyer 2017). Therefore, the concept of "soft law" seems relevant to associate Law to a "responsible" use of companies' reputations.

There is a debate around the very notion of "soft law." Two conceptual categories seem to characterize it. On the one hand, the standards are essentially marked by a flexibility of content that is relatively imprecise and indeterminate (in this case, we should rather talk about "fuzzy law"). On the other hand, there is the idea of standards whose main characteristic is to introduce a flexibility in their strength, either mandatory strength (rules formulated without obligation, involving that we evoke "gentle law") or binding strength (rules whose purpose or effect is to create little or no constraint; in this case, we should talk about "weak law") (Thibierge 2003).

In the background of these various normative realities, another more fundamental debate has crystallized to determine whether or not we are actually dealing with rules of law, in the way Kelsen has described them (1934), since their inclusion in this specific category questions the bossy and prescriptive traditional functions of Law.

Refuting the rigid approaches of Law, we consider that the concept of "soft law" introduces the idea of a graduation in the normative force of the law. This idea then brings us to consider that law is made of different textures, each one having a different impact on the conduct of the behaviors of the persons for whom the rules of law apply (Thibierge et al. 2009).

More fundamentally, we believe that the concept of "soft law" has the merit to renew the approach concerning the relationships between social values and the rule of law. Because as long as neither the obligation nor the constraint is imposed as the only determinant markers of what Law is, it is then possible to reconnect with this vision of a legal order whose only purpose is to transcribe in the social order, and with a variable force, what is acceptable or not in a given society; what contributes or not to preserve or strengthen the bonds of solidarity that cement the social body (Ailincai 2017).

In this perspective, the resolution of ethical violations committed by multinational companies takes another turn, particularly when addressing the relationship to the company's reputation. On the legal field, the question becomes: how can "soft law" help to better identify cases where this reputation could be questioned and legitimately blamed by the social body? In this configuration, one wonders whether or not the actions designed to question the reputation of companies are legitimate, or if they are not ultimately a temptation to substitute completely subjective moral orders for the objective legal order. This would be the case if there was no "soft law" at all. But "soft law" exists and has the main effect—according to us—to give birth to more objective judgments of values (and actions arising therefrom) that challenge reputations which traditional law does not always break when they are in contradiction with the acts. It is all a matter of legitimacy surrounding the "soft law" norm.

In this study, we will only consider the assumptions of "fuzzy law" (A) and "gentle law" (B) which both mobilize relevant functional legitimacies.

Confronted by a flexibility of the binding force of a standard ("weak law"), the configuration seems to us, indeed, radically different. A sanction that is not (or weakly) applied, even sometimes devoid of any form of punishment, the strength of a "weak law" standard—albeit mandatory—entirely depends on the idea of the "social justice" that it conveys. Thus, the mobilized legitimacy is above all ethical and permanently controversial; unlike a "hard law" standard, that is, a standard coming from authorities and procedures embodying constitutionally the will and the interest of the social body, its determination of what is "common good" will necessarily be discussed, with no possibility to "cut short" in a sufficiently objective and consensual way.[1] Reputation challenging, here, gains too little and is too nebulous to be relevantly presented.

"Fuzzy" Law: Using the Functional Legitimacy of the Interpreter of the Standard

"Fuzzy law" consists of standards in which the understanding of the content is flexible. In CSR, they are either internal company productions (charters, codes of conduct, recommendations, circular internal, etc.) or external productions (methodological repositories, recommendations, etc.), their purpose being essentially to guide the way in which the company is considering its ethical actions beyond its legal obligations.[2] In many cases, the flexibility of content is a deliberate choice in order to allow wiggle room for decisions based on the contextual realities. Its first aim is to incite the company to ask relevant questions upstream and to consider all aspects of the subject matter, without forcing them to adopt too early choices.

---

[1] Ideas that inspired the Rawlsian approach can nevertheless mitigate passions, especially the use of procedures of development of the standard which, according to Paul Ricoeur, have for purpose and for service "to ensure the rule of the righteous over the good, by substituting the procedure of deliberation to any commitment concerning an alleged common good." In other words, the more the standard of "weak law" will proceed a process that organizes the expression of the different initial designs, and decides in the most democratic way, the more it will gain opportunities to escape social protest.

[2] Particularly illustrative in this regard, the international repository of the United Nations "Global Compact" is designed in the form of ten principles deducted of different basic international standards that this institution carries. It aims to lead companies to wonder, in the early stages of the development process of their CSR strategy, on framework concepts or deliberately vague formulations that must guide their action. Note that other international repositories also use this flexibility in content, in particular the "Guiding Principles of the OECD to the attention of multinational companies," or even the ISO 26000 standard. Also, reviewing all of these texts, it appears their editors offer an "interpretation" of the stated principles, not so much to impose a unified approach, but to support the company in its questioning and make sure that it is considering all the dimensions of the mentioned subject.

But let us be cautious: if "fuzzy law" mainly intends to guide the company in its ethical process, to help formulate intentions in this area, it may also hide behind these intentions (voluntarily or not) legal commitments which, by nature, interact very differently with the observed behaviors.

For a lawyer, the fundamental question behind "fuzzy law" is, above all, one of interpretation. This is to clarify the meaning of the rule on the basis of a factual situation, unique in time and in space. Therefore, the existence of the standard is stable, but its application is subject to permanent, sometimes contradictory, contortions that involve many subjective factors which are initially foreign to the design of the rule. Among them are a given system of values, the emotional charge of a situation of fact, and a greater or lesser semantic complexity of language.

The importance of these outside factors positions the person who interprets at the heart of the problem, with the central issue of his own social legitimacy. One's interpretation of the rule will obviously not have the same impact on the social body, according to their social function. Thus, confronted by a vague provision in a code of conduct, one will not grant the same force to the interpretations given by respectively the manager, the employer, the administrative authority, or the judge. The social function of the interpreter is paramount before all, because behind each function are associated duties and identified interests which more or less effectively limit the risks of arbitrariness and change the perception that one can have of his skills.

For our problem, it must be concluded that the questioning of a business reputation gains legitimacy as soon as it is based on the interpretation of a "fuzzy law" provision made by an actor whose social function gives him a real credibility on the subject.

According to its social function, the interpreter will guide his analysis in different ways and use varying methods of interpretation (Champeil-Desplats 2014). He should first position himself on the level of discourse suitable for his purpose, by distinguishing what is part of the prescriptive speech and what is part of the descriptive or declaratory speeches. Indeed, the prescriptive speech makes it possible to detect what can be a commitment, either legal or simply moral (e.g. if the recipient of the commitment remains unclear, or if the rule does not meet the conventional criteria of generality, permanence, and abstraction). For its part, descriptive or declaratory speech reveals an intention which essentially serves an ethical purpose, but which can also sometimes enlighten a legal commitment.

The first approach is characteristic of the judges who will analyze the "fuzzy law" standard to try to detect possible legal commitments,[3] or to clarify the scope of a legal commitment. To that effect, he has a power of "discretion," confined by principles of method and very general designs of what a rule of law is and what should be his social mission (these limits being quite variable from one legal culture to another). But his social function, which he pulls from constitutional authority, remains in part to identify all these rules that should be included in the legal order if they are objectively eligible, regardless of the original intents that guided their production.

This approach leads one to consider that a company which would have failed in a legal commitment deducted by the judge from a "fuzzy law" standard can be very legitimately challenged on the ethical field since the first of any ethical obligations is to comply with applicable law. Companies will be blamed for having a conduct whose objective or effect were to escape its legal responsibilities—to emancipate itself from the rules applied to all of the social body, from the idea of the general interest in which the judge is functionally one of the guarantors.

The second approach is different and seeks other performers than the judge. The process is not to identify where Law can be (their social function does not allow them to) but to clarify content in order to find a socially eligible solution to a particular ethical issue. The interpreter looks for intentions, more or less explicit, in order to confront them with meta-legal principles, more or less clear about their purpose and their scope. From this confrontation, he will provide a way to correct the initial conflict situation, on the basis of values which he sees as shared by as many people as possible inside the social body.

This approach is particularly the one followed by the OECD throughout its "Guiding Principles," especially through the device of the "National Contact Points" (NCP) mechanism (Martin-Chenut et al. 2016). These authorities are not intended to state the law (they are not judges) but to bring together the actors of an ethical issue based on a possible breach of one of the Guiding Principles, with a view to conclude a mediation that engages the future. In this perspective, they are required to interpret the guidelines in light

---

[3] In French law, is often cited the judgment of 15 October 1998, by which the Court of cassation has deduced the existence of a contract of employment from the terms of the moral Charter of a humanitarian association, this text requiring indeed from its volunteers a number of principles which violations could be a cause of breach of contractual relationships. Even if a standard of "soft law," and despite relatively imprecise formulations that it could contain, the judge found that volunteers were submitted, by the effects of this Charter, to the control, the management, and the power of sanction of the association, three elements that constitute a salaried employment relationship.

of the facts that constitute the dispute. If there is no obligation to cooperate with the NCP, still less to subscribe to the arrangement proposed, the fact that these NCP mechanisms stem from an international institution and are placed directly under the coordination of the national governments gives them a legitimacy that allows them to seriously damage the reputation of a refractory actor.

In the same logic, we can assimilate all processes that imply a mediator, depending on who named him, his expertise, and his ability to influence opinion.

"Gentle Law": Using the Functional Legitimacy of the Author of the Standard

Faced, this time, with flexibility relative to the binding force of a standard, the approach is quite similar in many ways. Indeed, "gentle law" also specifies the path by which the company must achieve ethical goals. But they contain no obligations. They are standards of intention and never of commitment. The functional legitimacy of the interpreter therefore remains essential, when this interpreter is supposed to offer a socially eligible solution to an ethical problem when acting as a mediator.

But "gentle right" also leads us to wonder about the social legitimacy of its author. He does not command; he recommends, he advises, he encourages. What leads the social body to apply these standards, even in the absence of obligation, is mainly due to its author's functional credibility, his quality of expertise, and also to the reasons why he holds his function.

So confronted to a recommendation coming from an organization, this one will not be perceived in the same way whether this organization is private or public, national or international, or named or elected through a democratic process of designation. In the same vein, this recommendation will not have the same impact on behaviors depending on whether it comes from a unilateral production or a negotiation process.

Ultimately, one can say that "gentle law" interacts directly with the overall evaluation approach of "stakeholders" that underlies the concept of CSR. Somehow, one is positioned in a potential confrontation between several reputations; the company's on the one hand versus that of the standard's author on the other hand, the aim being to determine which will withstand the other, which will prevail over the other in the event of conflict to finally adapt itself in accordance. Should the author of the standard be the company itself, then the confrontation of reputations will take place in the same way, against the detractor's reputation (with a slight advantage in this case for the company as being the acting element of the confrontation).

But this interaction can create the risk of confining the company in a mostly defensive posture, the aim being no longer to rethink the perimeter of its social responsibility, but simply to justify and preserve as much as possible its own strategic objectives (Aquier 2013). Only a clearly stronger reputation can cause the redesign, in whole or in part, of the company's initial goals. We thus perceive the challenge to engage the public authorities in the definition and active promotion of "gentle law" standards that present a detailed and ambitious content. To this extent, the OECD's Guidelines, the UN's Global Compact and Global Reporting Initiative, as well as the ILO's Guidelines are particularly interesting and quite relevant to help challenge a company's reputation (or to consolidate it, if the company strictly followed their content when elaborating its CSR strategy).

Tomorrow's Legal Levers on the Issue of Law, Reputation, and CSR

If "soft law," throughout its dimensions of "fuzzy" and "gentle" law, allows the increase of the social legitimacy of a company's reputation, it is not the only component of Law able to do so. "Hard law" is also a particularly effective leverage that public authorities, or those acting on their behalf, can use, if they are themselves previously aware of their own social responsibilities for what concerns business ethics.

In other words, the economic power of multinational companies and the argument of frequent extraterritoriality concerning ethical disputes should not lead governments to abdicate their fundamental mission to protect individuals and their environment in the face of the market's logic. Rather, this new configuration of powers allows them to adapt themselves and to innovate in the law they generate, without ever losing sight that they are the only legitimate ones to define the general interest. They also act so that private interests, when they confront each other, ultimately marry this common horizon.

When observing the action of the States, and their relationship to the concept of CSR, it unfortunately appears that ethical disputes management has been deliberately conceded to the logic of private actors' self-regulation, which enjoys a quasi-exclusivity in this area. The examples of France and the European Union are particularly illustrative, especially with regard to the obligation to extra-financial performance reporting that, legally, causes burdens on businesses. Governments have indeed defined very vague, very incomplete, and often inconsistent information to communicate to the public, without real sanctions in case of breach. Generally, the law on CSR is essentially a cosmetic law, giving companies full control of their communication and their action, and governments creating the illusion that they have acted (Petit 2014).

Fortunately, recent years seem to follow the idea that the States and their delegates wish to be more effective in influencing companies' behaviors. These intentions and first initiatives must now be confirmed in time, with the idea to provide individuals more objectivity when they deal with companies' reputations.

Among the very many options that are available to governments, two seem essential. Firstly, the assertion that a CSR strategy is, by nature, eligible to commercial advertising law (A). Secondly, the constitution of a law of compliance which, while respecting the core spirit of the concept of CSR, must allow governments and their delegates to regain control on the extra-financial activities of companies (B).

The Lever of Misleading Publicity Law

A first lever is available to national governments to clarify the nature of CSR standards through the application of advertisement law, and more widely of deceptive trade practices law (Martin-Chenut and Tricot 2016). The idea comes directly from the United States, more specifically the Supreme Court of the State of California on the occasion of a resounding case: *Kasky v. Nike* (Trebulle 2004).

For the first time, indeed, a court of this magnitude had to pronounce itself on the legal consequences of a communication that could be likened to a CSR approach.[4] For the Nike company, these documents were part of its CSR strategy and were based on mere statements that could not lead to possible legal liability. The company thus opposed its right to freedom of expression, covered by the First Amendment, while Mr. Kasky exercised the provisions on misleading advertising.

---

[4] At the end of the 1990s, the reputation of the Nike company had been called into question by several associations because of its social practices in the countries of Southeast Asia. In order to defend itself against these attacks, which we measure easily the negative impact on its reputation, the company responded by developing a very active policy of communication, defending itself of having reprehensible behavior. A Californian community activist, Mr. Kasky, thus heard to call into question the responsibility of the Nike company claiming that it had lied in its communication campaign. In support of its application, he stated that the firm was committed to enforcing social and environmental regulations upon its subcontractors.

If the first California judges considered that Nike actually was protected by the First Amendment, the Supreme Court of the State of California noted that a message issued by a merchant, destined for a "commercial audience" and reporting facts within its activity in order to promote sales of its products, should be regarded as a commercial speech. By this decision, the Court admitted that voluntary claims which come from a logic of CSR are likely to be subject to the law of deceptive marketing practices.[5]

This decision raises several questions, whose scope goes beyond the world of Law. To put it simply: does a company really benefit from freedom of expression as conceived for an individual? Indeed, all of its communications have consequences on its position within the market. Depending on how the information will be collected by merchant actors—competitors, partners, consumers, regulators—the equation establishing the business opportunities of the company will be modified. Any public communication, including those that appear a priori innocuous, influence ultimately the reputation of the business, since it creates or deteriorates the conditions in which trust relationships are developed, and thus economic opportunities.

Conversely, in the case of a physical person, freedom of expression is conceived as the possibility for any individual to speak, without necessarily the idea of a profitable return (by convictions relating to the general interest, a person can also express a position that would be even contrary to its own interests). Social life, in contrast to market life, pursues much more varied and complex aims than economic profit. The reputation of the individual is certainly just as dependent on its expression, but it turns to interests and issues that are not necessarily and exclusively designed from the idea of economic enrichment.

Thus, one sees clearly the relevance of the decision of the Supreme Court of California: the possibility that mobilizing false advertising law, for the purpose of punishing incorrect, incomplete, or misleading statements made by a company on the occasion of its CSR strategy, leads to locking up the issue of its reputation within the strict framework of lucrative terms—legal, economic, social, environmental, and ethical—all of which are determined, controlled, and sanctioned by the social body. The image of the company does not fully belong to it anymore: its management is subject to the general interest.

But in this perspective, two major issues arise in law. The first concerns the content of the law on misleading publicity which, like in French law, is

---

[5] No more the California jurisdictions than the Supreme Court of the United States finally judged this affair, following a transaction concluded between the parties.

sometimes way too restrictive, concentrated on a good or service given, and not on the general context in which these goods and services have been designed and promoted. Certainly it can be referred to the "essential features" of that good or service, but the link with the content of CSR strategies remains too tenuous to hang it on a specific good or service. The law must evolve to explicitly target the information provided by the company with respect to its global extra-financial action, as one cannot deny that it influences indirectly (but surely) the development of that product or service.

The second concerns the ability of the government to broaden the spectrum of people who can call into question the illegality of the reputation of the company, to increase the frequency of this type of action, and to ensure stronger penalties. In other words, the question that arises here is the one of "class actions" (Laronze et al. 2016) and their circumstances—on this point, we welcome the current trend of broadening the terms of these actions—but also their consequences. When considering "class actions" as a real means of effective regulation of the market, we must design them not simply as corrective procedures (to stop a breach for the future), but as truly punitive procedures (compensation of a set of prejudices which, through additions to the individual injuries suffered by each victim of the group, results in important total damages and interests).

The Lever of Compliance Law

Some authors specializing in economic and regulatory law see another opportunity that would increase the accountability of companies via the issue of reputation: the development of a genuine compliance law (Frison-Roche 2016, 2017). They must nevertheless be very careful about the use of this new term, so that it is clear that it covers different realities but for now remains relatively imprecise. The law, in this area, is only in its infancy.

The idea of "compliance" becomes relevant to our topic if we exclude from this term the willingness of the company to ensure that its misconduct will not repeat in the future (self-regulation *after* sanction). In a particularly illuminating formula, Prof. Frison-Roche summed up the idea of "compliance" as being a kind of safe in which information is kept by the company, and that law will open on order (Frison-Roche 2016).[6] Confidence here is related not

---

[6] Frison-Roche, M.-A. (2017). The author defines compliance as "*the will of governments to impose rules which they do not have the strength to ensure the effectiveness of. (…) Regulators thus internalize the imple-*

toward the company, but toward the information kept; this mechanical confidence is the result of structural bonds. In other words, the issue behind compliance is certainly not to trust the willingness of businesses to act in accordance with ethical goals that they specify themselves as part of their CSR strategies, but to trust the function they occupy in the economic and financial system, which implies that they have information of which it is their duty to transmit to legitimate authorities.

Compliance therefore expresses an a priori defiance against the reputation that multinational companies builds, and all the procedures imposed from the outside which will force the company to reveal the adequacy report between their reputations and the cold reality of the objective information they hold.

We then face the States which, having almost no direct influence over the behavior of multinational companies (because they are multinational and economically overpowered), have found a way to regain control of them via the globalized market regulation authorities—which have the surface, the legitimacy, and the authority to act—as well as via the idea of compliance. We are also confronted with CSR strategies that cease to be the subjective view that companies have (and defend) of their own social sustainability to ultimately become more objective strategies, necessarily resulting from the confrontation organized by law, between the declared action (the company's reputation) and the relevant information to be revealed.

This finding opens nevertheless crucial issues for the future of CSR. The risk, indeed, is to reduce compliance to the idea of "comply and never explain." Compliance would thus build itself from a set of exclusive obligations of results, deaf to any justification and only animated by the cold mechanism of a sanction that could automatically fall if results do not "match" with a given aim. In this context, CSR disappears completely: reflection, introspection foresight, and efforts (and their virtues) clearly do not have their place in this configuration.

---

mentation of these monumental public standards into structures that are de jure *and* de facto *informed and powerful: multinational companies which operate international financial operations. Hence compliance is the global internalization of a local public regulation within supranational companies that are designated as effective agents of global, monumental goals. Since the goal set by public authorities is legitimate (fight against terrorism, crimes against children, drug trafficking, etc.), the company is bound. It can only outbid the 'compliance device' it is implementing to achieve the purpose of Regulation. If its organization and behavior is not consistent with the provisions taken by the laws in the very specific areas that are monitoring international and global financial flows to detect systemically harmful behaviors, then the company is sanctioned and cannot oppose neither any justification nor its own legal system: that is how regulation applies 'relentlessly.' Sanction is not the cause of compliance anymore, but rather its consequence."*

But it is also possible to think about the future in terms of "comply, then explain." Law, here, would constitute a set of obligations of means, which allows the company to assert the contextual elements of its action—to say the efforts that it has hired and to propose further efforts for the future. Companies will risk sanctions but ones that have a genuine educational function. That is a penalty that punishes, of course, but one that also makes you think before you act and before you punish and gets everyone to consider the contextual elements, not exclusively dogmatic assertions. In the end, law organizes a real liability regime, in the sense that the company is in a position to understand and to assume its mistakes and its failures, after having the opportunity to explain and to understand the path which led it in this situation.

In this context, CSR fully embodies the "explain" process. It remains a dynamic of risk-prevention and possible rebound after a failure. It remains, more than ever, a true ethical approach in that it values more efforts and the sincerity which underlies them than the results.

But CSR cannot be limited to just an explanation. It must also be the work of co-construction of the standards of compliance (Teubner 2015; Tricot 2016). If the regulatory authorities have, on the national and supranational levels, a mission to facilitate and ensure this "confidence pact" which unites them to companies, then there must be a normative space in which these companies participate beyond obedience in the extra-financial regulation of their sector of activity. If compliance is the process which leads to internalize, in market operators, the control system, if it requires to set, upstream, a duty of companies to structure themselves in order to meet the goals of general interest defined by the regulator, then the path leading to the satisfaction of those goals must also be drawn by companies according to their realities.

CSR thus retains this spirit of freedom—the "freedom-duty" concept so dear to the Dean Duguit—which, while preserving the ability of companies to shape the face of their reputation, nevertheless avoids the idiosyncrasy to shape masks behind which they hide their will to escape or destroy the general interest.

* * *

Notes

We strongly believe that Law and reputation-challenging are not to be opposed. They must work together to allow our societies to better protect themselves against strategies which, via CSR, can lead to manipulate information and create biased economic relationships or false representations of the commercial operators that can threaten the public interest. Law must admit it cannot do everything via "hard law," but that it can lead the actors to organize themselves differently, to decide in a more collective way, to rely on functional legitimacies to progress toward more ethics and more social responsibility. The challenge is to reposition each one in its original social function and to create constructive synergies otherwise than by punishment. The issue is, finally, to trust Humanity again without however ignoring its intrinsic part of inhumanity.

References

Ailincai, M. A. (2017). *Soft Law et Droits fondamentaux*. Actes du colloque du 4 et 5 février 2016, A. Pedone, Paris.

Aquier, A. (2013). Stakeholder vs Stockholder? In N. Postel & R. Sobel (Eds.), *Dictionnaire critique de la RSE* (pp. 434–439). Paris: Presses universitaires Septentrion, coll. capitalisme-éthique-institutions.

Boistel, P. (2014). Réputation: concept à définir. *Communication & Organisation, 2*(46), 211–224.

Cailleba, P. (2009). L'entreprise face au risque de réputation. *Annales des Mines – Responsabilité et environnement, 3*(55), 9–14.

Champeil-Desplats, V. (2014). *Méthodologies du droit et des sciences du droit*. Paris: Dalloz, coll. « Méthodes du droit ».

CIGREF. (2012). Étude des risques et opportunités liés à l'e-réputation des entreprises. Available from http://www.cigref.fr/wp/wp-content/uploads/2012/04/2012_E-reputation_Etude_des_risques_et_opportunites_lies_a_-l_e-reputation_des_entreprises_CIGREF.pdf. Accessed Apr 2017.

Cominetti, M., & Seele, P. (2016). Hard Soft Law or Soft Hard Law? A Content Analysis of CSR Guidelines Typologized along Hybrid Legal Status. *P. uwf, 24*, 127.

Corti-Varela, J. (2013). Les instruments d'exécution des décisions de justice dans les affaires environnementales internationales sont-elles efficaces ? Réflexions à partir de l'affaire Texaco-Chevron. *L'Observateur des Nations-Unies*, 2013-1, *34*, 198.

Delmas-Marty, M., & Supiot, A. (2015). *Prendre la responsabilité au sérieux*. Paris: Collège de France.

Dowling, G. (2002). *Creating Corporate Reputations: Identity, Image, and Performance*. New York: Oxford University Press.

Fombrun, C. J. (1996). *Reputation: Realizing Value from the Corporate Image*. Boston: Harvard Business School Press.

Frison-Roche, M.-A. (2016). Le droit de la compliance. *Dalloz*, p. 1871.

Frison-Roche, M.-A. (2017). *Compliance and Trust*. Available from http://mafr.fr/en/article/compliance-et-confiance/. Accessed Mar 2017.

Jestaz, P. (2016). *Le droit*. Paris: Dalloz, coll. « Connaissance du droit ».

Kelsen, H. (1934). *Reine Rechtslehre. Enleitung in die rechtwissenchaftliche Problematik*. Leipzig/Wien: Franz deuticke Verlag.
Laronze, F., Oliveira, C., & Saldanha, J. (2016). Tiers et victimes: l'outil des actions collectives. In K. Martin-Chenut & R. de Quenaudon (Eds.), *La RSE saisie par le droit. Perspectives interne et internationale* (pp. 545–557). Paris: A. Pedone.
Leroux, E. (2016). Sanctions économiques ou comment faire des acteurs du marché des militants RSE. In K. Martin-Chenut & R. de Quenaudon (Eds.), *La RSE saisie par le droit. Perspectives interne et internationale* (pp. 349–361). Paris: A. Pedone.
Martin-Chenut, K., & de Quenaudon, R. (2016). La RSE saisie par le droit: généalogie d'une recherche juridique sur la RSE. In K. Martin-Chenut & R. de Quenaudon (Eds.), *La RSE saisie par le droit. Perspectives interne et internationale* (pp. 1–14). Paris: A. Pedone.
Martin-Chenut, K., & Nord, N. (2016). La recherche d'un juge compétent: les défis posés par l'extraterritorialité. In K. Martin-Chenut & R. de Quenaudon (Eds.), *La RSE saisie par le droit. Perspectives interne et internationale* (pp. 625–642). Paris: A. Pedone.
Martin-Chenut, K., & Tricot, J. (2016). Loyauté des engagements: la RSE prise au mot par le Droit. In K. Martin-Chenut & R. de Quenaudon (Eds.), *La RSE saisie par le droit. Perspectives interne et internationale* (pp. 363–380). Paris: A. Pedone.
Martin-Chenut, K., de Quenaudon, R., & Varison, L. (2016). Les Points de contact nationaux: un forum de résolution des conflits complémentaire ou concurrent du juge ? In K. Martin-Chenut & R. de Quenaudon (Eds.), *La RSE saisie par le droit. Perspectives interne et internationale* (pp. 607–624). Paris: A. Pedone.
Mayer, A. E. (2009). Human Rights as a Dimension of CSR: The Blurred Lines Between Legal and Non-legal Categories. *Journal of Business Ethics, 88*, 561.
Mazuyer, E. (2017). Les relations entre 'soft law' et droits fondamentaux: une approche pragmatique par la RSE. In M. A. Ailincai (Ed.), *Soft law et droits fondamentaux. Actes du colloque du 4 et 5 février 2016* (pp. 265–283). Paris: A. Pedone, coll. "Fondation René Cassin,".
Petit, B. (2014). Reporting RSE: un nouveau coup d'épée dans l'eau. *Environnement*, No. 7.
Teubner, G. (2015). L'auto-constitutionnalisation des entreprises transnationales ? Sur les rapports entre les codes de conduite 'privés' et 'publics' des entreprises. In A. Supiot (Ed.), *L'entreprise dans un monde sans frontières. Perspectives économiques et juridiques* (pp. 75–83). Paris: Dalloz, coll. Les sens du droit, Dalloz.
Thibierge, C. (2003). Le droit souple. Réflexion sur les textures du droit. *Revue trimestrielle de Droit civil*, pp. 599–628.
Thibierge, C. (2004). Avenir de la responsabilité et responsabilité de l'avenir. *Recueil Dalloz*, pp. 577–583.
Thibierge, C., et al. (2009). *La force normative. Naissance d'un concept*. Paris: LGDJ/Bruylant.

Trebulle, F.-G. (2004). Responsabilité sociale des entreprises et liberté d'expression. Considérations à partir de l'arrêt Nike c/ Kasky. *Revue des Sociétés, 2*, 261.

Tricot, J. (2016). La conformité, outil de juridicisation de la RSE et de transformation du Droit. In K. Martin-Chenut & R. de Quenaudon (Eds.), *La RSE saisie par le droit Perspectives interne et internationale* (pp. 303–319). Paris: A Pedone.

Walker, K. (2010). A Systematic Review of the Corporate Reputation Literature: Definition, Measurement, and Theory. *Corporate Reputation Review, 12*(4), 357–387.

Part III

Representations and Practices of Responsibility in the European Context

9

Corporate Social Responsibility in Europe: Discourses and Practices

Sofia Imane Bouterfas, Stela Raytcheva, and Gilles Rouet

Introduction

The multinational companies that develop corporate social responsibility (CSR) strategies and internal ethical standards initiate a multitude of CSR actions. This chapter proposes a theoretical exploration of CSR and then an explanation of four cases of companies that have clearly defined a proactive CSR strategy on a European or global scale and aspire for each stakeholder to be directly involved, both in acts and in sensemaking.

It is indeed possible to question whether there is a universality of CSR "good practices" that are self-evident and to question the correspondence between discourses and behaviors. None of this is obvious; the same strategy at the level of a multinational group can generate discourses that may not have the same scope in all subsidiaries, and even if an explicit strategy refers to identical values, the hierarchies of these values are not necessarily identical in the different social, cultural, economic, and political contexts. Is the diversity

---

S. I. Bouterfas (✉) • S. Raytcheva
University of Versailles, Versailles, France
e-mail: stela.raytcheva@uvsq.fr

G. Rouet
University of Versailles, Versailles, France

Matej Bel University, Banská Bystrica, Slovakia

© The Author(s) 2019
A. Bartoli et al. (eds.), *Responsible Organizations in the Global Context*,
https://doi.org/10.1007/978-3-030-11458-9_9

of contexts decisive for the implementation of CSR strategies, and how? In order to provide answers, it is necessary to analyze some company cases and their businesses in different countries.[1]

CSR: Concepts and Strategies

Corporate social responsibility (CSR) is a "concept in which companies integrate social, environmental and economic concerns in their activities and in their interactions with their stakeholders on a voluntary basis" (European Commission 2001). It is a "fashionable" subject for both researchers and practitioners in the field of management. In spite of the more or less increasing involvement of organizations in the subjects of environmental protection and the improvement of social conditions in their locale, the CSR concept and its practices suffer from an instrumentalist imprint.

From the dawn of industrial capitalism in the United States, philosophers have questioned the relationship between business and morals, particularly in terms of corruption, false advertising, and bribes (Gendre-Aegerter 2008). At the end of the nineteenth century, executives began to evoke CSR, a theory that was formally defined in 1953 by Howard Bowen (Pasquero 2005; Gond 2006). In Europe too, since at least the nineteenth century, business leaders have been interested in the health, safety, education, and housing for workers. The Schneider, Peugeot, and Michelin families, for instance, have set up schools and built houses for their employees (Lépineux 2003). Nevertheless, practices and concepts do not follow same approach on both sides of the Atlantic, for while CSR comes from moralism in the United States, it is part of a tradition of social capitalism in Europe.

The model of the capitalist enterprise by Carr (1968) or Friedman (1970) is no longer predominant, that is, the pursuit of individual interests is no longer in contradiction with the collective interests and with the achievement of a social harmony. A positive climate facilitates personnel management, reduces the risk of conflict, and ultimately preserves capitalism itself. More generally, the "stakeholders" within companies understand and sometimes claim that production processes affect non-economic aspects of society, such as the well-being of employees and customers and the development of local communities and the natural environment. It is from this evolution, from the classic model

---

[1] This chapter is linked with the following one (Chap. 10), which examines the Veolia group in several European countries.

of M. Friedman (1970) to the "CSR" model of R. Ed Freeman (1984), that ISO 26000 became the international reference text on CSR. Following this standard, CSR acts as a source and framework for managerial innovations, and a company has the responsibility of meeting the interests of multiple stakeholders (Côme and Rouet 2015). The company and the society are bound by a contract, which ensures the company's legitimacy. It is thus possible to analyze the contribution of companies to the stakes of sustainable development. From their participation in the regulation of ecological and human crises through their implementation of responsible practices and processes, companies use CSR to satisfy the needs of various actors and maintain the primacy of traditional performance criteria (Mullenbach-Servayre 2007). It is also necessary to consider the overall performance of companies that integrate economic, social, and environmental performance into their management system. For Porter and Kramer (2006), CSR enables the creation of shared values and thus comes within the scope of company strategy. A company that follows CSR can contribute to a better society while maintaining its profit targets, especially by developing and advocating best practices, even if often normatively.

The stakeholders go beyond shareholders, employees, and customers; governments and citizens, in particular, must be considered. As integral parts of the company, employees have legitimacy, power (through their performances and claims), and action to solve their problems. These three criteria make possible to evaluate the "salience" of employees and their involvement in CSR (Mitchell et al. 1997). It is also interesting to study the influence capacities of the employees of the company (Barnett 2007). The employees, main actors in CSR, can be at the origin of CSR in practice. The economic actors are not independent and isolated from the citizen entities in which they operate. Thus, social responsibility practices of organizations are social constructions that transcend organizations and are shaped by the different entities of an organization and by stakeholders like governments, NGOs, consumers, and the media. Organizational citizenship, integrating CSR, is a source of competitive advantage because it contributes to the overall performance of the organization (Frimousse and Peretti 2015).

Multinational companies have been among the first to value their CSR actions—though not necessarily the first ones to put them into practice. Indeed, a determining factor of the internationalization of production sites abroad is often linked to constraints in terms of working conditions and environmental protections lower than those of the country of origin. At the same time, intensified global information flows can unveil ecological accidents and social problems and could undermine the reputation of some companies within a European or global scale. This problem can produce a negative opinion on the part of local populations and of their governments, particularly vis-à-vis the representatives of the countries from which the multinational groups originate.

CSR strategies are diverse and vary from one company to another depending on the sector of activity, the stakeholder pressure, or the organizational cultures. Some companies adopt defensive CSR in the face of regulatory constraints and stakeholder demands. Other companies consider sustainable development and CSR as opportunities and adopt offensive strategies; these companies integrate these opportunities into their overall strategy, setting up action programs to adapt new implicit standards of social and environmental responsibility while seeking to avoid risks and gain competitiveness by maximizing stakeholder expectations. However, multinational organizations are not monolithic: strategies and practices validated by headquarters may not have the same meaning, and local translations must be considered in local contexts (Raytcheva and Rouet 2016). Moreover, the complexity of the groups and the geographical and cultural remoteness of the sites are likely to make it more difficult to control the decisions and implementation of CSR practices at various sites. Finally, the different local contexts and the meaning for the local actors can make local constructions of CSR practices relevant.

It is important to study the processes from top to bottom (headquarters toward subsidiaries), from bases to top (subsidiaries toward headquarters), and between peers. These processes mix and develop from each other. Different factors, often difficult to demonstrate, stimulate these different translations, thus creating innovations that emerge from these processes of interaction between the entities of the multinational companies. Indeed, these processes are able to enrich not only the CSR practices of companies, but also those of the host countries. It is also possible to analyze the particular CSR concerns in each local context, both economic and cultural. The relationship between nature, business, life, and work is not the same from one country to another—even from one region to another—and a multitude of representatives of civil societies and the economy work to shape local practices according to the priorities and the values that make sense to them. These processes are not linear; they are multiple, contradictory, and complementary, and they define and redefine the meaning of the daily practices of CSR in each context.

Beyond the official discourse, over the last 25 years, CSR practices and programs, as well as the contributions of organizations to the challenges of sustainable development, have increased not only as a result of organizational and strategic changes but also with growing pressure from NGOs and trade union actions. This theme has been structured and affirmed within the European Union: 90% of European companies have developed a strategy for managing their environmental impacts, compared to 40% of North American companies and about 15% of Asian companies (Maanvilja and Lopez 2008).

It is possible to suggest the hypothesis of coherence, within the European Union, of CSR values, norms, and perceptions to the communications, meetings, studies, subsidized projects, and other initiatives thanks to the political role played by the community institutions. Under its presidency of the EU Council, Denmark ("the second most responsible country in the world" MacGillivray et al. 2007) has asserted "a responsible, dynamic, green and more stable Europe" (Mullerat 2013).

The policy formalized by the European Union, following the request of the European Parliament in 1999, led to the necessary establishment of a code of conduct governing environmental compliance and labor and human rights for EU companies around the world. In order to be socially responsible, companies must meet legal obligations and social and environmental responsibilities by integrating social, environmental, and ethical concerns and human rights into their operations and their strategies. It is about making Europe a center of excellence in CSR. After a "proactive" communication published in 2006, the European Commission renewed its CSR strategy with the communication titled "Corporate Social Responsibility: A New EU Strategy for 2011–2014" (European Commission 2011).

CSR becomes a defining goal of companies, as it is about maximizing the creation of a shared value for stakeholders and society as a whole. This new definition goes beyond the previous definition ("voluntary integration by companies of social and environmental concerns into their business activities and their relations with their stakeholders") (European Commission 2006, p. 2) and considers the responsibilities of companies regarding their effects on society as a whole.

If the word "voluntary" disappears from the definition, this does not mean that it is "mandatory" for companies to adopt a CSR approach but rather to become aware of societal change. The Commission intends, therefore, "to start a process in 2012 with companies and other stakeholders to develop a code of good practice on self-regulation and co-regulation, with the aim of improving the effectiveness of the CSR process" (European Commission 2011, p. 12). In addition, the Commission hopes to "give priority to internationally recognized principles and guidelines on CSR" (Ibid, p. 16). Compliance and regulation are thus the keywords of the new policy.

CSR Strategies and Practices: Four Examples

The integration of the principles of sustainable development and ethics through CSR makes it possible for the following four companies to produce and offer goods or services that are both "economically profitable" and "socially responsible," which may generate and maintain the trust of customers, employees, shareholders, and citizens.

These analyses are based on the three levels of CSR from the Wartick and Cochran (1985) model. The first is to show that the place of CSR and the classification of CSR principles and ethics change from one company to another, according to their sector of activity, their business model, and the will and the personality of their leaders. We must look at the upstream of the CSR strategy to highlight the company's perception of CSR, corporate citizenship, and business ethics, focusing on the motivations in terms of principles and value and considering the classification of responsibilities and the influence of institutional variables on the behavior of the company. So, given the resources of the company, its business, and its specific know-how, what are the problems that it can help solve?

A second approach consists of exposing the tools and procedures put in place in order to coordinate CSR principles with the traditional activity of the company. We look at what role the structures, processes, systems, and tools play in the integration of social and environmental issues in the "process of corporate social responsiveness" (Ackerman 1973). How does the company translate its principles into actions? To what environmental pressures should businesses respond?

The results of these actions on society and social actors must be highlighted in order to show the concrete impact of CSR policies and programs with reference to social impact theory (Blake, Frederick, and Myers 1976; Dierkes and Berthoin Antal 1986). The analysis thus considers three dimensions: societal responsibility, societal responsiveness, and societal performance of companies. These dimensions make it possible to show the passage from the discourse (*storytelling*) to the responsible practices (*sensemaking*) compared to the strategy put in place by the company (*the black box of CSR*).

These four companies have several points in common (such as at least one European location), and, above all, seek to build, maintain, or even increase their social legitimacy outside the framework of their economic activities alone.

Danone

Environment and human capital are at the very heart of Danone Group,[2] a leader in the food industry[3] with more than 100,000 employees and 160 production sites, whose main mission is to contribute to the maintenance of "good health by diet for the greatest number." Antoine Riboud, the founder of Danone, was one of the few leaders to announce the idea of CSR in a speech in 1972: "There is only one land, we only live once, the responsibility of the company does not stop at the threshold of factories and offices."[4] CSR for Danone is a value, a strategy, and a communication axis all at once, a daily commitment to a dual economic and social project whose main actions are to develop consumer confidence, attract quality employees, and maintain internal cohesion. Sustainable development is not a virtue but a corporate wisdom, and CSR must be intrinsic to business.

Engaging in a CSR-oriented strategy requires rethinking a company's value chain and impartially treating its main activities of support, the most involved in the creation of value. At Danone, and at each link of its value chain, societal objectives are set related to water pollution, risks related to refrigeration plants, storage of raw materials or hazardous products and electrical installations, and psychosocial actions. Social inclusion is at the heart of the action plan, and social innovation is present throughout the value chain.

Social commitment is also practiced with breeders, with a price commitment (more than the market)[5] and integration of producers' production costs in the calculation of the purchase price of milk, based on the expertise of third parties. Danone integrates concrete actions in logistics to reduce the environmental impact through transport optimization and storage actions. A new logistics base for low consumption building has been set up on all the sites. Furthermore, the "WISE" employee-training program embodies the commitment to employees' physical and mental safety.

The Danone Group has similarly set up Danone Way, a standard set of recommendations in terms of "sustainable development" practices for all

---

[2] Interview conducted at the CSR department, head office of Fresh Food Danone France.
[3] Danone is considered an "advanced performer" and remains the leader in the food industry in terms of environmental performance (Vigeo's Global Food Universe).
[4] Cf. https://www.lesechos.fr/25/09/2015/LesEchos/22031-040-ECH_danone%2D%2Dune-moderne-histoire-francaise.htm
[5] In 2016, Danone announced their decision to raise prices after the agricultural crisis, after discussions with producer organizations (press release, February 2016).

subsidiary companies. This compendium gathers 258 practices organized around 20 key themes structured around 4 categories: "to undertake differently," "for a healthier food," "for the service of all," and "for a more sustainable world."

Danone is moving toward more responsible social and environmental practices, not only to strengthen and improve its reputation or to stand out from the competition but also because this strategy is financially profitable and could assure the company's durability. Danone is one of the few ISO 50001 certified companies, which guarantees the control and management of energy performance with the main objective of reducing energy consumption and CO_2 impact.

To measure the performance and concrete impact of CSR policies and programs, key performance indicators have been put in place and linked to the four categories described above, both internally and externally. The CSR assessment (global and sectoral approach) by ISS-oekom Corporate Rating in May 2017 resulted in the B- score[6] and the "Prime Excellence" status.[7] The results with regard to equal opportunities, non-discrimination, the climate change strategy, and the reduction of food waste are often highlighted. Finally, the Access To Nutrition Index (ATNI) ranks Danone in the top three of the most successful agribusiness companies.

L'Oréal

One of the reasons for studying L'Oréal lies in its leadership in ethical practice and the group's initiatives for sustainable development. It is one of only two companies in the world, out of nearly 3000, to have received a triple A, the highest score awarded by the Carbon Disclosure Project,[8] for its actions in climate protection, sustainable water management, and the fight against deforestation.[9] These results can be explained by the strong autonomy granted to ethics and corporate responsibility. One of L'Oréal's main challenges is to make sustainable development a goal shared by the entire group and all stakeholders.

---

[6] Cf. http://www.oekom-research.com/index_en.php?content=pressemitteilung_26042007

[7] Cf. http://www.danone.com/pour-tous/rapport-integre/nos-chiffres/evaluations-par-des-tiers/

[8] Cf. http://www.loreal.fr/media/press-releases/2015/nov/loreal-reconnu-entreprise-leader-par-le-cdp-pour-sa-strategie-de-lutte-contre-le-changement-climatique

[9] Cf. 2016 Progress Report, on https://sharingbeautywithall.loreal.com/sites/default/files/cms/sbwa-progress-report-2016_english.pdf.pdf

The values and ethics charter is the result of a collective effort by 500 employees around the world who voluntarily participated in its creation. These employees of different generations believed that sustainable development must not be left to a small number of experts working alone to find some technical solutions and innovations. The ethical and CSR approach is voluntary for all employees concerned.

As part of its "Sharing Beauty With All" program, launched in 2013, L'Oréal has defined a series of commitments to be achieved by 2020, covering all of its impacts and mobilizing all of its teams. These commitments are concrete and organized into four pillars: innovate, produce, live, and develop sustainably to share growth with all of L'Oréal's stakeholders (employees, suppliers, and communities). The "Sharing Beauty With All" program has made substantial and lasting changes in the way products are designed, produced, communicated, and distributed, taking sustainability concerns into account from the beginning of the value chain.

At the end of 2016, in accordance with one of the commitments of this program, a consumer advisory committee was set up. Composed of people from different socio-cultural backgrounds, the committee members work to exchange their perceptions and to give their suggestions on the subject. This committee also proposes social and environmental responsibility activities, such as how to provide consumers with eco-designed products that have less impact on the environment and with marketing strategies and responsible communication.

Several strategic priorities were defined to evolve L'Oréal into a responsible company, in particular with a reduction of the impact of production on water, development of new raw materials by using green chemistry, and development of a soft and clean chemistry with less impact on the environment. In marketing, L'Oréal strives to make customers aware of the importance of sustainable development and the creation of relationships of trust. It has more than 200 programs of solidarity and sustainable supply, which have benefited more than 57,000 persons in 2015. In terms of production, 90% of the products are produced in-house, and the company has reduced carbon dioxide emissions by 50%, water consumption by 50%, and waste by finished product by 50%. L'Oréal has set a target for 2020 to help more than 100,000 people from disadvantaged groups gain access to employment by developing different projects in their host countries. Finally, 82% of new or renovated products in 2016 have an improved environmental or social profile, thanks to a new formula for reducing the company's environmental footprint.

L'Oréal has therefore put in place a proactive CSR strategy with a positive contribution to the environment, based not only on a necessary compliance process and obedience to the law and regulations but above all to become a creative enterprise integrating at all levels a logic of adherence and trust rather than a logic of obedience.

Michelin

Michelin's commitment to customers and to their safety can be traced back to the very creation of the company, when it was founded to find a solution for the cyclist who could no longer hit the road. The company is always faithful to its traditional values, as evidenced by the "Michelin Performance and Responsibility Charter" of 2002,[10] which clearly states its values, in the context of its activities, on the one hand, and its ability to evaluate the gap between intentions and actions, on the other hand.

Michelin's ambition is to improve the mobility of its customers—an objective that responds to a universal and fundamental need of people, based on innovations developed by its research and development department and key to its technological leadership. As a leader in the tire sector, the company is considered one of the most successful French companies in the exercise of all its responsibilities, through the design of new sustainable models to finding new ways to protect the environment. The responsibility of the company is to obtain good financial results, because the growth of the group ensures its durability. It is about sustainably increasing the value of the company by maximizing the profitability of operations and the return on investments.

Michelin is committed to its customers, with the main mission of customer service and the implementation of the safest possible transport. The company is also engaged in raising awareness on these issues and seeking to offer the best products and services at the best price in each market. Tires must be fuel-efficient and production must minimize energy, waste, and raw material consumption. It is also a question of integrating employees, setting up optimal working conditions, and ensuring their fulfillment in the exercise of their responsibilities, in particular by fully exploiting the diversity of the company and by developing the talents of the employees. This commitment is reflected in the recognition of the role of the company and its responsibilities toward the local community, particularly in terms of local and regional development.

---

[10] Cf. https://www.michelin.com/content/download/9218/79859/version/3/file/Charte-performance-et-responsabilite-Michelin_2002.pdf

With the implementation of the company's values—the exercise of its responsibilities and the maintenance of a strong, open, and shared corporate culture that is a source of social cohesion and motivation—Michelin is implementing its strategic orientations in CSR in the context of performance objectives. In 2002, it adopted societal initiative managed by the works council: "Performance and Responsibility."

With the creation of the Michelin Personnel Hygiene Society (SOHPEM), social services (social workers, psychologists, nursing home care, household helpers) and early childhood centers (day nursery and nursery assistants) are united in the same approach. Employees are encouraged to propose progress and improvements, with a system of suggestions named "ideas for progress," a "participatory innovation" approach that seems to be an important component of the corporate culture.

CSR is seen as an investment in many areas of community life: education, cultural and sports action, mobility of people and goods, and charity initiatives. In addition, Michelin is involved in the territories where it operates by respecting the cultures of the host countries and establishing relationships with local organizations in compliance with regulations. The company seeks to improve dialogue with local partners, create jobs, provide financial support, and participate in local life through training and development programs or through cultural and social exchanges, often in collaboration with the authorities.

Veolia

Veolia's CSR approach is part of a dynamic progress to integrate environmental, social, and societal performance into the overall performance of the company by 2020. Thus, taking the example of France, Veolia is positioning itself as a catalyst of attractiveness and an accelerator of economic and social development while contributing to the preservation of ecosystems and the fight against climate change. In 2014, the French economic magazine *Enjeux-Les Échos* ranked Veolia seventh in the CAC 40 companies most committed to CSR.

Since 2011, Veolia Environnement, the leading environmental services operator, has been engaged in adapting its businesses to the social and environmental ruptures induced by the reversal of scarcities and integrating the different dimensions of sustainable development into its activities. Thus, the challenges of sustainable development are an integral part of the contractual engineering that the company faces at the operational level. In this context of the "new Veolia," a sustainable development committee was created in 2012.

Veolia, like most multinational and transnational companies, has joined corporate coalitions on CSR and sustainable development[11] and has subscribed to training programs to learn and develop CSR best practices (e.g. the CSR-UK Academy). Veolia now develops more and more explicit CSR strategies.

Since 2003, Veolia has formalized its values for all its employees with the publication of the "Ethics, Belief and Responsibility" program, the purpose of which is to guide the behavior of employees of the company on a daily basis. Veolia supports its approach with awareness-raising and training actions aimed at rooting the ethical culture in its employees and preventing risks.

Veolia has defined its stakeholders in five main categories:

1. Economic partners (shareholders, investors, subcontractors/suppliers, banks, insurance companies, etc.);
2. Public institutions (governments, local authorities, European and international institutions, public institution organizations, etc.);
3. Customers (communities, industry, consumers, national states, regional states, etc.);
4. Internal actors (employees, managers, representative bodies of staff, unions, etc.); and
5. Civil society (associations/foundations, environmental organizations, development organizations, think tanks, extra-financial rating agencies, academic circles, media, entrepreneurs social, etc.).

Since 2014, Veolia has multiplied its partnerships with stakeholders from a wide range of backgrounds, from governmental and non-governmental organizations, considering that a co-construction of new models of relationships and value creation between stakeholders represents a real lever for growth and a source of innovation and differentiation.

Since 2004, Veolia has been listed every year in the FTSE4Good Index.[12] The regularity of this selection, in the context of the regular reinforcement of the inclusion criteria, illustrates the recognition of the company's long-term performance and commitment to sustainable development, particularly with

---

[11] For example, the U.K. Business community, CSR Europe, cf. http://www.csreurope.org/business-community-uk

[12] Cf. http://www.ftse.com/products/index-notices/home/getnotice/?id=1751208

regard to the objective of transparency. For its water business, in 2012 Veolia identified the number of facilities (drinking water production plants and wastewater treatment plants) that had set up an action plan to restore local biodiversity. In 2013, for instance, the company recognized 97 sites that had implemented 79 associated action plans). By reaffirming its commitment to biodiversity, Veolia changed its objectives to achieve a diagnosis by 2020 with the deployment of an action plan for all sites with a high biodiversity stake. This concerns water activity in addition to waste activity.

The group evaluated supplier relationships, diversity, and commitments to the local community. It also made donations and implemented charity practices and policies to promote, among other things, access to services related to health, education, the economy, and the arts. Thus, Veolia's CSR approach is similar to a strategic alignment approach because it integrates CSR and sustainable development practices at the heart of an operating model and in line with the company's strategy. These practices are pillars of Veolia. They are consistent with the sector of activity invested—a sector that is very sensitive to any transformation that influences the environment as well as public health, especially for the water sector—and which is directly subject to changes in the environment and the climate.

However, the peculiarity of this business sector does not fully explain why Veolia is moving toward practices that more in line with the implementation of numerous specific actions and with a renewal of mentalities, a particular "state of mind." Veolia is investing in eco-innovation and in strategic partnerships and is seeking to improve its value chain, not only to strengthen and improve its reputation or stand out from the competition but also to obtain financial profit and perhaps even a prerequisite for the very survival of the company. It is not a fashionable effect.

Table 9.1 presents a summary of CSR policies in the four studied companies.

Articulating Discourses to Practices, and Practices to Discourses

Some management science literature still sees CSR as a new attitude that responds to new needs that should be clearly identified in order to put in place effective actions. However, CSR strategies and practices are not fixed and rigid elements waiting to be studied by researchers. In other words, since the daily

Table 9.1 Summary—CSR among the four studied companies

	CSR: discourses and conceptions	Strategies and process	Results and outcomes
Danone (Fresh Products, France)	"Bringing health through food to as many people as possible" "Danone, the dual economic and social project," including six levels of commitment: – Continuously improve the nutritional quality of our products – Design healthier alternatives relevant to consumers – Reinforce our understanding of local nutrition practices and public health contexts – Contribute to addressing local public health challenges through partnerships – Develop even more responsible marketing practices, especially to children – Provide the most appropriate product labeling to encourage healthier practices	Danone Way framework introduces all the recommendations in terms of sustainable development practices, divided around three objectives: – Optimized production processes – Renewed recipes – Accompanied consumer	World leader in the food industry and is always trying to set an example in terms of CSR. May 2017, score B- by ISS-oekom Corporate Rating, corporate performance in CSR through a global and sectoral approach. One of the few ISO 50001 certified companies.
L'Oréal	"Share beauty with everyone," innovate sustainably, produce sustainably, live sustainably, and develop sustainably to share the growth with all of L'Oréal's stakeholders (employees, suppliers, and communities)	L'Oréal is developing highly innovative tools throughout the group to ensure that ethics and CSR are truly effective and real – Innovative human resources policies with suppliers and with the communities where they operate – Substantial and lasting changes in the way they design, produce, communicate, and distribute products	200 solidarity supply and sustainable supply programs, benefiting more than 57,000 people. 90% of their products are manufactured in-house and in 2015, a 50% reduction in carbon dioxide emissions, a 50% reduction in their water consumption, and a 50% reduction in waste per finished product.

Michelin	"Improve the mobility of its customers" through its collective responsibilities	Implement an engagement approach that has been renamed "Performance and Responsibility," and managed by the works council. Innovation capacity is the key factor in their ability to develop. Suggestion and incentive system, in particular through training.	Innovations: radial tire, green tire, PAX system, online travel itineraries. Between 2007 and 2013, reduction of the carbon footprint by 37%. Reduction of water consumption in factories by 60%. Care for families and participation in local development of the territories of implantation.
Veolia (Veolia Water)	Access to essential services and equitable distribution of resources	Sustainable Development Committee created in 2012. Veolia Water develops know-how with a view to achieving or approaching energy self-sufficiency, mainly for the treatment of effluents.	*Enjeux-Les Échos*: Veolia ranks seventh among the CAC 40 companies most committed to CSR. Veolia is listed each year in the FTSE4Good Index. More than 3.8 billion euros in revenue related to the circular economy. In 2014, the water business in France obtained the renewal of the label *Diversité*.
Comments	**Companies formulate their commitments, define their missions, and decide to engage in the context of their profession and their sector of activity, within their means and skills**	**Engaging in a CSR-oriented strategy involves rethinking the value chain, treating impartially its main activities and support.**	It is fundamental to measure the impact of CSR activity and the effects of implementing strategies, both internally (in terms of results) and externally (outcomes). Communication about results and outcomes is an integral part of the strategies.

reality of individual and collective actors is very complex and impossible to measure in a precise and detailed way, we propose to focus on the meaning that actors give to their CSR actions and on the dialogue between companies and their stakeholders.

However, making sense of a CSR dialogue does not necessarily make sense. The construction of meaning is not an individual act but always collective, and the "official" communication in its multiple forms (websites, conferences, advertisements, etc.) does not prefigure the reception and the interpretation that is made by people targeted by the communication department (Libaert 2014).

The complexity of everyday life and organizations makes it impossible to say with absolute certainty that one organization only adopts responsible behaviors, actions, and strategies and that another is totally irresponsible (Balmer et al. 2007). Indeed, CSR is a balance to be established between the interests of shareholders, employees, customers, citizens, democratically elected governments, and so on, which can be sometimes compatible, contradictory, or compatible and contradictory at the same time. It is necessary both to avoid idealizing organizations and their "official" CSR practices and to avoid giving the impression that any CSR is only manipulation, greenwashing, and serving the interests of the "powerful." Thus, an interpretative approach to CSR allows focusing on the construction of the meaning given to CSR on a daily basis.

The study of this construction of the meaning of CSR practices can be based on the analysis of official CSR communications. We see CSR communication texts produced as discursive acts. According to Lehtonen (2000), the "text" can come from all types of signifying practices (visual, language, behavior, etc.). A text is a social event that updates one or more discourses (Fairclough 2003). The analysis of discourses in the sense of social practices consists in identifying the themes that are supposed to make sense for the persons that communicate their interpretations and the acts they induce, in the sense of Gee (2009). Some examples of discursive acts include positioning oneself and positioning other persons as well as claiming power and expertise to naturalize one's activities.

We propose a semiotic framework of CSR communication analysis and the associated discursive acts. We distinguish two axes of analysis: the semiotic "quality" of information and the semiotic "international dimension."

The Semiotic "Quality" of Information From an informational perspective, CSR achievements seem to make companies more credible; their CSR attitude is supposed to be not only "discourse." Given the wide variety of sectors and contexts, it is very difficult to assess CSR achievements in a "universal" way. In a one-way communication on these "achievements," the goal is not so much to inform the stakeholders as to enhance the image of the organization (Crowther 2016). Some companies, however, emphasize their commitment and can focus on "engagements" to the detriment of actions. Other companies associate their commitments with a philosophy that gives meaning to their actions, strategies, products, commercial and non-commercial communications. This philosophy is not only embedded in CSR communication but also in all the signals issued by the company. However, the communication of "commitments *versus* achievements" should not be categorized systematically as "nice statements *versus* actions." Indeed, the reception of the messages is also influenced by the relationship between a company and its stakeholders and by the historical, political and cultural contexts.

Another semiotic dimension of the "quality" of information is the opposition of quantitative information to qualitative information. According to Hunter and Bansal (2007), quantitative information appears more credible than qualitative information in regards to CSR. With quantitative elements, the public can measure the specific evolution and achievements of CSR. Moreover, in a context where scientific and measurement culture dominates organizations, quantitative measurements are associated with neutrality, rigor, control, and possibilities of verification. They can be used as a decision-making argument by institutional actors who favor this type of discourse. However, quantitative measurements are simplifications of a more complex reality. In other words, a company that communicates with "quantitative" indicators that it defines itself and that is at the same time concerned by several CSR scandals, is no more credible than another that values the qualitative measurements, which give meaning to its global strategy and are not linked to environmental and social crises.

Combining CSR practices with scientific expertise allows a company to "universalize" its actions and CSR strategies and to obtain a status of technical leadership. On the other hand, examples of CSR practices and initiatives on a daily basis may be favored by some companies (or subsidiaries) involving local communities more than impersonal statistics. Companies can thus play the card of the proximity and emotion and put forward practices supposed to be consistent with the local and specific needs of each context of use.

It is also possible to put abstract principles and concrete practices into semiotic tension. Indeed, the ethical codes set up by the organizations represent general, positive principles and therefore allow the proclaimed adherence of all. It is a question of demonstrating the importance given by the company to CSR. For Bondy and Starkey (2014), the general principles facilitate the work of managers and allow them to save time in defining their CSR policy. However, these principles do not solve ambiguities in particular situations because everyone can have a personal understanding of each general principle. Thus, for Hunter and Bansal (2007), CSR communication is more credible when it consists of detailed information and illustrated examples to give the feeling of action and achievements.

Another semiotic opposition is that between positive externalities like "do well" (education missions, construction of new infrastructure for public use, etc.) and negative externalities such as "do no harm" (treatment of pollution due to the activity, etc.) caused by the organizations. According to Crilly et al. (2016), it is possible to distinguish the CSR practices adopted by internal (shareholders and managers) and external (outside stakeholders) pressures. The practices of "do no harm" would be induced rather externally, while practices "do good" are supposed to be initiated internally. Thus, "do no harm" practices would be considered as a mere compliance by managers, while "do good" practices induced by "internal motivation" would seem more credible.

The Semiotic Oppositions of CSR Specific to Multinational Companies The "standards" of CSR are often differentiated according to country categories. For example, a multinational company that adheres only to local standards in "non-Western" countries would not be seen as behaving responsibly on a global scale (Muller 2006). De Geer, Borglund, and Frostenson (2009) show that in Western countries with a "strong State," such as Sweden, CSR practices can be seen as causing employee and citizens' dependency on employers. Thus, the only way to balance the conflicts of interest of different business stakeholders is to make social and environmental legislation more demanding. Some practices considered as common in the home country of some Western multinationals are considered "CSR practices" in host countries where local social and ecological standards are less demanding.

Another semiotic opposition is between standardization and adaptation. In terms of communication, a global CSR could induce a sense of coherence and therefore make a CSR as "reality." For Hunter and Bansal (2007), a standardized CSR communication improves the legitimacy of multinational companies and reduces their disadvantages, like negative stereotypes. However, for De Geer, Borglund, and Frostenson (2009), the cultural and historical contexts being specific to each environment, the conception and the meaning of

CSR practices are also specific locally. CSR adapted to local contexts improves the image of subsidiaries as local businesses and brings greater proximity between subsidiaries and local stakeholders.

Another semiotic opposition is the increase of the socio-ecological standards of the host countries versus "neutrality." According to Wettstein (2010), multinational companies have an obligation to try to improve the legal, social, and ecological frameworks in contexts of local standards that are less restrictive. Some groups favor actions that value identical moral requirements regardless of the country (moral objectivism), but can be accused by some local stakeholders of neo-colonialism or lack of sensitivity to local contexts. Other multinational companies, under the pretext of adaptation to the local habits, try to claim political and cultural neutrality (moral relativism).

All of these tensions coexist in the process of making meaningful CSR. Trying to understand the trends and the style of CSR presentation is not useful for making typologies of strategies and companies. Typologies are too rigid to reflect the daily work of interpretation and negotiation of a fluid reality. On the other hand, the analysis of CSR communications makes it possible to identify the perceptions that the official communicators have of the needs of their audiences as well as the roles and statuses that they attribute to their organization, internal stakeholders, and various publics.

Conclusion

This research shows that while theoretical, social and political approaches can always be different from one country to another, particularly across the Atlantic, some multinational firms seem to be applying a new managerial paradigm integrating CSR. It is no longer (or not only) a marketing or communication argument. Corporate philanthropy, partnerships, and humanitarian activities are particularly characteristic of a new proactive orientation.

However, discourses and practices must be analyzed in perspective. This means that it is not enough to survey the "official" strategies. To be able to answer further questions, particularly about the effect of the discourses or the legitimization of the strategies in various countries, a further examination of the practices, processes, and policies is needed.

This is the purpose of the following chapter, which focuses on the case of Veolia Water company in three different European countries.

References

Ackerman, R. W. (1973). How Companies Respond to Social Demands. *Harvard Business Review, 51*(4), 88–98.

Balmer, J. M. T., Fukukawa, K., & Gray, E. R. (2007). The Nature and Management of Ethical Corporate Identity: A Commentary on Corporate Identity, Corporate Social Responsibility and Ethics. *Journal of Business Ethics, 76*(1), 7–15.

Barnett, M. L. (2007). Stakeholder Influence Capacity and the Variability of Financial Returns to Corporate Social Responsibility. *Academy of Management Review, 32*(3), 794–816.

Blake, D. H., Frederick, W. C., & Myers, M. S. (1976). *Social Auditing: Evaluating the Impact of Corporate Programs*. New York: Praeger.

Bondy, K., & Starkey, K. (2014). The Dilemmas of Internationalization: Corporate Social Responsibility in the Multinational Corporation. *British Journal of Management, 25*(1), 4–22.

Bowen, H. (1953). *Social Responsibilities of the Businessman*. New York: Harper.

Carr, A. Z. (1968). Is Business Bluffing Ethical? *Harvard Business Review, 46*, 2–8.

Côme, T., & Rouet, G. (2015). *Les innovations managériales*. Paris: L'Harmattan.

Crilly, D., Ni, N., & Jiang, Y. (2016). Do-Not-Harm Versus Do-Good Social Responsibility: Attributional Thinking and the Liability of Foreignness. *Strategic Management Journal, 37*(7), 1316–1329.

Crowther, D. (2016). *A Social Critique of Corporate Reporting: Semiotics and Web-based Integrated Reporting*. New York: Routledge.

De Geer, H., Borglund, T., & Frostenson, M. (2009). Reconciling CSR with the Role of the Corporation in Welfare States: The Problematic Swedish Example. *Journal of Business Ethics, 89*, 269–283.

Dierkes, M., & Berthoin Antal, A. (1986). Whither Corporate Social Reporting: Is It Time to Legislate? *California Management Review, 28*(3), 106–121.

European Commission. (2001). *GREEN PAPER: Promoting a European Framework for Corporate Social Responsibility*. Available from http://www.europarl.europa.eu/meetdocs/committees/deve/20020122/com(2001)366_en.pdf

European Commission. (2006). *Launch of "European Alliance for Corporate Social Responsibility"*. Available from http://europa.eu/rapid/press-release_IP-06-358_en.htm

European Commission. (2011). *Communication from the Commission to the European Parliament, The Council, The European Economic and Social Committee and The Committee of the Regions: A Renewed EU Strategy 2011–14 for Corporate Social Responsibility*. Available from http://www.europarl.europa.eu/meetdocs/2009_2014/documents/com/com_com(2011)0681_/com_com(2011)0681_en.pdf

Fairclough, N. (2003). *Analysing Discourse: Textual Analysis for Social Research*. London: Routledge.

Freeman, R. E. (1984). *Strategic Management: A Stakeholder Approach.* Boston: Pitman.
Friedman, M. (1970, September 13). The Social Responsibility of Business Is to Increase Its Profits. *The New York Times Magazine.*
Frimousse, S., & Peretti, J.-M. (2015). Regards croisés sur Engagement RSE & Performance. *Question(s) de management, 1*(9), 65–89.
Gee, J.-P. (2009). *An Introduction to Discourse Analysis: Theory and Method.* New York: Routledge.
Gendre-Aegerter, D. (2008). *La perception du dirigeant de PME de sa responsabilité sociale: une approche par la cartographie cognitive.* Thèse de doctorat en sciences économiques et sociales, Université de Fribourg, Suisse.
Gond, J.-P. (2006). *Contribution à l'étude du concept de performance sociétale de l'entreprise: fondements théoriques, construction sociale, impact financier.* Thèse de doctorat, Université Toulouse 1.
Hunter, T., & Bansal, P. (2007). How Standard Is Standardized MNC Global Environmental Communication? *Journal of Business Ethics, 71*(2), 135–147.
Lehtonen, M. (2000). *The Cultural Analysis of Texts.* London: SAGE Publications.
Lépineux, F. (2003). *Dans quelle mesure une entreprise peut-elle être responsable à l'égard de la cohésion sociale?* Thèse de doctorat, CNAM, Paris.
Libaert, T. (2014). *Communication et environnement, le pacte impossible.* Paris: PUF.
Maanvilja, L., & Lopez, J. (2008, March). CSR Europe. *European Agenda.*
MacGillivray, A., Begley, P., & Zadek, S. (Eds.). (2007). *The State of Responsible Competitiveness.* London: AccountAbility.
Mitchell, R. K., Agle, B. R., & Wood, D. J. (1997). Toward a Theory of Stakeholder Identification and Salience: Defining the Principle of Who and What Really Counts. *The Academy of Management Review, 22*(4), 853–886.
Mullenbach-Servayre, A. (2007). L'apport de la théorie des parties prenantes à la modélisation de la responsabilité sociétale des entreprises. *La Revue des Sciences de Gestion, 1*(223), 109–120.
Muller, A. (2006). Global Versus Local CSR Strategies. *European Management Journal, 24*(2–3), 189–198.
Mullerat, R. (2013). Corporate Social Responsibility: A European Perspective. *Miami–Florida European Union Center of Excellence, 13*(9). Available from http://aei.pitt.edu/43368/1/Mullerat_CSR_Europa.pdf
Pasquero, J. (2005). La responsabilité sociale de l'entreprise comme objet des sciences de gestion: Un regard historique. In M.-F. Turcotte & A. Salmon (Eds.), *Responsabilité sociale et environnementale de l'entreprise.* Québec: Presses de l'Université du Québec.
Porter, M. E., & Kramer, M. R. (2006). Strategy and Society: The Link Between Competitive Advantage and Corporate Social Responsibility. *Harvard Business Review, 84,* 78–92.

Raytcheva, S., & Rouet, G. (2016). Le partage culturel au service du développement à l'international de la "culture française". *Communication, 34*(1). Available from https://communication.revues.org/6659

Wartick, S.-L., & Cochran, P.-L. (1985). The Evolution of the Corporate Social Performance Model. *Academy of Management Review, 10*(4), 758–769.

Wettstein, F. (2010). For Better or for Worse: Corporate Responsibility Beyond "Do No Harm". *Business Ethics Quarterly, 20*(2), 275–283.

10

CSR Practices: The Case of Veolia in Three European Countries

Jana Marasova, Anna Vallušová, Elka Slavcheva Vasileva, and Delphine Philip de Saint Julien

Introduction

The subject of this study is a comparative analysis of the practices of corporate social responsibility (CSR) practices of at the multinational company Veolia in France, Slovakia, and Bulgaria. This chapter focuses on the semiotic oppositions of CSR specific to multinational companies mentioned in the previous chapter.

It examines how CSR strategies, practices, and tools that originated in a traditional market economy (France) have been adapted to the conditions of centrally planned economies (Bulgaria and Slovakia). We ask the question whether and how Veolia adopts its socially responsible practices to local conditions given their cultural and historical contexts. Furthermore, we observe how local management communicates the common corporate values to various company stakeholders and to the general public. We also analyze and evaluate the contribution of Veolia to increasing awareness of environmental values and respect for public interest.

J. Marasova (✉) • A. Vallušová
Matej Bel University, Banská Bystrica, Slovakia
e-mail: Jana.Marasova@umb.sk; anna.vallusova@umb.sk

E. S. Vasileva
University of National and World Economy, Sofia, Bulgaria
e-mail: elkav@unwe.bg

D. Philip de Saint Julien
University of Versailles, Versailles, France
e-mail: delphine.desaintjulien@uvsq.fr

Veolia CSR: An Explicit Strategy

The history of Veolia dates back to 1853, when Compagnie Générale des Eaux (CGE) came to existence. Its aim was to irrigate the countryside and supply water to cities in France. After changes in management, names, and strategies, including its entry into the stock exchange in 2003, the Vivendi Environment Group became Veolia Environnement and then only Veolia in 2005. Today, the company is divided into three major divisions: water, energy, and waste. It employs more than 160,000 employees worldwide, including more than 51,000 in France, 2500 in Slovakia, and 1500 in Bulgaria.

The study of the "official" CSR strategy of Veolia is based on a longitudinal analysis of CSR and sustainable development reports from 2012 (the year of transition to the "new Veolia") to 2017, highlighting the explicit elements of the CSR strategy to try to summarize the changes over time.

Since 2015, Veolia has focused its sustainable development strategy on three areas and nine commitments. First, "resourcing the world" addresses the sustainable management of natural resources by promoting the circular economy, contributing to the fight against climate change, and preserving and restoring biodiversity. Second, "resourcing the regions" consists of building new models of relationships and creating added value for a company, as exemplified in 2016 with Danone and IBM; contributing to the development and attractiveness of new regions; and providing and maintaining essential services for health and human development. Third, "for women and men in our company," Veolia aims to create a healthy and safe work environment through the professional development of each employee and a commitment to diversity and fundamental human and social rights within the company.

The Veolia CSR approach is part of a large-scale process to integrate environmental, social, and societal performance into the overall performance of the company by 2020. Thus, taking the example of France, Veolia is positioning itself as a catalyst for attractiveness and an accelerator of economic and social development, while likewise contributing to the preservation of ecosystems and the fight against climate change. In 2014, the French economic magazine *Enjeux-Les Échos* ranked Veolia seventh among the CAC 40 companies most committed to CSR (Veolia 2014); in 2017, EcoAct Cabinet ranked it third among the CAC 40 for climate performance.

As of 2011, Veolia Environnement, the leading operator of environmental services, is committed to adapting its businesses to social and environmental disruptions (Veolia 2011) and to integrating different dimensions of sustainable development in its activities. The company has the objective of strengthening management systems in the field of corporate social responsibility, developing contractual models, and initiating innovative partnerships in the social economy field in order to enable access to essential services for disadvantaged populations, particularly those in emerging countries. For example, Veolia Water designs, develops, and manages water, clean-up, and wastewater services for municipalities and industrial companies. In 2016, Veolia supplied water for 100 million people and provided sanitation for 61 million people worldwide. When the company confirmed its transition to "new Veolia" in 2012, a sustainable development committee was created.

The analysis of CSR/sustainable development reports and of scorecards from 2012 to 2016 indicates that Veolia Water France has developed an explicit and offensive CSR. This is not the typical position in the context of CSR in France and in Europe in general, where the academic debate is relatively young compared to America (Moon and Matten 2004). Indeed, the issue of the CSR practices in management, of CSR tools (Kolk 2005; Langlois and Schlegelmilch 1990), or of philanthropic donations for social and/or environmental causes (Brammer and Pavelin 2005) only recently became research subjects (Maanvilja and Lopez 2008).

According to Moon and Matten (2004), CSR is commonly used in liberal market economies where the firms address issues perceived as a part of corporate social responsibility. CSR practices typically consist of voluntary programs and activities realized for strategic reasons (Moon and Matten 2004). This strategy is motivated by the visible expectations of all stakeholders of the company and responds to the pressures from the stakeholders and partnerships with other organizations.

Veolia, like most multinational and transnational companies, joined corporate coalitions in CSR and sustainable development[1] and subscribed to training programs to learn and develop CSR best practices (e.g., the CSR-UK Academy). It began to adopt increasingly explicit CSR strategies.

Economic, Legal, Ethical, and Philanthropic Responsibilities

The Carroll's Pyramid of Corporate Social Responsibility (1991) is one of the most widely used theories to illustrate various aspects of CSR (Mardam-Bey Mansour 2011). The *economic responsibilities* of an organization are

---

[1] For example, the UK Business community or CSR Europe, cf. http://www.csreurope.org/business-community-uk

located at the bottom of the pyramid. Based on Veolia's financial reports, its turnover increased by 4% between 2012 and 2015, while net current income increased sharply from € 180 million to € 580 million (Veolia 2015). Therefore, we can say that Veolia is in very good financial health.

The second section of the Carroll pyramid is *legal responsibility*: an organization should comply with the law and should respect its agreement with society. The Group has set up group standards aimed at preventing legal risks, in particular (Veolia 2015):

- An internal criminal risk management procedure
- A procedure governing sponsorship and patronage actions
- A supplier charter and a code of conduct for purchases, including chapters devoted to ethical practices to be respected and promoted by all persons involved in the purchasing process
- A procedure for reporting cases of fraud committed by employees of Veolia
- An internal prohibition procedure applicable to payments and aids made during an election period
- A guide on protection of innovations and know-how

Carroll characterizes ethical responsibility in terms of activities that society expects: expectations of employees, consumers, shareholders, and communities. Since 2003, Veolia has formalized its values in the publication "Ethics, Conviction and Responsibility Program." Its objective is to guide behavior of the company's employees on a daily basis. Veolia supports these approaches by raising awareness and training activities designed to establish the ethical culture among its employees and to prevent risks. Moreover, to be considered as an ethical organization in terms of CSR, it is essential to develop good relations with all the stakeholders. Since 2006, the group has published a charter that affirms 12 principles (Veolia 2013):

1. Protect the environment, contribute to the preservation of natural resources and biodiversity, and combat climate change.
2. Promote, through innovation, research, and development, environmental, economic, and social solutions that meet the needs of future generations.
3. Sensitize the populations concerned by its activities to the environmental issues and to the behavioral adaptation that must result from them.
4. Adapt its service offer to the needs and expectations of clients through dialogue, quality of its advice, and expertise.

5. Ensure the safety and health of its employees and contribute to improving public health.
6. Ensure working conditions in which fundamental human rights and international labor standards are respected.
7. Promote diversity and fight discrimination to ensure equal opportunities.
8. Promote the development of skills and the social promotion of employees throughout their working lives.
9. Define gradually its own environmental and social standards imposed on all its locations all over the world.
10. Base its corporate governance on a transparent communication, an anticipation of risks, and a setting of rules of vigilance and good conduct.
11. Contribute to local economic and social development, and achieve international goals in access to essential services.
12. Encourage its partners, subcontractors, and suppliers to adhere to its values and contribute to sustainable development commitments.

The fourth element is the set of *philanthropic responsibilities* of the organization, which considers all activities that present the organization as a "*good corporate citizen.*" These activities may include programs that improve well-being and goodwill.

Stakeholders and Partnerships

Veolia has developed a definition of its stakeholders based on some academic works (Freeman 1984; Porter and Kramer 2011) with five broad categories: economic partners (shareholders, investors, subcontractors/suppliers, banks, etc.), public institutions (governments, local authorities, European and international institutions, public institutions, etc.), clients (communities, industry, consumers, national states, municipalities, etc.), internal actors (employees, managers, employee representative bodies, trade unions, etc.), and civil society (associations/foundations, environmental organizations, development organizations, think tanks, extra-financial rating agency, academic circles, media, social entrepreneurs, etc.).

According to Porter and Kramer (2006), CSR became a tool that organizations use to gain a better reputation. Therefore, organizations should try to create shared values with local communities and other stakeholders. As Veolia's 2015 global performance report describes, during the previous four years, Veolia increased its partnerships with a wide range of governmental and non-governmental organizations. Veolia believes that co-construction of new models of relationships and value creation between stakeholders is a real lever for growth and a source of innovation and differentiation. The company has established numerous partnerships; for example, Veolia collaborates with Ashoka, the world's largest network of social entrepreneurs, to develop a model ("POP UP") that aims at creating incubators of social entrepreneurship in all major metropolises in France and the world.[2]

Transparency, Innovation, Climate, and Biodiversity

Since 2004, Veolia has been included in the FTSE4Good[3] Index every year. The regularity of its selection for the Index illustrates the recognition of the company's long-term performance and commitment to sustainable development, in particular to the objective of *transparency*.

Veolia developed the Water Impact Index to help companies implement the necessary measures in water and sanitation management. This indicator, presented for the first time at the Milwaukee Water Summit in 2010, gives information about the effects of human activity on water resources. Compatible with ISO 14046 on water footprint, the Water Impact Index incorporates data on the quantity of water used, level of stress upon water resources, and overall water quality. This new instrument enables Veolia to go further in the evaluation of the water footprint of anthropogenic activities.

Veolia Water regularly asserts its intention to reduce the quantities of water taken from a natural resource (substituting it with recycled water), both for its facilities and for those operating on behalf of its customers. The aim is to manage natural resources sustainably by promoting the circular economy, which represents more than 3.8 billion euros of its turnover. The objective is also to contribute to the fight against climate change through the activities of water protection. The company participated in the GHG Protocol's experiment on the assessment of greenhouse gas emissions throughout the supply chain and was involved in the development of a new version of the

---

[2] Cf. http://www.veolia.com/fr/groupe/medias/actualites/veolia-lance-pop-une-nouvelle-plate-forme-d-incubateurs-d-entreprenariat-social
[3] Cf. http://www.ftse.com/products/index-notices/home/getnotice/?id=1751208

methodological guide for the assessment of greenhouse gas emissions from water and sanitation services.

For its water business, in 2012, Veolia identified a number of drinking water plants and wastewater treatment plants that had carried out a diagnosis and put in place an action plan to restore local biodiversity. In 2013, 97 sites for water treatment or drinking water production carried out the biodiversity diagnosis and 79 of them implemented the associated action plan. By reaffirming its commitment to biodiversity, Veolia evolved its objectives in 2014 to deploy an action plan on all sites with high biodiversity stakes by 2020. This now concerns the water business, in addition to the waste business.

Social and Societal Strategy

The CSR strategy includes objectives and actions focused on employees. Policies for the development of remuneration, training, and good practice in terms of access to shareholding are planned, as well as those for the company's working environment, evaluation of the management, internal communication, flexibility of work, corporate culture, health, and safety. Veolia's objectives are threefold:

1. Ensure a safe and healthy working environment: in particular, achieve a workplace accident frequency rate of 6.5 or less.
2. Promote the professional development and commitment of each employee: deliver training each year to more than 75% of employees. Sustainability principles and practices are integrated into the training of new employees and managers. Training and information for employees in environmental matters are an integral part of the company's efforts in each of the countries in which it operates.
3. Ensure respect for diversities and fundamental human and social rights within the company: cover more than 95% of employees with a social dialogue mechanism. In 2014, the activity "Water in France" obtained the renewal of the label "Diversity."

The group evaluates its relationships with suppliers, to diversity, and to its commitments in local communities. It also measures donation and charity practices and policies to promote, among other things, access to services related to health, education, economic opportunities, and the arts. For Veolia, it is important to:

- Build new relationships and value creation models with stakeholders.
- Contribute to the development and attractiveness of regions by participating in the development of the local fabric through aid and humanitarian emergency, social bonding, and support for employment and environmental protection and for biodiversity. For example, in the framework of contracts for the delegation of public services provided by Veolia, an educational animation for biodiversity was developed, in addition to establishment of "educational pools," ecopastures, and apiaries. This work enabled approximately 2500 children living in these communities to be exposed to these subjects each year (Veolia 2014).
- Provide and maintain essential services for health and human development.

Veolia's CSR in France

From the Europress database and an Internet search using two keywords "Veolia Water" and "CSR," we have collected about 40 newspaper articles published between January 2012 and March 2017. The analysis of these texts enables us to determine various fields of discourses about Veolia's CSR policy in this area, similar to "gusts" (*rafales*)[4] in a cognitive-discursive analysis (Ghiglione et al. 1998).

Like many CSR policies developed by the CAC 40 companies, Veolia communicates about its CSR policy in three major lines. First, the company offers a formalized program on respect for human, social, and environmental rights and the fight against corruption. Second, it implements proactive measures concerning protection of biodiversity, addressing disability, seniors, young people, and diversity. Third, it monitors its suppliers regarding their working conditions and their supply chain. These three lines are organized around three main "gusts" in the collected newspaper articles: environment, human resources, and economy.

Over the past five years, *environmental issues* have been the main thrust of Veolia's CSR policy, which was intensified at the time of COP 21 in Paris in December 2015.[5] One of the issues addressed at the conference concerned global warming, and Veolia proposed three fields of action: to change its production and consumption patterns by turning to the circular economy, to use

---

[4] "Gusts" include "occurrences of words tending to occur with significant concentration in a part of the text" (Ghiglione et al. 1998).
[5] Veolia was present at the "One Planet Summit" in Paris in December 2017.

methane with significant heating power, and to create a carbon-based fee to promote a low carbon economy.

The company has entered into agreements with non-profit organizations in connection with its water management business, enabling access to water and adequate sanitation for nearly 10 million people between 2002 and 2015 in India, Africa and China. Veolia has established a number of ecological partnerships that involve a reduction of pollution thresholds and the prevention of harmful substances being released into the environment. They enable Veolia to enhance its strategic objectives for sustainable development. Moreover, the "Environment" criterion is included in the calculation of remuneration of managers, as well as to the incentive bonus paid to employees, depending on their compliance with the environmental requirements. However, one of the company's fears is to be accused of "greenwashing," or eco-laundering, that is, the misuse of ecological messages in order to give a responsible image.

One of the major tools of Veolia's CSR policy is its foundation, which has one of the largest budgets in France. It is both a tool for managing the company's relationship with its environment, a tool for dialogue with stakeholders, and a means of capturing weak signals sent by society. One of its most publicized actions was the scientific expedition "Tara," which studied coral reefs between 2016 and 2018.

The second theme revolves around the company's social and *human resources* (HR) policy. Veolia enhances the internal mobility to its regional sites to promote the quality of life of its employees: its intranet site, in particular, lists internal offers of professional mobility. Veolia also supports the mobility of employee spouses, and it uses promotions and wage increases as incentives.

Moreover, while the Copé-Zimmermann law (la loi Copé-Zimmermann) required boards to provide for 40% of women before the end of 2016, Veolia seeks to integrate different profiles of employees to facilitate professionalization, internationalization, and rejuvenation of its board, while favoring internally the development of women's networks.

In order to strengthen both its social responsibility and its reputation, Veolia also signs charters of commitments and joint resolutions known as "global" agreements with its trade unions via its European group committee, as these alliances and agreements are highly observed by employees of the company.

Veolia encourages "social entrepreneurs." Driven by a vision and an acute sense of general interest, these employees, are looking for "meaning" in their work. They work to develop an innovative activity capable of bringing a durable solution answering a problem of society. In this way, employees have the opportunity to create new career paths based on societal missions, in cooperation with local NGOs on projects with a strong social impact. For example, in Bangladesh, water is contaminated by arsenic. After Veolia cleans the water, the villagers sell it, which contributes to the development of the local economy. Through its training campuses and "skills patronage,"[6] Veolia is helping people who are in the process of reintegration into the labor market with the objective to recruit a certain number of them over time in order to meet their skills needs. In this way, Veolia sensitizes its managers on disability, a financial penalty being attributable to the results of any regional management that does not reach the legal threshold of 6% of total number of employees. Considering gender equality, the wage gap was 15% in 2014 (the female population representing 22% of the workforce).

The third "gust" deals with the *economic theme*. Veolia tends to combine its own interests, the interests of the country where it develops its activities, and international interests linked to the Millennium Development Goals set by the United Nations for the development of poor countries. It is materialized by a "social business," associating philanthropic and business methodology with a principle of "neither loss nor profit." Veolia's CSR policy also incorporates the "Bottom of the Pyramid" (BOP) concept and creates new sources of growth and develops new customer segments within the poorest socio-economic groups. These populations can only become potential consumers if a radical innovation policy is pursued (Prahalad 2004). Integrating this concept is seen as the key to winning the "right to operate" in poor and emerging countries. It is recognized as a form of relocation of revenue and as a stimulus for so-called inverted innovation, that is, innovations created in the conditions of developing world, subsequently spread in the Western world.

Two different approaches to analyze the field of CSR can be employed. One, focusing on the company and its managers, CSR demonstrates the positive link among the company's approach, its financial performance, and its relations with external stakeholders. Two, focusing on corporate governance, a company seeks a positive link between its actions and its interests, along with its potential for self-regulation and legal regulation to ensure effective social responsibility (Acquier and Aggeri 2008). This latter approach is favored by Veolia based on information gleaned from the press papers.

Four CSR strategies can thus be put in place: a "cosmetic CSR" where the company only complies with legal obligations; a "peripheral CSR" where it

---

[6] The "patronage of skills" allows a company to make available to a body of general interest the skills of its volunteer employees during their working time (Vuillequez 2012).

implements actions that are not directly related to its activity; an "integrated CSR" where it implements actions related to the activity of the company, financial and social indicators being integrated into the dashboards; a "CSR-BOP" (Martinet and Payaud 2008) where the company develops an activity for the needs of the poorest (Prahalad 2004). According to the press articles, we can consider that Veolia CSR is both "integrated" and "BOP."

Beyond a legal obligation, the reports on CSR by Veolia tend to favor transparency and disclosure requirements for practices implemented within the company (De Serres and Ramboarisata 2012). It is also characterized by a commitment to integrate the views of the various stakeholders of the company on the long-term basis (European Commission 2001).

Its relatively intense communication reflects the interests of both economic actors and social actors to CSR (Acquier and Aggeri 2008). Moreover, Veolia's communication about its social and environmental responsibility is supposed to help protect it in case of accusations of irresponsible behavior. At the same time, however, in case of irresponsible behavior, it would be even more damaging for Veolia, which communicates around its responsible activities (Vanhamme et al. 2015).

Veolia's CSR in Slovakia

The concept of CSR was not known and used during the period of communism; however, state enterprises practiced certain socially responsible activities (Koleva 2006). Among others, they developed numerous activities concerning employee care, such as building crèches, providing housing, and financing cultural or sporting events. Since these activities were mandatory in its nature, it cannot be seen as social responsibility in the sense in which CSR is defined and perceived by the European institutions. After the transition to a market economy, the social pillar of CSR was not unknown for companies.

Considering the environmental pillar of CSR, the 40 years of the planned economy and orientation of Slovakia to heavy industry within COMECON left serious environmental problems. The awareness about the need for environmental protection is increasing only gradually. Unlike Western countries, the social dialogue, which is generally considered to be the driving force of corporate social responsibility, is underdeveloped in Slovakia. The main reason for this is the lack of a tradition with participatory democracy (Lacová 2016), and a poorly developed third sector, which is often funded by corporate sources, therefore cannot be expected to play a critical role for businesses.

Veolia Slovakia: Organization, Activities, and CSR

CSR is an essential and inseparable part of Veolia's business. Veolia increasingly perceives its core business—central water and heating supply—as a public service. Therefore, it also tries to act in such a manner—not only toward its customers but also toward its partner cities, policy-makers, and local authorities that affect its business environment. The company takes part in several professional associations through which it helps to shape the wider business environment.

The values on which Veolia's CSR is based have been defined at a group level—they were selected by a forum of around 5,000 employees through an intranet questionnaire. They include responsibility (toward employees, the environment, municipalities, clients), solidarity (toward customers and other partners), respect (to the law, internal regulation, and to other people), innovation (toward renewable resources, energy efficiency, and savings), and consumer care (orientation on consumer expectation to deliver quality and efficient product or service).

Context of the Slovak Subsidiary CSR has been part of the Veolia strategy since the beginning of its 25-year history in Slovakia (before 2015 Veolia acted as an owner of Dalkia, predecessor of Veolia Energia). The strategic line is guaranteed by Veolia International in Paris, and the management of the Slovak subsidiary maintains and develops CSR by its own measures.

The strategy of Veolia Slovakia (mainly Veolia Energia) is based on the above-mentioned values of Veolia Group and contains seven main objectives for the next five years, of which the last three are focused on CSR: to act as a responsible partner for municipalities, to support the community in which the company operates, to be responsible for sustainable development and to protect the environment, to be an attractive employer, and to create motivating working conditions for all employees.

Veolia Slovakia focuses on the environmental pillar, which is directly related to its core business. The company uses high-efficiency technologies. The flagships are technological appliances in Bratislava and Žiar nad Hronom. The facility in Žiar is unique of its kind—the gas is produced by gasification of biomass, and then electricity and heat are produced. This is widely considered to be a highly eco-friendly approach.

The context of the Slovak subsidiary differs from the French environment. To provide heating, producers have to meet strict criteria for its production and supply, specifically in terms of control of resources, technical parameters, and emissions. While in France, it is perceived as an instrument of quality of life; in Slovakia, there persists a certain aversion to a former socialist monopoly. The result is an effort of residential houses in towns to be separate from the central supply and ensure their own heating, which "appears" to be cheaper but can differ in any given individual case. The opportunity costs of increased environmental pollution are often not considered by the inhabitants in these cases.

Relationship Subsidiary: Headquarters

The Veolia Group has its legal and business structure. The owner of Veolia Slovakia is from the legal perspective Veolia International based in Paris. Veolia International owns Slovak Veolia Energia (Energy) based in Bratislava and Veolia Voda (Water) based in Banská Bystrica and Poprad. Veolia Energia has 16 individual companies in 27 towns in Slovakia in addition to its headquarters in Bratislava, and Veolia Voda also has an additional structure. It is managed not from Paris but from Prague, where the Central and Eastern Europe Central Office covers these types of activities in the given European region. Prague represents the intermediate management level ("zone" level) between France and Slovakia.

HR Practices Management perceives HR practices as linked primarily to the environmental and social pillars of CSR. However, the organization of activities and thus CSR have to adapt to the labor market situation. Veolia Slovakia addresses the question how to increase its attractiveness as an employer. It seems to be more efficient for the management to prioritize targeted searching for quality people who are motivated to work in an environmentally friendly firm and then to solve specific technical requirements for each job position.

The Course of Social Dialogue The company is convinced that collective bargaining takes place before it starts officially. It has well-established cooperation between operational and regional directors and their employees. It is a permanent preparation for collective bargaining itself, where the debate is already focused on what needs to be solved: remuneration, benefits, or some issues of the labor code, which are the specific subject of a collective agreement.

Prognostic Management of Job Positions and Competencies For Slovak managers, this is a bit of a technocratic concept; however, working with age structure is seen as important. The average age of Veolia Slovakia employees is 47 years. As Veolia International focuses on building long-term technical competencies, national-level managements have to transfer it to their level and address the age structure to ensure that the company's knowledge remains preserved.

Remuneration Issues Veolia Slovakia is a regulated entity. The state limits its costs, including payroll, through the Network Regulatory Office. Therefore, this company will never be a top employer in terms of remuneration. However, remuneration is always a result of several factors, for example, combinations of employee training, certain social benefits, or investments in the working environment. In a period of increased pressure on performance and growing stress, employees can appreciate the healthy attitude of managers, their humane approach, and a fair mix of remuneration that contributes to their satisfaction in addition to wages.

HR and Environmental Responsibility In the headquarters of Veolia Energia Slovakia in Bratislava, the signs of environmental responsibility are present everywhere. By introducing ISO standards, especially ISO 50000 concerning energy management, the company has committed itself to act to protect natural resources and increase awareness about environmental protection. This is also reflected in the relationship with employees. The environmental awareness is necessary not only for employees who work directly, for example, with the boilers, but also for the white-collar employees, who have to understand that not only heat production but every single human activity has an impact on the protection of resources and the environment.

Within "Ecoweek," organized annually, Veolia Slovakia runs its own programs focused on how to save paper; how to print less and more economically; how to save electricity, water and fuel; how and where to buy organic products; and more.

Management supports employee initiatives through employee grants. The assumption for acquiring the grant is an employee's personal involvement in the implementation of the project. Employees come up with interesting suggestions, often educational in its nature in relation to the environment. Some examples include an interactive exhibition about bees and building a workroom for a retirement home.

According to the questionnaire survey among the employees, all of the respondents are convinced that the business activities of Veolia have an impact on the environment. Most of them agree that the protection of the environment concerns every firm. They also think that CSR enables people to become familiar with an ethical approach to the protection of the environment.

HR and Responsibility for Community Issue Several managers noted during the interviews that their work at Veolia changed their lives in terms of sensitivity to environmental values and responsibility for community issues. What they have learned in their work is automatically transferred to their personal life, and they promote respect for scarce resources in their surroundings through energy saving, waste sorting, and adapting to central heating supply.

Veolia Energia Slovakia contributes to maintaining employment in the localities where it operates. In several towns, its activities are based on cooperation—joint ventures with municipalities that have a 25–35% share in them and have supervision over economic issues. Mutual contracts (for 5–20 years) define precisely the rights and obligations of the company, for example, the obligation to invest annually specific amounts into the maintenance, safety, and renewal of facilities or distribution networks. Veolia also invests in environmental programs that municipalities cannot afford.

The Veolia's product line itself has a built-in community-based responsibility: central heating supply is a solidarity system that contributes to sustainable growth. By emphasizing the environmental dimension of heating production and supply, including waste recycling, and securing the appropriate protections for purifying and distributing water, Veolia is committed to the day-to-day implementation of corporate social responsibility, at both the management and executive level.

Veolia's CSR in Bulgaria

The introduction of the concept of CSR in Bulgaria is seen mainly as a consequence of the expanding business activities of multinational corporations in response to globalization in recent decades in the national context of the emerging economy. At the same time, it can be stressed that the enactment of public policies in the field of CSR has been linked to the country's membership in the European Union (EU) since 2007, following the outlined European framework of CSR initiatives.

A comparative study (Slavova 2013, 2015; Slavova et al. 2014) on the implementation of priority public policies of CSR in Bulgaria and other EU member states shows the proximity of the situation in the country to that of the so-called new members of the EU in 2007. In the developed national strategy, Bulgaria is seen as a country still at an early stage in the development of the social and environmental practices with a focus on promoting and strengthening the CSR concept. However, the government policy in the field of CSR has begun to be manifested in a more explicit form.

The analyses made in the recent years showed a significant increase in the CSR activities of the companies operating on the Bulgarian market after Bulgaria's accession to the EU (Peycheva et al. 2016, Slavova 2015; Slavova et al. 2014). Various forms of corporate social initiatives have been identified, and a number of companies which are subsidiaries of multinational companies stand out with an integrated approach to the implementation of CSR programs and projects (Slavova 2013, 2015). Unlike other Western European countries, global companies operating on the Bulgarian market, often supported by international institutions such as the UN Development Program, have a defining role in the emergence of CSR initiatives in Bulgaria (Simeonov and Stefanova 2015).

The research of the CSR discourses and practices of Veolia in the Bulgarian market will help to reveal the impact of the global, and in particular European, practices in the field of CSR in Bulgaria.

Similar to the situation in Slovakia, Veolia operates in the country in the water and energy fields through Sofiyska Voda AD and Veolia Energy Bulgaria. The focus of the study in Bulgaria is the Veolia affiliate in the water sector.

CSR in Sofiyska Voda AD: Part of Veolia Group

Sofiyska Voda AD was established in October 2000 under a 25-year concession contract. Through it, the Sofia Municipality ceded the exploitation and maintenance of its water supply to the company. Sofiyska Voda is a joint stock company, and Veolia Voda S.A. holds 77.1% of the shares. The remaining 22.9% of the shares is held by the Sofia Municipality. Since November 2010, Sofiyska Voda is part of the Veolia Group and is the exclusive provider of water and wastewater services in the area of Sofia Municipality. It is important to emphasize that the water supply and sewerage assets are public municipal property and all newly built facilities with the investment of Sofiyska Voda also belong to the city.

Applying the methodology for studying CSR in Sofiyska Voda through a "press search" did not help us determine the various fields of discourse around Veolia's CSR policy in Bulgaria. An Internet search was conducted on two keywords "Sofiyska Voda" and "CSR," and newspaper articles, publications on the Sofiyska Voda website, presentations, and other press releases were collected in January 2010 and May 2017. As a result, relatively little information on CSR policy and company practices was found. Despite the limited amount of information gathered and the impossibility of a detailed analysis, the three major axes of the CSR policy established above for Veolia France (environment, human resources, and economy) are generally confirmed.

In-Depth Interviews with Representatives of Sofiyska Voda AD

In order to expand and focus the study, in-depth interviews with representatives of Sofiyska Voda were conducted to reveal new aspects, other viewpoints, and opinions related to the enactment of CSR policy and the instruments for its implementation in Bulgaria. Among the four participants were the Communications Senior Manager, responsible for CSR activities in Sofiyska Voda; two Communications Specialists in the public relations department; and the Director of "Purification and Water Management." For the purpose of the survey, a 45- to 60-minute direct personal interview was conducted by one interviewer with one respondent on pre-established, core CSR thematic areas, with open questions. For this purpose, the team of this international study developed a "questionnaire" containing general questions that guide the conversation with the respondents. The questions were related to CSR in the national context, Veolia context, Veolia—Sofiyska Voda context, and CSR policy and practices.

The interviews were held in May 2017 at the head office of Sofiyska Voda AD, Sofia, according to a preliminary agreement (time, place, and other details). All interviews were audio recorded.

National Context The interviews revealed country specifics in enacting CSR in Bulgaria. Respondents stressed that Sofiyska Voda AD does not face challenges in offering new products or services and in this sense conducts "regulated business." Yet the company still faces problems related to "water reform conditions," such as old and inefficient networks, huge investment needs, and limited funds for investment, which are provided by the tariff and EU funds. Other specific attitudes related to public understanding of water services were noted such as "the second, or third generation of city population that thinks of water as a 'gift of God,' not a subject of commercial activity."

The respondents' answers were also focused on communication issues related to "the decline of traditional media while social media is fragmentizing public opinion" and "the huge rate" of "Net haters that make senseless public debate." This provides some explanation for CSR's external communication in Sofiyska Voda. The views expressed in the context in the country, and more precisely the media environment, forces external CSR communication to be indirect. Very often in the media, CSR news is "distorted" by focusing on the celebrities present at an event and not the results of an initiative. In order to avoid this "distorting" effect, Sofiyska Voda uses an "indirect" or "hidden" form of communication of CSR practices. During the interview, the following expressions were used: "do not boast"; "it is important that there is a contribution to society and there is no need for it to be publicized"; "they will recognize us by the effect of activity – e.g. when we receive a prize from 'SOS – Children's Villages.'"

The Bulgarian media are strongly focused on the lifestyle of Bulgarian celebrities. As a result, critical journalistic studies are less common and/or have a more limited impact on the Bulgarian media market. In this context, the results of the in-depth interview show that the press and CSR practices are partially opposed. At the same time, the communication of CSR practices within the organization is direct and intensive, using primarily the intranet.

Veolia: Sofiyska Voda Context

Unlike the Veolia Group, there are no formal CSR and sustainable development reports for Sofiyska Voda. Respondents highlight the importance of "Sofiyska Voda's Annual Reports – Figures and Facts," as well as of the internal monthly reports to the senior management on CSR policy activities and practices. The interviews revealed that in the Bulgarian context, there are formal certified management systems. Sofiyska Voda AD has an integrated quality management system (providing quality services), environmental management system (environmental protection), and healthy and safe working conditions management system (health and safety of workers). The mechanisms of internal and external audit, management report, improvements, and so on applied in this regard enable the achievement of effective and efficient quality management and environmental protection and the provision of healthy and safe working conditions for workers in the organization. This is in line with other studies by Bulgarian organizations regarding the motivation to introduce quality management systems and the environment related to external factors, such as clients, suppliers, partners, NGOs, financial institutions, and the media (Ivanova et al. 2016; Vasileva et al. 2012).

CSR Policy and Practices

Despite the lack of a formal (explicit) system, respondents' answers confirm Veolia's CSR approach and policy typology. In Bulgarian practice, initiatives are developed under the 12 principles of the Veolia Code (Veolia 2013). These principles have been adopted, and there is a desire to employ practices that share common values such as customer orientation, innovations, solidarity, responsibility, and respect.

Sofiyska Voda AD has identified stakeholders and partnerships within the integrated management system. There is an emphasis on the relationship with the institutions and the main company's stakeholders (state bodies such as the Energy and Water Regulatory Commission, the Ministries and State Agencies, and Sofia Municipality; universities, high schools, and elementary schools; EU institutions; and other partners).

Respondents provided multiple confirmations of activities on the other axis of Veolia's CSR approach and policy, namely, "transparency, innovation, climate and biodiversity." This direction is also supported by the activities that strengthen the connection with the scientific circles: a round table organized by Sofiyska Voda about the climate conference COP 21 and the fight against climate change; the Veolia Campus initiative; the "Water of Life" Project—a two-year research project for the exploration of biodiversity in the Iskar River, in partnership with the Biology Faculty of Sofia University; the Academy for Business Leaders; and others.

In connection with the social and societal component of Veolia's CSR strategy, interviewees revealed a variety of practices that can be classified into the following groups: "care from the employees" and "with care for people and environment."

In the first group of "care from the employees" practices, respondents described a number of practices related to corporate philanthropy and voluntary community work, such as voluntary city cleaning, payroll donation to help the "SOS Children's Villages," a Christmas charity lunch (for the "Our Children" Foundation), financial help for suffering people (those reeling from the impacts of floods and forest fires), an Annual Sport Weekend, and *Spartakiada*.

In the second group "with care for people and environment," Veolia presented practices related to the care for people of the community. This includes giving out freshwater in the hottest summer days, live laboratory demonstrations to ensure the best water quality, showing of gratitude with a

Martenitsa[7] for every customer in the consumer offices on March 1, a raffle for loyal employees, discounts from the bills each month, and large summer and Christmas gifts every year. The company likewise focused on helping people in need, which includes working with associations for disabled children, helping other cities in natural disasters, and sponsoring a foundation focused on the integration of Roma youth. The Veolia Foundation and "Eau et Vie" intend to contribute to activities for creating social skills and practices to limit water waste in local Roma communities. There was also an emphasis on practices for environment protection (the "trees for greener life" initiative, where for each 1000 subscriptions for electronic invoices, the company plants a new tree; care for the city; and an annual volunteer spring cleaning).

The results of the interviews describe a variety of CSRs in the Veolia—Sofiyska Voda context. They confirm the conclusions from other authors about CSR practices identified in Bulgaria, mainly "corporate philanthropy," along with "socially responsible business practices" and "corporate social marketing" (Slavova 2013; Slavova et al. 2014).

The CSR policies and practices of the global company Veolia play a motivating role in developing the socially responsible behavior of business organizations in Bulgaria and in particular of Sofiyska Voda AD. As a subsidiary of a multinational company, Sofiyska Voda adopts an integrated approach to the implementation of CSR programs and projects and successfully adapts them to the national context. On the other hand, the organization can contribute to enriching the CSR practices of other affiliates in Central and Eastern Europe regarding the inclusion and integration of the young Roma population into the social environment and local economy. This could lead to the transfer of social skills practices to limit waste of water as a natural resource in the local Roma communities in Central and Eastern Europe.

Conclusion

Based on examination of the official documents of the Veolia Group on the application of CSR in three countries, we have arrived at the conclusion that the level of CSR approach, largely determined by the European standards, is approximately the same in each of these countries. Interviews with managers

---

[7] A "Martenitsa" is a small piece of adornment, made of white and red yarn and usually in the form of two dolls, a male and a female. "Martenitsi" are worn from Baba Marta Day (March 1) until the wearer first sees a stork, swallow, or blossoming tree. The holiday and the wearing of "Martenitsi" are Bulgarian traditions related to welcoming the spring, which, according to Bulgarian folklore, begins in March.

and information from questionnaire surveys and the media have shown that the approaches to CSR differs only in the ways to meet these standards. For example, unlike France, management of Veolia in Slovakia and Bulgaria needs to focus more intensively on communication about the importance of the central distribution of heating and water and about environmental protection. This communication to employees, town authorities, and municipalities, as well as to the wider society, still has some aspects in which improvement is necessary.

CSR of Veolia is based on the transparently declared corporate values. Both the headquarters and local managers consistently require compliance to these values. However, they also consider the cultural and historical context of the local environment. In particular, the local management team has a significant area of freedom in terms of how to encourage motivation of employees and the public to socially responsible activities. Past experience shows that, for example, the system of awarding grants to their own CSR staff projects greatly awakens their initiative and leads to the realization of interesting programs that have a positive impact on the environmental awareness of the broad local community.

Running the core business of Veolia assumes a close cooperation with municipalities of the country. This cooperation provides the most important space for Veolia to contribute to raising awareness of sustainable development. It communicates its values, informs the public about existing environmental standards and perspectives for their development, and brings top expertise and invests in technologies that municipalities cannot afford.

The specificity of the development of CSR in post-communist countries is the fact that it was brought to this region by multinational firms, as the existing institutions were not able to shape the business environment at that time. In this respect, Veolia is the actor that constantly contributes to development of the business culture in its host countries.

References

Acquier, A., & Aggeri, F. (2008). Une généalogie de la pensée managériale sur la RSE. *Revue Française de Gestion, 1*(80), 131–157.

Brammer, S., & Pavelin, S. (2005). Corporate Reputation and Social Performance: The Importance of Fit. *Journal of Management Studies, 43*(3), 435–455.

Carroll, A. B. (1991). The Pyramid of Corporate Social Responsibility: Toward the Moral Management of Organizational Stakeholders. *Business Horizons, 34*(4), 39–48.

De Serres, A., & Ramboarisata, L. (2012). Gouvernance des banques canadiennes et gestion des ressources humaines responsables. In J. Allouche (Ed.), *Encyclopédie des ressources humaines* (pp. 712–724). Paris: Vuibert.

European Commission. (2001). *GREEN PAPER: Promoting a European framework for Corporate Social Responsibility*. Available from http://www.europarl.europa.eu/meetdocs/committees/deve/20020122/com(2001)366_en.pdf

Freeman, R. E. (1984). *Strategic Management. A Stakeholder Approach*. Boston: Pitman.

Ghiglione, R., Landré, A., Bromberg, M., & Molette, P. (1998). *L'analyse automatique des contenus*. Paris: Dunod.

Ivanova, D., Haradinova, A., & Vasileva, A. (2016). Environmental Performance of Companies with Environmental Management Systems in Bulgaria. *Quality – Access to Success, 17*(172), 61–66.

Koleva, P. (2006). *Nouvelles Europes. Trajectoires et enjeux économiques*. Belfort: Université de Technologie Belfort-Montbéliard.

Kolk, A. (2005). Corporate Social Responsibility in the Coffee Sector. The Dynamics of MNC Responses and Code Development. *European Management Journal, 23*(2), 228–236.

Lacová, Ž. (2016). *Politique monétaire et investissements des entreprises en Slovaquie*. Saarbrücken: Éditions universitaires européennes.

Langlois, C. C., & Schlegelmilch, B. B. (1990). Do Corporate Codes of Ethics Reflect National Character? Evidence from Europe and the United States. *Journal of International Business Studies, 21*(4), 519–539.

Maanvilja, L., & Lopez, J. (2008, March). CSR in Europe. *European Agenda*.

Mardam-Bey Mansour, F. (2011). La Responsabilité sociale de l'entreprise: Définitions, théories et concepts. Available from http://www.fgm.usj.edu.lb/files/a112011.pdf

Martinet, A.-C., & Payaud, M. (2008). Formes de RSE et entreprises sociales. *Revue Française de Gestion, 180*, 199–214.

Moon, J., & Matten, D. (2004). *Corporate Social Responsibility Education – How and Why Europe is Different*. Research Paper Series ICCSR Nottingham.

Peycheva, M., Veysel, A., & Dineva, V. (2016). *Corporate Social Responsibility – Theory, Accountability and Auditing*. Sofia: IK ATL-50 Publishing House.

Porter, M. E., & Kramer, M. R. (2006). Strategy and Society: The Link between Competitive Advantage and Corporate Social Responsibility. *Harvard Business Review, 84*, 78–92.

Porter, M. E., & Kramer, M. R. (2011). Creating Shared Value. *Harvard Business Review, 89*, 62–77.

Prahalad, C. (2004). *The Fortune at the Bottom of the Pyramid*. French translation: *4 milliards the nouveaux consommateurs*. Paris: Village Mondial.

Simeonov, S., & Stefanova, M. (2015). Corporate Social Responsibility in Bulgaria: The Current State of the Field. In S. Idowu, R. Schmidpeter, & M. Fifka (Eds.), *Corporate Social Responsibility in Europe. CSR, Sustainability, Ethics & Governance*. Cham: Springer.

Slavova, I. (2013). Corporate Social Responsibility and Public Policy: Focus and Trend in Bulgaria. *Economic and Social Alternatives, 2*, 51–65.

Slavova, I. (2015). Corporate Social Responsibility in Bulgaria: Development, Constraints and Challenges. *Economic and Social Alternatives, 2*, 113–126.

Slavova, I. et al. (2014). *Corporate Social Responsibility in Bulgaria – Part of European Social Practices*. Sofia: University of National and World Economy. I. Slavova (Ed.). Sofia: Publishing Complex of University of National and World Economy.

Vanhamme, J., Swaen, V., Berens, G., & Janssen, C. (2015). Playing with Fire: Aggravating and Buffering Effects of ex ante CSR Communication Campaigns for Companies Facing Allegations of Social Irresponsibility. *Marketing Letters, 26*(1), 565–578.

Vasileva, E., Ivanova, D., & Nikolov, B. (2012). The Specificity of Management Systems According to the Bulgarian Producers from Selected Sectors. *Club Library, 9000*(29), 3–27.

Veolia. (2011). Rapport Responsabilité sociale & environnementale. Available from https://www.veolia.com

Veolia. (2012). Cahier de la performance RSE. Available from https://www.veolia.com/sites/g/files/dvc2491/files/imported-documents/2016/11/Veolia-cahier-performance-RSE-2012_0.pdf

Veolia. (2013). *Cahier de la performance RSE 2013*. Available from https://www.veolia.com/sites/g/files/dvc2491/files/importeddocuments/2016/11/veolia_rse_fr_2014_0_0.pdf

Veolia. (2014). *Cahier de la performance RSE*. Available from https://www.veolia.com/sites/g/files/dvc2491/files/importeddocuments/2016/11/RSE-2014-FR_0.pdf

Veolia. (2015). *Rapport d'activité et de développement durable*. Available from https://www.veolia.com/southwark/sites/g/files/dvc2491/files/imported-documents/2016/11/rapport-activite-developpement-durable-2015_0_0.pdf

Vuillequez, E. (2012). Mécénat de compétences: trois exemples réussis: l'implication citoyenne au coeur des performances RH. *Personnel ANDCP, 534*, 72–73.

11

Social Costs of Non-Responsible Research

Sylvie Faucheux, Caroline Gans Combe, Catherine Kuszla, and Martin O'Connor

Introduction

Responsibility in science and for the uses of science is a complex amalgam. There are matters of integrity in research practice, knowledge quality assessment, administration, and governance. But there are also matters relating to the use and abuse of scientific knowledge in society; and these engage questions of economic and political power, societal purposes, institutional arrangements, and individual values.

This chapter addresses the question of the social costs of non-responsible research. These are "costs" having incidence, in various ways, across the four capitals—that is, produced assets, human capital (including health), social capital, and the biophysical environment. They can in part be considered in

---

S. Faucheux (✉)
Inseec U Paris, Paris, France

C. Gans Combe
Reihoo, Paris, France
e-mail: cgc@reihoo.com

C. Kuszla
University of Paris Nanterre, Paris, France

M. O'Connor
University of Paris Saclay, Paris, France

monetary terms but must also be investigated in qualitative and relational terms—notably for the dimensions of societal capacities and cohesion, and biosphere integrity.

The opening section "Responsibility in Science: Who, What, Why?" introduces our key topics of, first, research misconduct (i.e., misconduct of persons and organisations directly engaged in the practice of scientific research) and, second, responsible research (meaning activities of research, development, and demonstration—and, by extension, of innovation—that are respectful of defined societal norms or values). These two topics are intertwined; but they are not the same. Drawing on results of the recently completed European DEFORM Project (2016–2018), we clarify the distinction between, and the inter-relations of, these two concepts, and then investigate the complex challenges of quality assurance and governance that arise from their inter-penetration.

The section "Research Fraud and Its Costs" addresses the incidence and social costs of research fraud—that is, omissions, deformations, and falsehoods in the production and exploitation of results in scientific research. This is research misconduct relative to "internal" standards of good science; but it may also be considered as delinquent relative to wider concerns for creation of wealth and social cohesion.

The section "Responsible Innovation in the Context of Sustainability" addresses the theme of responsible innovation, notably with reference to contemporary ecological and societal challenges of sustainability. We situate this within the ongoing debate about quality in science and technology relative to societal values "external" to science.

The section "The Paradoxical Case of Dieselgate" discusses the inter-penetration of these two issues. The example of the "Dieselgate" scandal of falsified vehicle emissions measures is used to illustrate feedback loops between research misconduct in the narrow sense (such as fraud) and wider debates about science in society.

The final section "Towards Integrative Quality Assurance Procedures" concludes with a short discussion of effective procedures of quality assurance in science and technology assessment. We add our voices to the call for radical (and responsible) innovation specifically in the knowledge quality assessment and governance domain.

Responsibility in Science: Who, What, Why?

As a methodological frame, we exploit and adapt the typology proposed in O'Connor et al. (2018), itself drawing on DEFORM Project findings. That paper introduced demarcations along three axes:

- WHO?—The relevant actors include individual researchers and research teams "internal" to the scientific community, and also those "external" to the research sector exercising investment, policy, regulatory, evaluation, and civil responsibilities.
- WHY?—As criteria of performance or acceptability, we must consider quality criteria that are "intrinsic" to science in the sense that they are espoused by and for the scientific community itself but also quality considerations that are "extrinsic" societal priorities and purposes.
- WHAT?—The situations and actions whose quality or acceptability is to be judged are sometimes located inside the research process (i.e., inside the "knowledge sector"); but a wide range of actions and impacts are situated outside of the knowledge sector itself.

We build on this, by adding some further demarcations leading to a fuller 3×3×3 typology. Look first at the domains of action. The "research life cycle" is characterised, on the one hand, by activities taking place "inside" the knowledge sector (such as proposing, performing, reviewing, and reporting research) and, on the other hand, by activities "outside" the knowledge sector itself. These "outside" activities can be split into two sub-categories:

- The decision-making and resource allocation activities "upstream" that provide for the material, human, and financial resources that feed into research activities; and
- The domains of activity "downstream" including innovation, decision support, and educational uses of knowledge.

In a corollary, we can distinguish different broad classes of "stakeholders" around the knowledge sector. It would seem relevant to distinguish two sub-categories of "external" stakeholders:

- Those entities or institutions having a well-defined "contractual" *engagement* with the research activity—for example, as a funding agency, a private sector investor, an actor in the exploitation of research and development (R&D), a consumer, or another sort of client of the knowledge, product, or derivative services; and
- Those persons within *civil society* "at large," who are not directly engaged with the knowledge production process but perceive their interests "at stake" along any dimension of the environmental, health, or societal implications of the research taking place.

With this typology of "internal" and "external" (contractual and wider civil society) stakeholders of the knowledge sector, we open the door to exploiting models of stakeholder responsibility developed in the recent literatures on CSR (corporate social responsibility) and social acceptability (e.g., in technology risk appraisal), in this way treating research as a sector of economic activity susceptible to governance and quality control considerations analogous with other sectors (Faucheux and Nicolaï 2004; O'Connor and Spangenberg 2007; Barré 2011).

We can expect finally some correlation between domains of action, stakeholder categories, and quality considerations. R&D activities in both private and public sectors are subjected to multiple expectations. These performance imperatives include, first of all, the "intrinsic" quality considerations—norms of methodological integrity and quality that, by conventions set in place progressively since the eighteenth century, are supposed to be assured by, on the one hand, the "scientific spirit" of individual researchers and teams and, on the other hand, by various "peer review" processes conducted within the research community. They also include "extrinsic" quality considerations which are expressed across multiple institutions, notably:

(a) legislative frameworks that require research entities to address, over and above pure scientific outputs, their "ethical" status and their potential impacts in terms of environmental protection, employment, health benefits, or other social progress;
(b) funding conditionality that, in public as well as in private sector domains, incites researchers to focus on fields and forms of analysis that correspond not only to knowledge production criteria but more particularly to politically determined priorities in environmental, employment, health, technology, or other domains; and
(c) the pressures, codified, for example, in business reporting and performance rating procedures, of demonstrable commercial value and market success.

And finally, we must consider value statements expressed, individually and collectively, by people as participants in "civil society"—for example, about the acceptability of a project, product, or innovation. Such value statements may have their roots in diverse moral, religious, cultural, political, or existential concerns, and may be quite disparate relative to the legislative, contractual, and financial considerations evoked in (a), (b), and (c) just above.

Table 11.1 Framework for analysis of responsibility in and around research

WHO?	WHAT?	WHY?
The classes of actors around science	*Categories of actions or events*	*Criteria of quality and responsibility*
Policy and funding institutions	"Upstream" activities providing for R&D capacity	"Extrinsic" institutional performance imperatives
Researchers and immediate associates	"Inside" the research sector (proposing, performing, reviewing, reporting)	"Intrinsic" considerations of scientific integrity
Civil society "at large"	"Downstream" actions (uses of knowledge in society)	"Extrinsic" considerations of societal acceptability

We thus refer to scientific integrity, institutional performance, and societal acceptability as the three major classes of quality considerations. In this way, we establish a schematic 3×3×3 typology in Table 11.1.

We have not yet specified the position of regulatory/governance agencies. This is intentional. The question of where to locate the exercise of responsibility is one of the controversial questions of the "crisis in science" today (Kuszla 2019; O'Connor et al. 2018). Our Table 11.1 typology provides for the characterisation, along each of the three axes, of events or situations of alleged research misconduct or other contention about knowledge quality and responsibility. It may be used as a framework for attributing costs and responsibilities associated with such events or situations, distinguishing "costs caused" (Whose responsibility for creating these costs?) and "costs borne" (Whose responsibility towards the victims in terms of liability, reparation, or compensation?).

"Research fraud" (discussed in section "Research Fraud and Its Costs") is misconduct taking place inside the knowledge sector, relative to "internal" standards of good science, and so falls in the middle row in Table 11.1. But when discussing causes and consequences of such fraud, and questions of governance responsibility and liability, we address actors, domains, and quality considerations across the whole 3×3×3 spectrum. "Responsible innovation" (discussed in section "Responsibility in Science: Who, What, Why?") poses the question of quality in science and technology relative to societal values and so corresponds immediately to the top and bottom rows in Table 11.1. The inter-penetration of these two themes is highlighted with the "Dieselgate" scandal of falsified emissions measures affecting millions of motor vehicles (in section "The Paradoxical Case of Dieselgate").

Research Fraud and Its Costs

The topic of misconduct in scientific research is most often addressed as a deviation relative to established norms of research integrity (Funtowicz and Ravetz 1990; Petousi and Sifaki 2019). A benchmark was provided by sociologist Robert Merton (1973), who suggested a set of norms (subsequently referred to as the Mertonian Norms) with the acronym CUDOS: Communalism, Universalism, Disinterestedness, Originality, Skepticism. Many recent characterisations have built on this. The European Science Foundation (ESF 2011) proposes the following principles of research integrity:

> "Honesty in reporting and communicating, reliability in performing research, objectivity, impartiality and independence, openness and accessibility, duty of care, fairness in providing references and giving credits, and responsibility for future science generations…"

Relative to these considerations of integrity, research misconduct (henceforth RM) is then defined as the intentional implementation of "deviant" practices such as[1]:

- Mistreatment (of people and animals as research subjects),
- Fabrication (the invention, recording, or reporting of data),
- Concealment, whether partial or complete, including incomplete presentation or distorted interpretation of findings, insufficient recordkeeping,
- Falsification (refers to the alteration of research materials, equipment, protocols, data, or results),
- Piracy, understood as the unauthorised reproduction or use of ideas, data, or methods from others without adequate permission or acknowledgement,
- Plagiarism and other forms of inappropriate attribution of authorship,
- Unlawful use of funds,
- Undue influence of funding companies/sponsors,
- Biases and carelessness in peer review activities (including funding and publication contexts),
- Sabotage of research activities.

---

[1] This list is a composite from typologies provided during the first DEFORM International Workshop (O'Connor et al. 2018). Analogous lists can be found in published and unpublished literature (see Petousi and Sifaki 2019).

An inspection of the various categories shows the proximity of RM with the general notion of fraud.[2] This is important for the question of possible sources of statistical data on the RM incidence, as criminology statistics in many countries are abundant.

Estimating the incidence of research fraud is not a trivial task. Research data on the incidence of RM are fragmented and heterogeneous. Academic researchers themselves seem historically reluctant to implement statistical research on their peers' misconduct (Titus et al. 2008). Overall, the available data from academic sources are:

1. Limited in volume: for example, the analysis by DuBois et al. (2013) is focused on 120 cases; the different databases studied by Fanelli (2009) draw on 3247 participants, mostly located in the Anglo-Saxon world (18 out of 21 data sources), with 2/3 being US based (plus 14% in the UK, 5% in Australia, and 14% from other sources).
2. Focused on publications retraction data (even when looking from the criminologist point of view, as in Hesselmann et al. 2014), a restricted scope that does not take into consideration either the full spectrum of RM or the full population of researchers.[3]

The modest academic output contrasts with mediatised statements about the possible scale of the RM problem. A recent *The Lancet* Editorial (*The Lancet* 2015), titled "Rewarding true inquiry and diligence in research," highlighted the immense scale of putatively "wasted resources" in key publicly funded research sectors. According to this article, an estimated US$200 billion might be considered as "wasted" R&D money in the US alone, for the study's reference year of 2010.

In fact, not all of the US$200 billion figure signalled by *The Lancet* is attributed to RM. Nonetheless, major international conferences are devoted to research integrity (or the lack of it), and hardly a week passes without news in the world of retractions, failed replications, fraudulent peer reviews, or supposedly misinformed science-based policies.

---

[2] Fraud is, in a dictionary definition, *an act of deceiving or misrepresenting*. In most RM definitions, poor research is not considered as misconduct unless the "intention to deceive" can be demonstrated.

[3] Institutional data from the UNESCO database for 2017 show that only about 16% of academic researchers are actively publishing in scholarly journals; and, in turn, academic researchers make up only one quarter of researchers in the world (the majority now being employed in the private sector).

So how can we get a handle on the incidence and magnitude of the phenomenon, in physical or monetary terms? In particular, what might we hope from a more aggregate statistics approach based on considering RM as occupational fraud?

The category "RM" itself is not recorded per se in national and international crime statistics. What is recorded, in most countries, is the incidence of various types of "occupational crime." In the DEFORM Project, inspired by precursors such as Hesselmann et al. (2014), Friedrichs (2010), and Gee and Button (2015), we looked therefore at ways that statistics for occupational fraud might be exploited to obtain estimates of research misconduct costs more particularly.

As an initial step, we conducted semantic analysis to check our underlying hypothesis that research misconduct (RM) could reasonably be considered as falling (fully or partially) within the perimeter of occupational crime (OC).[4] This analysis showed that RM descriptions have about 70% semantic correspondence with occupational crime descriptions. This appears plausible, as some domains of occupational crime such as bank fraud are clearly not within the perimeter of research misconduct.

The attempt was then made to exploit occupational crime statistics as a basis to estimate the incidence of RM. The full results and methods are presented elsewhere (Gans Combe et al. 2019); here we give an overview of the main steps as considerations for estimation of categories and magnitudes of RM-related costs.

The uncovering of research fraud cases depends on their observation and then also on the willingness of people to report instances of fraud—and, thereafter, on institutional follow-up, including police practices, categories of offence under prevailing laws, and court practices. Occupational fraud is among the penal/civil instances that frequently go unreported. Nevertheless, a percentage of fraud cases do get reported, some of these cases do go to court, and penalties are assigned to convicted fraudsters. So, there are databases available which do provide data on a wide spectrum of occupational crime categories, including (implicitly or explicitly) instances of research fraud.[5] On this basis, the DEFORM approach was to define parameters and estimation procedures as follows.

---

[4] Occupational fraud is typically classified as "theft" which means *unlawfully taking or obtaining of property with the intent to permanently withhold it from a person or organisation without consent and without the use of force, threat of force or violence, coercion, or deception.*

[5] Work in DEFORM has used data from the US BJS, crime data in England and Wales, French Interstats, Trac Reports, COPE, UNODC, ACFE report to the nations, Advisen Cybercrime handbook. Concomitantly, for statistical analysis and validation, pre-existing public databases from Eurostat, the World Bank, OECD, UNESCO, BJS, IODS, and Ortis were used. Gans Combe et al. (2019) provide details.

Suppose data on the population of researchers and *the number of research projects*. From occupational crime statistics (taken as a proxy for RM) and with available samples, an estimation is made of the *frequency of fraud occurrences* in this population of projects. Assuming a probabilistic framework, the [frequency of fraud occurrences] is formalised as:

[Freq. fraud occurrences] = [No. research projects] × [fraud occurrence ratio]

According to DEFORM data and models, the fraud occurrence ratio for RM in Europe is estimated to be about 0.6%. That is, the probability of some form of RM happening on a given project/set of projects is about 0.6%. Then, the frequency with which RM wrongdoers' actions become known, the fraud visibility rate, can be estimated with another parameter, the discovery ratio, as follows:

[Fraud visibility rate] = [Frequency of fraud occurrences] × [Discovery ratio in fraud cases]

We take the discovery ratio (sometimes referred to as the elucidation rate) in fraud cases in Europe[6] to be about 25%.

This means that the % of projects for which RM is revealed is estimated (with rounding to two significant figures) to be 0.6% × 25% = 0.15%.

So, if an institution (such as the European Commission) finances 25,000 projects during a set time period, the estimated number of projects tainted with misconduct will be about 0.6% of 25,000 = 150. And, the number of projects where a RM matter is elucidated in the justice process would be 25% of this, that is, 150 × 25%, or some 35–40 projects.

Turn now to the question of costs to society associated with RM. It is a simple matter to go from estimates of the number of projects, to estimates of financial resources involved. Using the above parameter of 0.6% for the percentage of projects for which RM is revealed, and assuming that RM incidence is independent of the funding scale of the project, we can estimate that about 0.6% of project funding is tainted by RM.

Taking the European FP7 programme from 2007 to 2013, the total project funding was (in round figures) about 56,000 million euros.[7] So, if 0.6% of the

---

[6] This is our current estimate for the discovery ratio (sometimes called the elucidation rate or the clearance rate) for fraud cases in brought to courts in Europe. As a model parameter, this must be used with caution. This clearance rate (*C*) is calculated by dividing the number of crimes that are "cleared" (a charge being laid) by the total number of crimes recorded. Clearance rates are far from homogeneous across crime categories and from country to country. Our figure of 25% is a median clearance rate for 2012–2013 for six European countries: Sweden, Norway, Denmark, Netherlands, Germany, and England and Wales (see Gans Combe et al. 2019). But inclusion of data from other countries could modify this estimate.

[7] Source: https://ec.europa.eu/research/fp7/pdf/fp-1984-2013_en.pdf.

financed projects were tainted by fraudulent behaviour, up to 340 million euros (i.e., 56,000 million × 0.6%) of EU monies may potentially have been spent on "corrupted" research activities during those seven years.

During the same period, according to OECD figures, business enterprise R&D spent about US$123,000 million. So, following the same sequence of calculations, we can estimate the "RM risk" at 123,000 × 0.6% = US$740 million worth of R&D projects.

We are more than two orders of magnitude down from *The Lancet* figure of US$200 billion for US R&D "wastages" from all causes combined. But of course, the EC framework programmes are not the only sources of Europe's public research funding. For an aggregate estimate of the public "RM risk" in Europe, we must look at the total resources invested in research, including public funding of universities and specialised research institutions. Depending on accounting conventions for fixed capital and major equipment as well as human resources and running costs, annual European R&D expenditure might be as high as 300 or even 500 billion euros. With the same estimation process as before, we bring the estimate for the RM risk of wasted R&D funding up to the order of three billion euros—still nearly two orders of magnitude below *The Lancet* figure, but nonetheless significant.

These numbers are obtained with primitive estimates for model coefficients. They should all be used with care. But quite apart from the statistics base for our parameter estimates, we need to ask if the financial resources visible as institutional sources of funding are telling the whole story about the risks and costs associated with RM. Of course, they are not. To form a picture of "full costs," we must make an inventory of the full spectrum of impacts of the RM, across the full spectrum of stakeholders. Each stakeholder, whether a cause or a victim of the RM, is engaged in the use of resources, may lose opportunities, and may bear damages of various sorts. In an institutional context, the obvious cost categories include human resources, direct operating expenses, and capital expenditures for the compromised research project. The question may also be asked if RM corrupts or compromises the worth of prior human capital investment (i.e., training of the researchers and the formerly useful knowledge capitalisation). There may also be significant costs associated with audit, enquiry, hearings, and judiciary procedures.

Going beyond the lost funding (which may need to be repaid in whole or in part) and other direct costs to individuals and research sector institutions, there may be negative consequences in terms of lost reputation and lost future opportunities (e.g., ineligibility for funding or reduced attractivity to students or other clients). They may also be "external" costs involving third parties. Quantification of these latter may depend on legal procedures (including fines or obligations of compensation) or agreements (after mediation or litigation). In section "The Paradoxical Case of Dieselgate," we illustrate the necessary breadth of the RM cost analysis with the example of "Dieselgate."

Responsible Innovation in the Context of Sustainability

Science and technological advances, seen widely as motors of competitiveness and as the cornerstones of the new "knowledge society," bring benefits and attractive novelty. But new knowledge also contributes new risks.[8] In parallel with discourses promoting new technologies and innovation, there has emerged a new "social demand" to reappraise the place of science and technology as a vehicle for society's aspirations. Translated into economic and managerial terms, R&D processes are not necessarily creating "responsible value" in the sense of results in compliance with declared societal considerations of (for example) individual and collective wellbeing, justice, or environmental sustainability.

But, if "social responsibility in science" is a specific normative consideration and not an automatic corollary of science itself, then the question arises, by what criteria or principles, and by whom, should this responsibility be ascertained?

For van den Hoven (2015), the innovation process is responsible if "risks, potential harms, wellbeing, values, needs, rights and interests of relevant parties ... are ... taken into consideration"—which, in his view, means that there exist effective mechanisms permitting different stakeholders to share information and knowledge and to participate in the evaluation ex ante and ex post of research projects and their outcomes. For analysts such as Taebi et al. (2014), Owen and Goldberg (2010), and Von Schomberg (2011), responsible innovation is an engagement for public values and carries with it a requirement for interdisciplinary research and the confrontation of diverse perspectives including value considerations.

Of course, concern for social responsibility in science is not new. What is perhaps distinctive about the contemporary responsible innovation theme is the accent placed on longer-term economic and environmental considerations. Seminal work by Ravetz (1971) on *Scientific Knowledge and Its Social*

---

[8] See: Wilsdon et al. (2005), Faucheux and Hue (2000, 2001), Faucheux and O'Connor (2000), Gallopin et al. (2001).

Problems had placed issues of uncertainty and ethics at the centre of the social practice of science and was an early attempt to reflect on the challenges of "industrialised science." Such themes have penetrated gradually into public policy and governance discourses, notably in correlation with sustainability concerns. Technology assessment, territorial planning, and economic analysis literatures now refer universally to "externalities" of resource use, production, and consumption decisions. The unintended "side effects" may, over time, come to be far more significant than the original purposes (e.g., radioactive wastes whose management has a much longer time horizon than the power generation itself).

The extent to which the social problems of science are located in science itself, or in human nature, or in putative abuses of science, is a matter of permanent dispute. What is clear, nonetheless, is how attention to "external" societal risks now influences both companies' and public bodies' research and innovation processes.

- In the private sector, one pattern of response is the formulation of CSR (corporate social and environmental responsibility) principles in application to innovation strategy and thus concomitantly to R&D. This can be a pro-active strategy of positioning in new or changing markets; or it can be a reactive positioning in response to legal obligations; or of course a circular causation where businesses may seek to anticipate and to influence legislation. Businesses active in R&D are confronted with the emergence of new legislative or normative frameworks that require the declaration—and demonstration—of compliance with an increasingly comprehensive array of ethical, public health, safety, risk management, and environmental conditions.
- In the public sector, the various government agencies, publicly funded research entities, and public-private partnerships benefiting from public monies are, analogously, required to include ethical and "societal" considerations in their workflows, and to justify the hoped for or expected results not only in scientific quality terms but also in terms of their profile of societal and environmental impacts. Multi-year R&D investment programmes are negotiated at a high political level (e.g., in ministries or at the European Commission), often with consultation processes engaging both business and civil society, defining "public good" priorities considerably wider than simple consumer satisfaction and productivity gains.

How, then, should we judge the performance, the likely yield, the value to society, or the societal acceptability of an R&D? Our response is to insist on the need to compose an inventory of the harmed parties and the harms. This may be a complex task, especially when we include consideration of value creation and destruction in a wider society and across space and time (Frame and O'Connor 2010).

Then we need to decide if, and to what extent, any of these harms or prejudices are evidence of non-responsibility. Not all non-responsible R&D involves researcher misconduct in the narrow sense. Some R&D is conducted with adequate method, tools of observation, and so on; but results are then distorted in subsequent policy or project evaluation process. Research procedures that are epistemologically and methodologically sound may nonetheless have purposes that violate societal values—for example, respect of the person, animal rights, ecosystem health, or long-term sustainability.

In practice, there will be movement back and forth—along scientific, legal, political, and societal avenues—from characterising effects (or feared effects) and attributing responsibilities. We must (1) identify the chains of cause-and-effect and the parties (present or future) that bear the costs of (or are at risk by) the research/innovation, (2) trace these back to the research/innovation action, and (3) locate (to the extent justified) the authors, forms, and places of any alleged non-responsibility. Once this scoping process is completed, the next step is to estimate the severity of the prejudice or harm for the parties due to these different responsible or non-responsible activities.

Who decides what constitutes an unacceptable loss or an adequate compensation? This is the question of "sustaining what, why and for whom?"—to which we return to the section "Towards Integrative Quality Assurance Procedures," after a passage through the "Dieselgate" case study.

The Paradoxical Case of Dieselgate

Misconduct may sometimes be wilfully delinquent behaviour by a "rogue" individual or organisation (Power 2013). But misconduct can arise without there being prior intent, in the face of a perceived (or real) gap between a research results promise (a value creation engagement) and the likelihood or capacity to achieve this promise. The DEFORM Project results highlight that fraudulent claims within the research sector, and with the use of research results, may sometimes arise when there is (1) the desire to obtain benefits that can accrue to well-conducted research and then also (2) the desire to avoid consequences of failure, for example, exclusion from a status group, loss of face, loss of revenue (jobs, clients, institutional funding, etc.).

"Misconduct" in this sense engages individual researchers. But where they arise and the ways in which they develop depend on the institutional environment and wider societal condition perpetrators (DuBois et al. 2013; Kuszla 2019; Petousi and Sifaki 2019). In the case of funded or other contracted research, several different pathways might be open to researchers, and to research projects' owners/promoters/sponsors, when faced with a "gap" between promise and likely real outcome. These include:

- Retraction and restart;
- Redesigning the research project or simply ending it;
- Fraudulent actions to disguise or cover up the gap.

If the choice of fraud is made, this might be influenced by perceptions of a low likelihood of detection or only light penalties if caught. Or it may be because the institutional environment is not propitious towards alternate paths of action.

Moreover, in the wider political, economic, and societal context, there can be "misconduct" by people outside the research sector itself, such as the wilful misrepresentation of research methods and results for commercial or political motives. The phenomenon of "delinquency" in and around the research sector, both public and private, is considered by many analysts and commentators (e.g., Saltelli 2016), as directly related to the penetration of commercial, military, and other "strategic" interests into the financing and rewarding of R&D activities. In schematic terms:

- Publicly funded higher education and research institutions facing demands of high societal relevance, commercial value, and impact respond to pressures for visible outputs, but sometimes in defiance of espoused scientific integrity standards.
- Private companies, increasingly important worldwide as vehicles for scientific R&D, face pressures for market success that may override the declared precepts of "social responsibility" in investment, innovation, and communication.

We now review the paradoxical case "Dieselgate" where a seemingly virtuous engagement for "responsible research" tipped over into major industrial and product fraud.

On 18 September 2015, the United States Environmental Protection Agency (EPA) issued a notice of violation of the Clean Air Act to the Volkswagen Group. The saga started, for Volkswagen, with the expression of a performance promise. In 2012, Martin Winterkorn, Chairman of the Board of Management of Volkswagen Aktiengesellschaft, announced the group's expectations: "Our pursuit of R&D and perfection and our responsible approach will help to make us the world's leading automaker by 2018 – both economically and ecologically" (VW Aktiengesellschaft, Experience D[r]iversity—Annual report 2012).

This promise was unrealistic. On the one hand, for VW, the US market opportunity was paramount, and internal policy had introduced a strong incentive for strategists whose bonuses relied on financial outcomes. On the other hand, the commercial strategy relied on "old" technology—motor and exhaust systems on which no new R&D investments had been planned as this was considered a dead end in view of the next generation of electrically powered engines. So there was no innovation strategy permitting to reach the emissions performance levels newly required under the Clean Air Act. Faced with imminent non-compliance, the company had chosen since 2009 the solution of implementing and installing software in the cars that induced misleading test signals about emissions performance of the cars. This fraud was unmasked, incriminating millions of cars worldwide, and the visible costs to VW are now very large.

- Human resources costs: Six high-level employees were condemned including to jail terms, for fraud and for tampering with evidence (in all, some 40 VW employees were suspected of participation in the destruction of proof).
- Direct financial costs to the VW group: Civil resolutions are expressed, so far, in three settlements. The first resolved the EPA (Environmental Protection Agency) claim; the second involved the U.S. Customs and Border Protection (CBP) claim; and the third regarded the violation of the FIRREA (Financial Institutions Reform, Recovery, and Enforcement Act). In June 2016, a US$14.7 billion settlement addressed one engine type (the 2.0-litre engine); this was followed by a further $1 billion settlement in December 2016 (the 3.0-litre engines). Nearly $3 billion for environmental mitigation projects came as a corollary. In January 2017, US$1.45 billion was announced to resolve the EPA and the CBP claims. VW has agreed to pay $50 million in civil penalties for its alleged violation of FIRREA. Thus, while VW succeeded in terms of its market share acquisition strategy in 2016, being the world number one car provider (number of cars sold), with 10.3 million units sold, it suffered significant balance sheet damage relative to its value creation objectives.
- Indirect financial costs to the VW group: At the peak of the crisis (in 2016), when the IT group had admitted to installing the technology that enabled

diesel cars worldwide to understate harmful emissions, VW affirmed that the firm had sufficient liquidity to resist the shock. This was true in a sense, but the company had no remaining capacity to invest in future developments. By the end of 2017, the scandal had cost the company $30 billion. On top of this, VW during 2016 (and until March 2017) had no capacity to obtain funds from the European bond market, whereas it had been the largest issuer of corporate bonds in Europe. This constituted a financial opportunity loss.

- Compensation to "victims" of the fraud? Penalties applied by the EPA under the Clean Air Act are based in part upon evaluation of the lost value of the VW cars. The reference figure was established at about $37,500 per car. This does not preclude that, under European, US, or another law, there may still be class actions seeking compensation directly to car owners.
- Costs to shareholders: There are several distinct interests amongst shareholders. VW's controlling shareholders are the Porsche and Piëch families, in addition to the German state of Lower Saxony. These families' first decision was to impose the resignation of Winterkorn and the elevation of Pötsch to the chairmanship of the board. This choice (of a senior inside manager) only enhanced suspicions of cover-up. This suspicion was reinforced further when a whistle-blower from VW's US operations alleged that he had been fired after he warned IT employees against the destruction of evidence. In September 2015, 1400 shareholders sued VW in Germany for investment losses. Damages are claimed at around 8 billion euros: 3.3 billion euros in compensation for a group of institutional investors and the remainder for modest shareholders.
- Damage to image and reputation: The company being under scrutiny, the scandal has led to the unveiling of other questionable practices such as the tests of diesel fumes' impact on animals including non-human primates without respecting the different legal provisions in that respect.
- Energy and ecological transition: The VW scandal created a systemic suspicion on the car industry, specifically its continued use of diesel. Old debates were reopened. In time, "Dieselgate" may well have ushered the end of diesel engine usage in individual cars. Major car manufacturers around the world have announced intentions to halt diesel engine production, and this has already impacted the second-hand value of existing such vehicles (not just VW).

R&D fraud here is not a minor phenomenon. The direct and indirect impacts appear across different timescales through systemic effects transmitted by a wide spectrum of vectors: material, legal, financial, reputation, and public opinion.

Towards Integrative Quality Assurance Procedures

The so-called Mertonian Norms (CUDOS) included, among others, Disinterestedness and Skepticism. The actors of present-day scientific research and its management are subjected to radically dissonant operating conditions. Various commercial, legal, and other societal mechanisms act to supplement, and sometimes to supplant, the "internal" science quality considerations. Maintaining traditionally established beliefs in, and self-declarations of, the disinterestedness of scientific endeavours, separated from vested interest (whether political agenda, business objectives, or cultural context), is increasingly difficult.

For the actors in the research sector, this cross-fire can induce dilution or abandonment of traditional ideals of scientific community.[9] We do not examine this sociological dimension here. But it is plausible that the dissonance and fragmentation within research institutions themselves is a degradation in social cohesion, trust, and "social capital" contributing significantly to the sentiment of "crisis in science."

Are there ways out of this crisis? Our chapter has proposed a heuristic framework (Table 11.1) for the identification of the full spectrum of actors, issues, and impacts associated with research and its uses in society. We advocate the development, in an experimental way, of innovative approaches to the appraisal of business—and also public sector—R&D performance across the full spectrum of quality criteria and the full spectrum of stakeholders. This will necessitate new competencies in auditing tools and in knowledge quality assessment as professional practice.

Our 3×3×3 system has several functions. First, it is a frame for the characterisation of events or situations of alleged research misconduct or other contention about knowledge quality and responsibility. Second, for a given institution or controversy, it may be used as an "audit" framework for the inventory and attribution of costs. The audit questions to be answered are:

---

[9] The work of Vasiliki Petousi and her University of Crete colleagues in the DEFORM Project, documenting the perceptions and opinions of a wide range of actors in the research sector, provides examples on this point (Petousi and Sifaki 2019). Reflections on a possible typology of people's "fallback strategies" (patterns of withdrawal, disengagement or denial) are found in Douguet and O'Connor (2019) as a part of their investigation into publicly accountable deliberative multi-stakeholder approaches to knowledge quality assurance.

- Costs Borne: that is, costs to WHOM (across the stakeholder categories), relative to WHAT type of event or action (located at one or more of the stages upstream, inside, or downstream of the R&D life cycle), and WHY (i.e., relative to the various performance and quality considerations).
- Costs Caused: WHO (across the stakeholder categories) has caused the damages, relative to WHAT type of event or action (located at one or more of the stages of the R&D life cycle), and WHY (relative to the performance and quality considerations).

The costs caused/borne inventory may then be exploited for posing (and answering) the multi-faceted question of responsibility, with responses to the following considerations:

- Societal conventions about knowledge quality assurance responsibilities: WHO holds responsibility (across the stakeholder categories), relative to WHAT facets of the event or action (located at one or more of the stages upstream, inside, or downstream of the R&D life cycle), and WHY (in relation to which performance and quality considerations).
- Societal conventions about liability: WHO (across the stakeholder categories) is considered to have an obligation to submit to a punishment, pay, or otherwise provide compensation, relative to WHAT facets of the event or action (located at one or more of the stages of the R&D life cycle), and WHY (in relation to which performance and quality considerations).

For any given situation under analysis, there will be correlations between these four considerations of costs borne, costs caused, KQA responsibilities, and liability. Nonetheless, these are four conceptually distinct dimensions or layers of information that can be built up for any given research misconduct or other controversy.

In consideration of costs borne and costs caused, we have sought to demonstrate the pertinence of this framework through discussion of two facets of research fraud: the full direct costs approach for funders (in section "Research Fraud and Its Costs") and, through the VW case study, a micro-focused cost analysis process dedicated to companies (in section "The Paradoxical Case of Dieselgate"). Different classes of prejudice require distinct procedures of observation and evaluation as to their severity, and may, as a function of societal conventions, engage very different forms of liability, penalty, and compensation. In conclusion, we offer the following points as considerations for audit and governance design:

- In extending to four capitals, we admit fundamental measurement challenges as well as normative complexities. We do not imagine an implementation of this "full cost" accounting in fully monetary, or even fully quantified non-monetary terms.
- The "internalisation" of costs caused on parties outside the sphere of a company's (or government's) immediate concern can be achieved only by building a "duty of care" as a collectively enforced societal norm.
- Further work is required to characterise incentive systems that could be engaged to discourage fraudulent behaviour and to encourage honour and virtue—that is, integrity in both the narrow Mertonian sense and in the wider sense of "duty of care" endorsed in ethics for sustainability.

This new generation of KQA for R&D in society cannot be envisaged as a process of secluded expertise. Evaluation tools and reporting procedures will need to break with the habits of in-house self-governance traditions common to both business and academia. New conventions of reciprocal accountability are required. Certainly, the different stakeholders' concerns—business managers, company shareholders, public research funding agencies, academia—must be addressed with language and formats corresponding to their respective needs. But this cannot be obtained by inward-looking processes; rather there must be transparency in the engagement of accountability from each stakeholder toward the others.

Clearly, in all this, there is an ethical and societal dimension. Competence and responsibility cannot be established only in managerial terms. Key considerations lie at the level of the quality of the relationships to be sought for all the parties concerned.

Benessia and Funtowicz (2015), discussing the relationship between framings of sustainability and techno-scientific innovation, have insisted on "…the need to shift from predicting and promising what to do (in the future) to a political resolution of how we want to live together (in the present)." Our didactic schema can here be envisaged as a framework for supporting multi-stakeholder deliberation—that is, for the presentation of multiple views in confrontation or dialogue (Douguet and O'Connor 2019). Coexisting multiple views may arise in several ways, including (a) in a situation of uncertainty about the facts of costs caused and costs borne and (b) as controversial opinions about what "should" be the responsibilities and/or liabilities. The articulation and confrontation of multiple views can then be envisaged, in prolongation of the audit process, as the basis for a transparent multi-stakeholder approach to knowledge quality governance.

References

Barré, R. (2011). Des concepts à la pratique de l'innovation responsable: à propos d'un séminaire franco-britannique. *Natures Sciences Sociétés, 19*(4), 405–409.

Benessia, A., & Funtowicz, S. (2015). Sustainability and Techno-science: What Do We Want to Sustain and for Whom? *International Journal of Sustainable Development, 18*(4), 329–348.

Douguet, J.-M., & O'Connor, M. (2019, forthcoming). Publicly Accountable Dialogue and Deliberation: Building Integrity Around the Question of Quality in Knowledge? *IJSD* Special Issue on Integrity and Quality in Science. *International Journal of Sustainable Development, 22.*

DuBois, J. M., Anderson, E. E., Chibnall, J., Carroll, K., Gibb, T., Ogbuka, C., & Rubbelke, T. (2013). Understanding Research Misconduct: A Comparative Analysis of 120 Cases of Professional Wrongdoing. *Accountability in Research, 20*(5–6), 320–338.

European Science Foundation. (2011, March). *The European Code of Conduct for Research Integrity.* ISBN: 978-2-918428-37-4.

Fanelli, D. (2009). How Many Scientists Fabricate and Falsify Research? A Systematic Review and Metaanalysis of Survey Data. *PLoS One, 4*(5), e5738.

Faucheux, S., & Hue, C. (2000). Politique environnementale et politique technologique: vers une prospective concertative. *Natures Sciences Sociétés, 8*(3), 31–44.

Faucheux, S., & Hue, C. (2001). From Irreversibility to Participation: Towards a Participatory Foresight for the Governance of Collective Environmental Risks. *Journal of Hazardous Materials, 86,* 223–243.

Faucheux, S., & Nicolaï, I. (2004). La responsabilité sociétale dans la construction d'indicateurs: l'expérience de l'industrie européenne de l'aluminium. *Natures Sciences Sociétés, 12*(1), 30–41.

Faucheux, S., & O'Connor, M. (2000). Technosphère versus Ecosphère: quel arbitrage ? Choix technologiques et menaces environnementales, signaux faibles, controverses et décision. *Futuribles, 251,* 29–59.

Frame, B., & O'Connor, M. (2010). Integrating Valuation and Deliberation: The Purposes of Sustainability Assessment. *Environmental Science and Policy, 14*(1), 1–10. January 2011.

Friedrichs, D. O. (2010). *Trusted Criminals: White Collar Crime in Contemporary Society* (4th ed.). Belmont: Wadsworth Cengage Learning. 496pp.

Funtowicz, S., & Ravetz, J. (1990). *Uncertainty and Quality in Science for Policy.* Dordrecht: Kluwer Academic Press.

Gallopin, G., Funtowicz, S., O'Coonor, M., & Ravetz, J. (2001). Science for the 21st Century: From Social Contract to the Scientific Core. *International Journal of Social Science, 168,* 209–229.

Gans Combe, C., Faucheux, S., & Kuszla, C. (2019, forthcoming). The Societal Costs of Research Misconduct: Some Method Considerations from the DEFORM Project. *IJSD* Special Issue on Integrity and Quality in Science, *International Journal of Sustainable Development, 22.*

Gee, J., & Button, M. (2015). *The Financial Cost of Fraud*. London: PKF Littlejohn.
Hesselmann, F., Wienefoet, V., & Reinhart, M. (2014). Measuring Scientific Misconduct – Lessons from Criminology. *Publications, 2*, 61–70.
Kuszla, C. (2019, forthcoming). Organisation & Governance of Research. *IJSD* Special Issue on Integrity and Quality in Science, *International Journal of Sustainable Development, 22*.
Merton, R. K. (1973/1942). *The Sociology of Science: Theoretical and Empirical Investigations*. Chicago: University of Chicago Press, 605 pp.
O'Connor, M., & Spangenberg, J. (2007). A Methodology for CSR Reporting: Assuring a Representative Diversity of Indicators Across Stakeholders, Scales, Sites and Performance Issues. *Journal of Cleaner Production, 16*(13), 1399–1415.
O'Connor, M., Gans Combe, C., Faucheux, S., & Petousi, V. (2018). Responsibility within Without: The Challenges of Misconduct and Quality Assurance in Scientific Research. *Revue Française d'Administration Publique, 166*.
Owen, R., & Goldberg, N. (2010). Responsible Innovation: A Pilot Study with the U.K. Engineering and Physical Sciences Research Council. *Risk Analysis, 30*, 1699–1707.
Petousi, V., & Sifaki, E. (2019, forthcoming). Narratives and Discourses about the Causality of Research Misconduct: An Interdisciplinary Perspective. *IJSD* Special Issue on Integrity and Quality in Science, *International Journal of Sustainable Development, 22*.
Power, M. (2013). The Apparatus of Fraud Risk. *Accounting, Organizations and Society, 38*, 525–543.
Ravetz, J. (1971). *Scientific Knowledge and its Social Problems* (449pp). Oxford: Oxford University Press.
Saltelli, A. (Ed.). (2016). *The Rightful Place of Science: Science on the Verge*. Tempe: Published by The Consortium for Science, Policy and Outcomes, Arizona State University.
Taebi, B., Correlje, A., Cuppen, E., Dignum, M., & Pesch, U. (2014). Responsible Innovation as an Endorsement of Public Values: The Need for Interdisciplinary Research. *Journal of Responsible Innovation, 1*(1), 118–124.
The Lancet (2015). Editorial. Rewarding True Inquiry and Diligence in Research, 385, p. 2121.
Titus, S. L., Wells, J. A., & Rhoades, L. J. (2008). Repairing Research Integrity. *Nature, 453*, 980–982.
Van Den Hoven, J. (2015). Value Sensitive Design and Responsible Innovation. In P. Kawalec & R. P. Wierzchoslawski (Eds.), *Social Responsibility and Science in Innovation Economy*. Lublin: Learned Society of KUL.
Von Schomberg, R. (2011). Prospects for Technology Assessment in a Framework of Responsible Research and Innovation. In M. Dusseldorp & R. Beecroft (Eds.), *Technikfolgen abschätzen lehren: Bildungspotenziale* (pp. 39–64). Wiesbaden: Springer-Verlag.
Wilsdon, J., Stilgoe, J., & Wynne, B. (2005). *The Public Value of Science: Or How to Ensure that Science Really Matters* (67pp). London: DEMOS.

Part IV

New Forms of Responsibility to Address Societal Challenges

12

Social Networks and Professional Communities: A Fair Governance?

Christophe Assens and Jean-Pierre Bouchez

Introduction

This research focuses on social relationship management within networks and workplace communities in which the softening of institutional boundaries and the development of a digital and collaborative economy becomes as important as financial resources and skills management. Yet relationship management is certainly the most problematic task as it is difficult to foresee and control another person's response. To minimize uncertainty, businesses tend to organize relationships among colleagues in a social network or a professional community in which the principles of trust and reciprocity prevail.

An Issue of Governance

One of the major topics of this research is the governance of a network or professional community, namely, how decision-making power and tasks are shared. In other words, what is the best way to manage the collective interest

---

C. Assens (✉)
University of Versailles, Versailles, France
e-mail: christophe.assens@uvsq.fr

J.-P. Bouchez
University of Versailles, Versailles, France

Planet S@voirs, Versailles, France

without threatening independence, individual responsibility, and equality among members? This is not an easy problem to resolve because traditional governance theory, such as Board of Directors' control of private companies or state supervision of public bodies, cannot be applied to the network; the parameters of a network's territorial, legal, or capital limits are not always clear. On the one hand, no clear legal, territorial, or capital boundaries have yet been established. On the other hand, the network may evolve into a hybrid public/private entity. Further, the network is not always represented by a collective agent with the legitimacy to discipline its members. Finally, the network does not always have a predetermined objective for its existence (Kilduff and Tsai 2003).

In order to explore this issue of network and community governance, we shall base our analysis on the work of Provan and Kenis (2007) by successively examining three forms: the participant-governed network, the lead organization-governed network, and the network administrative organization. This classification will enable us to determine, in the chapter's conclusion, whether governance is socially responsible based on certain criteria that could limit its implementation: transparency of information that is able to give legitimacy to a decision; equal treatment of members with equitable power sharing, which acts as a gauge of efficiency for democratic government; and equity in the distribution of tasks and payment, which effectively empowers each member.

Networks, Communities, and the Governance Model

In order to fully understand the challenges of our subject, it is important to establish the difference between the networks and communities that exist, particularly within organizations in the form of social networks (SNs) and communities of practice (CoP).[1]

A social network is defined by Powell (1990) and Williamson (1991) as a collaborative organization of institutions or actors whose rules of exchange depend neither on market nor on hierarchy. The network is formed of fiscally and legally independent associates who self-govern and rely on one another for the achievement of a common goal.

---

[1] It is worth noting that these concepts of community and network, which have come back into vogue over the last years, are probably as old as the history of mankind itself....

So that one could ask oneself whether digital communities are based on an intermediate form between traditional, human-sized communities and wide social networks.

Much like an ecosystem, as described by Moore (1996), the network thrives on an exchange with its environment, which urges it to further extend its sphere of influence and constantly challenge its own limits. However, the more the network expands, the more difficult it is to regulate, as the number of interacting components increases. Conversely, when the network stops growing, it loses flexibility and modularity, giving way to rigidity between its connecting parts, thus causing an imbalance of power between its members.

Furthermore, by continuing to rely on the work of Lave and Wenger (1991), Wenger (1998), and Cohendet et al. (2008), we will consider that a CoP is characterized by the voluntary and regular involvement of its members. They take part in the sharing and exchange of knowledge and practices, based on a shared interest in a given field. This in turn leads to the development of a shared identity while complying with the group's social norms. Also, a distinction between the two emerges through the deployment of a key variable based on the intensity of ties (Bouchez 2015, 2016), by referencing the work of Granovetter (1973) on "the strength of weak ties." Taking this perspective, SNs inherently rely on the logic of "weak ties." The internal rules of engagement and operation are—a priori—much looser and more relaxed, and concern peripheral relationships that fall outside the primary circle, such as neighbors, work colleagues, business associates (or sports buddies), friends of friends, and so on. As Granovetter consistently illustrates, the strength of these ties is that they lead to a breakdown of boundaries, thanks to the potential for joining new circles and new communities, for example. This perspective also increases individuals' potential for accessing information that is quantitatively, and often qualitatively, superior to that offered by close relationships alone. In this way, these weak ties are "bridges" that provide members gateways to the members of other networks or social groups, thus building a greater social capital than that open to individuals with only strong ties. Similarly, we shall argue that CoPs more typically rely on "strong ties" in that they rely on a very close primary and direct network in the familial, intellectual, and cultural spheres, that is, those found in affective relationships. The strength of these ties in fact correlates with their closeness and the trust they generate. But very intense links can also contribute to the creation of relationships that isolate the members of a group, as shown below. Further, we will outline how Bogenrieder and Nooteboom (2004) present four criteria with which to assess the strength of ties. The first refers to their "intensity," explicitly their "strength," considering the amount of effort each party puts into the relationship. The second relates to the "frequency" of interactions. The third relates to the "degree of openness" of communication, and the fourth to the relationship's "longevity." These criteria highlight that the weak/strong ties polarity is graded. In this way, some digital CoPs within large firms bring together many thousands, sometimes tens of thousands of members (as with IBM). In this instance, the CoPs in reality resemble an SN.

It is however important to note from the outset, the network and the community frequently appear together within organizations. In this way, the largest digital network corporations, such as Facebook or LinkedIn, encourage their millions of members to organize themselves into "groups" that resemble communities of interest with minimal organizational effort. Equally, in large organizations that now have digitalized social networks, CoPs attach themselves to SNs, particularly as groups that share a professional interest.

With regard to the governance model, taking the work of Moreau Defarges (2003), we will examine three dimensions in order to understand the mechanics of governance. In other words, one has to address three dimensions that explain the power struggle between networks or communities of participants and the distribution of their bargaining power:

- **The founding principle**: the network is viewed as a regulated collaborative space based implicitly or explicitly on a founding principle of solidarity. In other words, it is necessary to understand the common denominator of its members and the sense of affiliation that unites them. This will help us to understand the strategic issues of governance.
- **The network architecture**: the issue is to examine how network boundaries change as members join and leave, whether by co-option or by "decree." This may prove useful for understanding network properties.
- **The rules of relational games**: this leads us to examine the informal or formal code that governs relationships within the network, guides collective action, and arbitrates conflicts between its members. This will help us understand how decision-making power is distributed and how the benefits of the common relational capital are shared.

Based on these dimensions, Provan and Kenis (2007) recommend distinguishing three types of network, each with specific governance mechanisms that apply to communities: the participant-governed network, the lead organization-governed network, and the network administrative organization. We undertake to present these in the three sections that follow.

The Participant-Governed Network: Self-Governance

Within this form, as with the lead organization-governed network that follows, we will sequentially present the network (RS) and community approach (CoPs), always bearing in mind that the third form, the network administrative organization, is more dependent on network than on community.

Network Perspective

This is based on a dense network, with members who occupy symmetrical and interchangeable positions. This means that no single member exercises control over another. In other words, no member is able to fill the network's structural gap by becoming an intermediary or pivotal connection. In this type of network, collective power is equally shared between all individuals.

Within the participant-governed network, governance has certain specific features. In so far as no member occupies a central position, governance is a self-regulatory process (Accard and Assens 2010). The self-governance process is a social structure based on exchange conventions. Through their interactions, the members together establish conventions that will either empower or restrict their subsequent interactions. These conventions also provide interactions with a spatial and temporal framework. In other words, the network develops a "structure" (Giddens 1984).

This type of self-governance exists mainly in networks with a founding principle based on corporatism, local rooting with a strong sense of belonging to a common territory, and shared working practices. Participant-governed networks correspond, for instance, to a "community of practice" as defined by Wenger et al. (2002). Specifically, this means that the network operates in a community-like way, regulated by peers who transmit the codes and adopt unwritten conventions (Gomez 1994). These conventions give meaning to collective action by ensuring legitimacy of action and equitable sharing of resources. Thus, deviant or over-opportunistic behavior is proscribed by peer pressure.

Community Perspective

Taken from a community perspective and its focus on self-government, we will look at the case of Communities of Practice (CoPs), known as autonomous communities. The first CoPs, whose characteristics we highlighted above,

Table 12.1 An illustrative example: the originally "self-organizing" CoP of maintenance technicians at Xerox

In the above contribution, the American anthropologist Julian E. Orr (1996) presents the community of maintenance technicians at Xerox, after having observed them closely in situ. These technicians, who worked on site at Xerox clients' premises, had the habit of meeting informally before and after work, as well as during their lunch break, to exchange information and share "war stories," which created a real narrative, generally around the subject of machinery malfunctions that "strangely" weren't covered by the company's very extensive documentation … These informal, professional exchanges gave technicians the opportunity to share their collective knowledge and practices in order to resolve problems created, in particular, by unforeseeable or unusual malfunctions.
In this way, the group effectively becomes a "self-organized" or "autonomous" CoP: one that is based on an area of common and shared interest as well as mutual, voluntary, "free" and virtually invisible interaction. Over time, it develops a collective memory based in particular on the sharing of an operational repertory of contextualized practices (under the form of a shared passion), thus effectively replacing the official manual.
Management's attitude was initially hostile, but evolved; particularly after finding that when the informal meetings were suspended, practices were no longer shared and client calls increased significantly, especially with regard to unforeseeable malfunctions … In order to overcome this problem, the firm launched a project called Eureka, designed to provide structure and supervise the diffusion of tacit practices relating to these technical repairs, and finally recognize the CoP by creating a database able to store and preserve useful ideas, making them accessible to all. After the Eureka project had been running for a few years, Xerox estimated that it had saved the company close to 100 million dollars.

appeared progressively; thus, in some corporations from the 1990s on, they took on a spontaneous form. Table 12.1 describes an example of a community of maintenance technicians at Xerox who were initially autonomous but then developed into a neo-hierarchical group (see part 2 of the text).

Too Much Solidarity Kills Solidarity

The self-governed CoP provides the first real-life experience of a participant-governed network thanks to its two-core governance-related characteristics: first, the equal treatment of members regardless of their social status, their size, or skills, and second, the limiting of individual opportunism through peer pressure.

More precisely, a lack of anonymity leads to a form of self-discipline for all the links in a chain of solidarity. In other words, in a participant-governed network, trust cannot be broken without negative consequences to the originator. By leaving the group, he loses access to the network resources on which he depends. Indeed, if one party tries to mislead another, the offending party is punished by all members of the network, not only by the victim or a transaction partner. Therefore, the transaction becomes equitable not because of the balance in interactions between parties, but rather the reciprocity, with its shared vision of solidarity.

However, this sense of solidarity is weakened when the network expands haphazardly and allows access to trespassers. Indeed, like any shared property that is used individually and paid for by the community, solidarity is beneficial for everyone and no one in particular (Hardin 1968). Yet, the management of a common asset is a sensitive issue, because its use cannot be refused to any member within the network, including those who exhibit trespassing behavior, thus depriving other users of the shared benefit of its use. This is why it is sometimes necessary to introduce a more formalized mode of governance to avoid deviant behavior among peers that may transform the network into a lead organization-governed network or a network administrative organization.

The Lead Organization-Governed Network: Hierarchical Governance

Network Perspective

The characteristic feature of a lead organization-governed network is a hierarchy that exists between a member who is at the pivot of exchanges and the group's peripheral members. The central member acts like a pilot regulating the behavior of other members (Assens 2003). Specifically, the network pilot has three particular competencies: a strategic vision of the network's future through a set of specifications and contracts with various members of the network; the ability to create and consolidate an atmosphere of trust and reciprocity (McEvily and Zaheer 2004); and lastly, the means to canvass and select new associates. In this capacity, he defines the network's boundaries and pools its resources like a master architect. He secures solidarity within the network because, as project manager, his objective is to constantly consolidate relationships between entities. To do this, he monitors and contributes to the development of relationships in many ways: he shares information, educates newcomers, and disciplines members who fail to comply with the rules he introduces.

Thus, the unity of a lead organization-governed network relies on the intangible assets belonging to the pilot (Assens and Bouteiller 2006): brand image, relational capital, access to market players, and technological know-how. They give meaning to the founding principle and explain the solidarity between partner manufacturers within the network. Ultimately these assets unite network members around a pilot situated at the core of all exchanges.

Community Perspective

Since the 2000s, there has been a progressive shift from "self-organizing" to "sponsored" communities. The main reason behind this is the common need of large, enlightened organizations to develop an original, hybrid form of governance that is advantageous for all participants. The sponsored communities of practice (SCoPs), via their less-remote leaders, gain official recognition from their sponsor leaders, as well as a certain amount of resources (time, meeting areas, financing), once their projects and work appear relevant.

SCoPs have in fact multiplied, sometimes bringing together many thousands of members through the use of digital supports. In his annotated review, Bootz (2013) states that Siemens, British Petroleum, IBM, the Council of Europe, GDF-Suez (now Engie), Hydro-Quebec, the World Bank, Hewlett-Packard, EDF, Clarica, and Schlumberger have all undertaken a knowledge management initiative centered around sponsored communities of practice (SCoPs). For their part, Cohendet et al. (2011) confirm this trend by classifying the different types of sponsored communities: "apprenticeship groups" (Hewlett-Packard), "family groups" (Xerox), "peer groups" (British Petroleum), "knowledge networks" (IBM Global Services), "knowledge sharing groups" (Siemens), and "internal knowledge management group" (EDF GDF—former name). The objective remains the same: these companies recognize that communities are capable of making a big contribution to performance.

Too Much Monitoring Kills Practice Sharing

The sponsored communities referred to as "institutionalized," that is, those that form part of and are integrated into an organization, can be likened to a type of deviation. We have observed two approaches that must be differentiated from this point of view: "project communities" and "hierarchical communities."

The first case refers to a return to classic and formal functioning, particularly in the guise of qualified, collaborative "project" communities that in reality operate in a way that is analogous to traditional collaborative project groups. They function by mobilizing digital tools and constrained processes to the point of losing any identity and specificity. Managerial governance and procedural devices therefore strip them of all "community spirit" in a type of "recycling," hijack, or deviation. However, we have observed an increase in the existence of project manager communities. The second case can be seen in the deployment of what are referred to as "hierarchical" communities; inevitably closed, they extend a service or department's reach. But this fusion of a hierarchical team and a community (the team leader is also the community group leader), even when it includes exchanges that are both extraprofessional (sharing of holiday videos and curiosities, etc.) and professional (calendars, document libraries, information on current activities, capitalizing exchanges and document monitoring, etc.) carries a real risk of clouding boundaries and heightening embarrassment.

The Network Administrative Organization: "Democratic Governance"

By its very nature and extent, the administered form creates more of a network than a community, although this does not stop communities from forming or attaching themselves to these vast networks.

The network administrative organization has specific characteristics. Collaboration among members falls under the jurisdiction of institutional rules, that is, the charter of rights and duties required for network membership. The governance structure, led by elected members, is responsible for changing these rules and ensuring their implementation with compliant members.

This governance structure embodies the legal nature of the network. It engages the network's legal responsibility and has the legitimacy needed to resolve bottlenecks, mediate conflicts, and define the axes of expansion. Consequently, the network administrative organization is a real joint venture based on *affectio societatis*, that is, on the intention of its members to be considered equal within the governance structure (Hatchuel and Segrestin 2007). This model is dominant in the social and solidarity economies, associations, NGOs (non-governmental organizations); in the mutual banking sector, the social capital of which is distributed among member customers; in mutual health organizations where solidarity becomes apparent in the distribution of contributions made by the sick and the healthy; in the private sector with its economic interest groups; in the public sector through the example of public interest groups (PIG) which have a limited life span and a legal entity aimed at implementing a public interest project by pooling member resources.

We can complete this assessment by citing the cooperative entity, which appears in many production sectors such as banking, crafts, trade, industry, and services. It is likewise prevalent in the agricultural sector, which has a total turnover of 4 billion euros and employs 42,000 employees who are affected by this status.

One of the specific features of the network administrative organization, the examples of which we mentioned above, is the fair distribution of property rights, and, therefore, the democratic distribution of decision-making power within the governance structure. According to Parrat (2003), the relational capital within the network is distributed in a "democratic" manner. The right of ownership over the governance structure is assigned solely to network members. Thus, no individual owner may appropriate the benefit of relational capital, which is a membership benefit, at the expense of other partners. The right to use social capital or a network membership benefit, in order to gain from it or transfer its ownership, therefore belongs to the network as a whole. Despite these theoretical arguments, the "democratic" dimension of a network's governance is often challenged in practice.

Too Much Democracy Kills Democracy

In associations or cooperatives, all members are entitled to an equal share of property rights in order to better apply the principles of solidarity and reciprocity. In theory, this rule is intended to reinforce the network's democratic nature, with the election of representatives to the Board of Directors being part of the governance structure. In practice, in the case of very large cooperatives or associations with several tens of thousands of voting members, the power of representation becomes so diluted and remote from its original purpose that elected representatives of the Board lose the legitimacy of their authority. This loss of legitimacy occurs most often in a technostructure in the case of the managing director, who enjoys the status of employee but not of elected member. In fact, in the end, the managing director, who remains untouched by the outcome of a vote, has the real power within a network, without ever being subject to the political alternation of elected representatives. In these circumstances, members of a network administrative organization may gradually lose "democratic power" in favor of a technostructure.

Conclusion

In theory, both networks and communities operate according to democratic standards, with a transparency and collegiality in decision-making that is in line with the universal principles of good governance (Graham et al. 2003) as defined in the United Nations Development Programme (UNDP). On the one hand, it concerns the legitimacy that gives any actor a voice in decision-making in order to achieve consensus despite divergent interests, the orientation that it benefits all and not just some. On the other hand, it concerns the efficiency that results from a rational use of resources to produce the best possible result; the accountability practices that apply to members in charge of transparency of information; and the equity of coming together around the principles of equality and impartiality.

According to our framework of interpretation based on three forms of governance—participative, lead, and administrative—the network and community are not always untarnished examples of good governance that are unwaveringly respectful of democratic principles. We will review these principles to discuss the limits of their practical application within the network.

The *legitimacy* of network members to participate in collective decisions is at question, particularly in the lead organization-governed network where only the pilot has the legitimacy to make decisions on behalf of everyone, with the inherent risk that he will exploit the organization for his own interests. As for the legitimacy of a community of practice, and in particular that of its leader, the institutional integration into a classic organization amounts to a deviation that has the effect outlined above, specifically, a distortion of the "community spirit."

In practice, the *orientation* of a network, and of a community, is not always beneficial to the majority of network members. In the network administrative organization, the founding members retain the prerogative to steer the network's development and prioritize their own specific interests before considering the stakes of new members.

Efficiency is not always guaranteed either within the network or the community. Peer control as in a participant-governed network can cause adverse effects because of the crossbreeding of members acting as judge and judged, especially when network membership operates by the "reproductive cloning" of its existing members. This can lead to inertia or the desire for a soft consensus on collective decisions, thereby resulting in a loss of individual accountability and the paralysis of the network as a whole.

Accountability practices are not always established. In a participant-governed network, for example, operating without a pilot or compliance with a charter of best practices, self-governance can lead to the appearance of "trespassers" who do not wish to get involved in the community but enjoy the benefits that it provides. Responsibility is no longer fairly distributed but is based on a compromise between active and inactive members. If there are no regulatory mechanisms to correct the perverse effects of this self-governance, the network may become discriminatory and rapidly lose efficiency.

Equity is another principle of good governance that can be jeopardized under certain circumstances. In a network administrative organization, the more one advocates equity with a fair distribution of decision-making power between all members of the network, the higher the risk of diluting this collegial power until it finally becomes a technostructure (too much democracy kills democracy). In the lead organization-governed network, particularly in the network form, the peripheral members' proximity to the pilot is more likely to sharpen relational asymmetry than reduce an imbalance of power (too much proximity kills proximity). Finally, in a participant-governed network, solidarity that is based on goodwill has its limitations because of the existence of active members and those who benefit from the structure without getting involved (too much solidarity kills solidarity).

Further, network governance does not depend on the nature of geographical boundaries. In network administrative organizations, local roots can be a good indicator of solidarity only if physical proximity is important for cognitive proximity—for the ability to exchange information and remain supportive. In lead organization-governed networks or participant-governed networks, territorial boundaries are not enough to understand the true limits of solidarity within a network. This solidarity can be extended by means of telecommunication tools, due to the geographical migration of agents (diasporas), without raising issues of sharing and pooling. Therefore, the true limits of a network or a community are often intangible; they are based on a sense of belonging to a club, with specific rules of co-optation and control. Governance issues are thus dependent on the rules of exchange that are established through conventions and based on a balance of bargaining power, for which a member's location is less important than his or her position within the network. This reflects his influence over others as an intermediate or a pilot, even if this influence is exercised remotely.

References

Accard, P., & Assens, C. (2010, mars-avril). La dynamique des réseaux non hiérarchique. *Gestion 2000, 2*, 81–93.

Assens, C. (2003). Le réseau d'entreprises: vers une synthèse des connaissances. *Management International, 7*(4), 49–59.

Assens, C., & Bouteiller, C. (2006). Mesurer la création de valeur réticulaire. In W. Azan, F. Bares, & C. Cornolti (Eds.), *Logiques de création: enjeux théoriques et management* (pp. 159–182). Paris/Budapest/Kinshasa: L'Harmattan, Collection Gestion et Economie, Chapter 7.

Bogenrieder, I., & Nooteboom, B. (2004). Learning Groups: What Types Are There? A Theoretical Analysis and an Empirical Study in a Consultancy Firm. *Organization Studies, 25*(2), 287–313.

Bootz, J.-P. (2013). L'évolution du manager: un pilote de communauté de pratique entre l'expert et l'intrapreneurs. *Management & Avenir, 5*(63), 115–139.

Bouchez, J.-P. (2015, septembre). Vers l'émergence progressive d'un nouveau cycle de management hybride ? Le cas des communautés de pratique 'pilotées'. *Gérer et Comprendre, 3*(121), 51–60.

Bouchez, J.-P. (2016). *L'entreprise à l'ère du digital. Les nouvelles pratiques collaboratives* (Méthodes & Recherches). Louvain-la-Neuve: De Boeck.

Cohendet, P., Grandadam, P., & Simon, L. (2008). Réseaux, communautés et projets dans les processus créatifs. *Management International, 13*(1), 29–44.

Cohendet, P., Roberts, J., & Simon, L. (2011). Créer implanter et gérer une communauté de pratique. *Gestion, 35*(4), 31–35.

Giddens, A. (1984). *The Constitution of Society: Outline of the Theory of Structuration*. Berkeley: University of California Press.

Gomez, P. Y. (1994). *Qualité et théories des conventions*. Paris: Economica.

Graham, J., Amos, B., & Plumptre, T. (2003). Principles for Good Governance in the 21st Century. Policy Brief No 15, Institute on Governance.

Granovetter, M. S. (1973). The Strength of Weak Ties. *American Journal of Sociology, 78*(6), 1360–1380.

Hardin, G. (1968). The Tragedy of the Commons. *Science, 162*(3859), 1243–1248.

Hatchuel, A., & Segrestin, B. (2007). La société contre l'entreprise ? Vers une norme d'entreprise à progrès collectif. *Droit et Société, 65*, 27–40.

Kilduff, M., & Tsai, W. (2003). *Social Networks and Organizations*. London: SAGE Publishing.

Lave, J., & Wenger, E. (1991). *Situated Learning: Legitimate Peripheral Participation*. Cambridge: Cambridge University Press.

Lorenzoni, G., & Baden-Fuller, C. (1995). Creating a Strategic Center to Manage a Web of Partners. *California Management Review, 37*, 146–163.

McEvily, B., & Zaheer, A. (2004). Architects of Trust: The Role of Network Facilitators in Geographical Clusters. In R. Kramer & K. Cook (Eds.), *Trust and Distrust in Organizations* (pp. 189–213). New York: Russell Sage Foundation.

Moore, J. F. (1996). *The Death of Competition: Leadership and Strategy in the Age of Business Ecosystems*. New York: Harper Business.

Moreau Defarges, P. (2003). *La gouvernance*. Paris: Presses Universitaires de France.

Parrat, F. (2003). *La gouvernance d'entreprise*. Paris: Éditions Dunod.

Powell, W. W. (1990). Neither Market Nor Hierarchy: Network Forms of Organization. *Research in Organizational Behavior, 12*, 295–336.

Provan, K. G., & Kenis, P. (2007). Modes of Network Governance: Structure, Management and Effectiveness. *Journal of Public Administration Research and Theory, 18*(2), 229–252.

Snow, C. S., & Thomas, J. B. (1993). Building Networks: Broker Roles and Behaviours. In P. Lorange (Ed.), *Implementing Strategic Process: Change and Cooperation* (pp. 217–238). Oxford: Blackwell.

Wenger, E. (1998). *Communities of Practice. Learning, Meaning, and Identity*. Cambridge: Cambridge University Press.

Wenger, E., McDermott, R., & Snyder, W. M. (2002). *Cultivating Communities of Practice: A Guide to Managing Knowledge*. Boston: Harvard Business School Press.

Williamson, O. E. (1991). Comparative Economic Organization: The Analysis of Discrete Structural Alternatives. *Administrative Science Quarterly, 36*(2), 269–296.

13

Corporate Social Responsibility in Times of Internet (In)security

Anna Tarabasz

Introduction

The year 2016 signaled a new phase in the growth of digital technology. For the first time in history, the penetration rate of Internet users reached 4.16 billion, exceeding half of the world population (Internet World Stats 2017). Yet this trend, though emblematic of the global reach of modern technology, exposed the underbelly of Internet usage. With more and more people voluntarily submitting sensitive data to online networks, often with little to no knowledge of cyber threats and privacy management, hackers secured unprecedented access to personally identifiable information (George Washington University 2017; Fidelis Cybersecurity 2016; Kupczyk 2016; Centrum Badania Opinii Społecznej (CBOS) 2015; Smith 2014; Tarabasz 2017; Symantec 2015; Trim and Lee 2014; Ulsch 2014; Gharibi and Shaabi 2012). In 2014 alone, more than one billion social media accounts were reportedly hacked and overtaken (Fereira 2016). By 2017, an additional 6 million accounts on Instagram and 2.2 million accounts on Facebook were compromised (Chekalov 2018). One in every ten social media users claim to fall victim to cyber-attacks, and the numbers are on the rise (Zaharia 2016).

What is the cause of this careless nonchalance among Internet users? In an era of widespread social media use, users thrive for "likes, comments, and re-tweets" to the point of social narcissism, and many ignore threats to their

A. Tarabasz (✉)
SP Jain School of Global Management, Dubai, UAE

© The Author(s) 2019
A. Bartoli et al. (eds.), *Responsible Organizations in the Global Context*,
https://doi.org/10.1007/978-3-030-11458-9_13

digital security. Such negligence must be eradicated in order to combat the increasing activity of hackers. For this reason, corporate social responsibility (CSR) may act as a panacea to the lack of education and awareness of cybersecurity among average Internet users. Many researchers have already emphasized the importance of CSR in the process of communication (Ihlen et al. 2011; McKean 2014; Cohen-Almagor 2015; Visser et al. 2015; Diehl et al. 2017), and some authors have indicated the necessity of companies to be proactive against cybercrime (Trim and Lee 2014). Unfortunately, this work largely falls under the umbrella of information technology, and incorporating systematic cyber threat awareness at the corporate level usually comes only after a cyber-attack has occurred.

Based on a robust literature review, this chapter uses data to visualize the scale of cyber threats and the costs involved. It proves that the most vulnerable point in security strategies is the human factor, with exiting employees surprisingly becoming the largest source of data leakage (Arabian Marketer 2016; Shambler 2017). It also presents the functioning regularities of contemporary social media and describes possible cyber threats within a turbulent online environment. An in-depth analysis of case studies from mBank (a digital retail bank in Poland) and du (a mobile network provider in the UAE) follows.

Defining the Scale and Cost of Data Breaches and Cyber Threats

There are two main approaches to defining cyber threats in relation to Internet insecurity. The first focuses on a single malevolent occurrence, or what the *Oxford English Dictionary* (under cyber threat) (2018) defines as the possibility of a malicious attempt to damage or disrupt a computer network or system. In contrast, certain authors perceive cyber threat (or cyberthreat and cybercrime) from a process perspective, where computer technology threatens a society's ability to maintain internal order (Antonucci 2017; Griffor 2016; Brenner 2009).

In their investigation of cyber threat, cyber hate, and cyber terrorism, Awan and Blakemore (2012) purport that "cybercrime has become part of everyday business for organized crime [...] that ranges from the most minor to the most serious of crimes and from affecting one individual to large populations." In fact, a 2018 PricewaterhouseCoopers report reveals that top CEOs around the world consider terrorism and cyber threats as two of the most significant problems in running a business. Yet the threat level of cyber menace is perceived differently across regions. Its importance is most visible in the Middle East (54%) and North America (53%), followed by Africa (45%), the Asia-Pacific region (44%), and Western Europe (33%). Cybercrime is not listed among the top ten threats by CEOs from Central and Eastern Europe and Latin America. The higher the level of perceived cyber threats, the more complex the problems that are mentioned in the list, with many issues oscillating around security threats, government overregulation, and imposed taxes.

Internet insecurity is likewise visible among average breadwinners. A 2017 Sophos report reveals that among home users vulnerable to different types of threats, those surveyed indicated that they were extremely or somewhat worried more about cyber-attacks than with financial loss caused by a computer breach (63%); hackers taking over personal computers to send spam (61%); or hackers rendering personal computers useless (58%). The loss of personal computer files or private information followed (56%), with fears of burglary (52%), car accidents (49%), and physical assault or stolen cars (46%) thereafter (Sophos 2017).

Regardless of the level of threat awareness, cyber menace exists and is rising exponentially. According to the Breach Live Index (2018), 2.6 billion data records were compromised in 2017. This number equates to more than 7 million lost or stolen records every day. Sixty-nine percent of these breach incidents involved identity theft, and 72% were caused by a malicious outsider. Less than 4% were considered to be secure, rendering the encryption process useless. With each successful attack, the average cost in damages totaled upwards of $1 million (Chekalov 2018).

But data leaks are not spread evenly across industries. The majority of the leaks impacted the healthcare industry (27%), with smaller amounts affecting the financial (12%), education (11%), retail (11%), government (11%), and technology (7%) sectors. Of these attacks, 93% involved cyber criminals who took mere minutes to compromise systems. Four out of five victims were not aware of the attack for multiple weeks, and in 7% of the cases, the breach went undetected for more than a year. Moreover, 63% of the data breaches were caused by a weak, default, or stolen password. This data comes from companies who, in the majority of cases, have more than 1000 employees, IT departments, and security specialists.

With these statistics in mind, Chekalov (2018) predicts that by 2020, organizations will spend $101 billion on cybersecurity software, security, and hardware in order to curb data leaks. But as big market players have the financial means to institute these measures, small and medium-sized enterprises

(SMEs) lack the resources. Only 5.6% of SME budgets are spent on cybersecurity, regardless of the fact that 43% of attacks are aimed at SMEs and 60% of SMEs shut down six months after a cyber hacktivist event. Indeed, companies still do not understand how impactful and severe a cyber strike can be, whether it be reputation loss, simple theft, or fines for failing to comply with data protection legislation.

Individual ignorance on cybersecurity further puts digital users in peril. Up to 97% of people are unable to identify phishing mail, and 35% of people use weak passwords. In one notable example, a 2016 attack on Mark Zuckerberg's data exposed his "open sesame phrase" as a simple "dadada." Furthermore, mobile-oriented security risks include the lack of screen locks or passwords, with only one-fourth of people using a pin code and 24% using a fingerprint scanner (Chekalov 2018).

Data loss or leakage has deep financial consequences for companies, and simple ransomware, privacy breaches, or social engineering may impact an individual with proportionally the same or even larger cost. Following their corporate responsibility, companies should take the lead to educate and prevent additional threats.

Possible Cyber Threats

The lack of awareness and cybersecurity education undertaken within company CSR leave organizations vulnerable to the Trojan Cyber Horse. According to multiple reports (PricewaterhouseCoopers 2018; Verizon 2018; International Telecommunication Union (ITU) 2017; AMEinfo Staff 2016; Fidelis Cybersecurity 2016; Bada et al. 2015; Centrum Badania Opinii Społecznej (CBOS) 2015; Eurobarometer 2015), cyber threat awareness remains low despite recent preventive activities. As a result, the number of breaches continues to rise, leaving more individuals and more companies fearful of their Internet security. But basic education aimed at enhancing security methods could alter these startling reports.

Acting against existing cyber threats is similar to combatting the Lernaean Hydra. Even if finally manageable, *natura horret vacuum*, and cyber criminals will develop innovative and more harmful techniques to obtain sensitive data. For instance, Japanese researchers have identified a new threat from flashing the "peace" sign (AFP 2017; Harthorne 2017). Digital cameras in smartphones are now powerful enough to zoom in and retrieve a person's fingerprint.

From data leakage to unauthorized banking transactions to snooping on official documents and full identity theft, the possibilities of vulnerability are enormous. The overall list of cyber threats awaiting individuals is presented in the following table (Cf. Table 13.1).

Table 13.1 List of possible cyber threats awaiting individuals

No	Threat type	Threat description
1.	Botnet	Also known as zombie army. Refers to a number of Internet-connected devices used by a botnet owner to perform various tasks. Can be used to perform DDoS (distributed denial of service) attacks, steal data, send spam, or simply give the attacker access to the device and its connection
2.	Child predator	A person who uses the Internet with the intention of contacting minors below the age of consent, soliciting sexual relations
3.	Cyber bullying	Type of cyber harassment using electronic forms of contact. Increasingly common especially among teenagers. Identified by repeated behavior and intent to harm. May include rumors, threats, sexual remarks, pejorative labels, and disclosing the victims' personal information
4.	Cyber stalking	Use of the Internet or other electronic means to stalk or harass an individual, group, or organization. May include false accusations, defamation, slander, and libel. Often includes monitoring, identity theft, threats, vandalism, solicitation for sex, or the gathering of information that may be used to threaten, embarrass, or harass
5.	Identity theft	Deliberate use of someone else's identity, usually as a method to gain a financial advantage or obtain credit information and other benefits in the other person's name
6.	Phishing	Exploiting fear, anxiety, and system vulnerability by urging unaware users to share their funds. Often combined with stealing passwords, credit card numbers, bank account details, and other sensitive information
7.	WiFi Pineapple	The automatic stealing of passwords and credit card data from WiFi users
8.	Ransomware	Type of malware that blocks files and system access unless victims pay a ransom to their attackers
9.	Site compromise	Compromising a social network site with malicious code. Any visitor to a compromised site would be susceptible to attack. Often combined with phishing, like-jacking, or link-jacking, in which a user, referred to a "like" or redirected to a desired page, may download the malware or infect a device

(continued)

Table 13.1 (continued)

No	Threat type	Threat description
10.	Snooping/ spoofing/spying	Snooping (synonymous with sniffing) occurs while logging in to a website without encryption by acquiring a person's username and password and monitoring a person's website movement (i.e. capturing the network traffic between the affected user and the web). Can describe unauthorized access to another person's or another company's data, akin to eavesdropping. More sophisticated snooping uses software programs to remotely monitor activity on a computer or network device
		Spoofing refers to those who actively pretend to be another person or device on network traffic. Can refer to data transfer or sent emails
		A spying third party may use both snooping and spoofing
11.	Spam/malware	Unwanted messages in an email inbox. Junk mail is considered annoying and harmless. However, spam messages may contain links that, after activation, redirect a user to a website that will infect a computer with malicious software (malware)
12.	Unauthorized access/ information leak	A combination of theft, burglary, and/or revealing seemingly uncritical technical information to the public

Source: Tarabasz (2017)

Social Oversharing in the US, Poland, UAE, and Worldwide

Today's digital users make themselves easy targets for cyber criminals by oversharing sensitive data on social media. According to Leiter (2016), the most popular social networks include Facebook (1 billion users), Twitter (560 million users), Google+ (400 million users), LinkedIn (250 million users), Instagram (150 million users), and Pinterest (70 million users), with numbers of monthly active users continuing to rise. The sweeping presence of social networks offers more opportunities to disclose personal information. From the publication of birthdays, email addresses, photographs, marking locations, and relationship statuses to regular posts on hobbies, interests, and beliefs, personal data becomes forever imprinted with names and digital identities.

A general lack of understanding about privacy policies contributes to this oversharing. Research conducted by Joseph Turow, Ph.D., a specialist in digital marketing and privacy issues at the University of Pennsylvania's Annenberg

School for Communication, offers solid proof that 52% of Americans do not understand the purpose of privacy policies.[1] Indeed, ordinary users do not grasp the scope of the data that is being collected on them. They are not at all cognizant of the manner in which small amounts of data can be used to create much more detailed portraits when matched with information from third-party sites that collect and share customer information. As Turow rightly points out: "The general sense among marketers is that people understand that their data is being used, but we've found in our research that people don't truly understand how data mining works. They may realize that one or two pieces of their information are being given out; what they don't realize is that those one or two data points can be linked with other sources to uncover information they would have never given out in the first place" (Smith 2014).

A recent study by the Pew Research Center articulates the scope of Turow's thesis (Pew Research Center 2015; Dewey 2015). Conducted in English and Spanish, this survey reached a nationally representative sample of 1060 teenagers aged 13–17 and their parents or guardians. According to its results, 92% of surveyed teens have shared their real name publicly, 91% have shared photos, 84% have shared their interests, and 82% have shared their birthday. Moreover, 71% of respondents published their city, and the same number revealed their school affiliation. Sixty-two percent disclosed their relationship status. Fifty-three percent posted their email address. Only 20% shared their cell phone number.

Such data should without a doubt be a cause for concern. Yet social media oversharing will continue to be an unstoppable force in this era of public exhibition, new media, and social narcissism (Agger 2015; Bałdys 2014; Twenge and Campbell 2013). Many experts believe that privacy challenges will only continue to worsen as the Internet of Things expands and people become increasingly enticed (if only begrudgingly) to share personal information in return for the conveniences afforded by digital technology. Oversharing is not only a domain of the cradle-countries of social media, but a "sin-confessed" obsession around the world.

Poland is not immune to social media oversharing. According to Centrum Badania Opinii Społecznej (Centre for Public Opinion Research) (2015), 40% of Internet users shared at least one of the aforementioned examples of privacy information, and 71% shared this information to companies and institutions. Almost all Internet users aged 18–24 publicly publish information about themselves on social media websites. Further surveys from CBOS uncovered that

---

[1] According to initial part of the survey, they were willing to claim that the statement "When a company posts a privacy policy, it ensures that the company keeps confidential all the information it collects on users" is true, while it is simply a legal document that discloses how customer data is managed and used (Smith 2014).

only 20% of Internet users do not make public any information about themselves, and upwards of 40% share information only with a limited audience. Especially among young users, a lingering belief exists that sharing statuses, photos, and comments will only be viewed within a "narrow circle of friends and family." But this approach is misleading. Assuming that a person only has 300 followers on Facebook and each of these friends has a similar number of contacts, any updates to his profile can become visible to 90,000 people.

AMEinfo.com (2016), a provider of online business information in the Middle East, presents a similar picture. In the UAE, 75% of social media users do not interact with people that were previously added to their contact lists, yet 49% of respondents accepted 50% of unfamiliar contact requests. Furthermore, 58% of respondents share friends' pictures on social media, while 50% share family pictures and 39% check in at their location. In addition, 31% admit that they have posted something online that they have later regretted. Lastly, 97% have experienced at least one form of cyber-attack in the form of spam links, inappropriate messages from strangers, fake accounts, viruses from downloaded files, or an account hack.

According to research conducted by the International Computer Driving Licence (ICDL) Arabia (2015, 2016), the governing body and authority for the ICDL certification program, social media strongly influences young Arabic minds, and users are not aware of the dangers of exposing their information online. A 2015 report revealed the ubiquity of smart devices among Arabic youth. Their unsupervised Internet access on smartphones raised serious concerns about their online safety and their exposure to cyber addiction, cyber bullying, and cyber exploitation. Sixty-four percent of those surveyed did not know the meaning of cyber bullying, and when given an explanation, 60% found it applicable to themselves. Respondents were likewise unaware about the difference between posting as public and private and what kinds of consequences may be involved.

These examples are more than disquieting, as they show a lack of common sense and basic knowledge on cybersecurity among adults and youth. Companies likewise face multiple online threats. In order to combat this general disregard for safe Internet usage, innovative approaches to cybersecurity must be developed and implemented.

Innovative Approaches to Corporate Social Responsibility

Corporate social responsibility (CSR) is a catchall term to represent the activities and projects of corporate strategy building. It considers the interests of social and environmental protections as well as relationships among various stakeholder groups (Visser et al. 2015). Many researchers equate CSR to the process of corporate communication (Ihlen et al. 2011; McKean 2014; Cohen-Almagor 2015; Visser et al. 2015; Diehl et al. 2017).

Contemporary scholarly literature highlights the importance of CSR in helping companies meet and exceed market expectations. In particular, researchers point to the necessity of companies to be proactive against cybercrime and to educate the larger public about possible threats (Trim and Lee 2014). Even though such requests may not directly comply with the Prerequisites for the SA8000® Standard (SAI 2017), they do ally with AccountAbility's AA1000 Series of Standards with particular emphasis on the principle of continuous improvement and a willingness to contribute to society on the basis of benevolence (AccountAbility 2017). Companies acting in such a manner may avoid potential expenses caused by cyber criminals and thus provide better resistance to cyber crises. This would in turn increase shareholder confidence, brand awareness, and even profits.

Socially Responsible Online Campaigns

Presenting an innovative CSR approach and increasing customer awareness is indeed challenging. Customers seem to trivialize the matter, claiming it either not to be applicable to their lives or simply denying the existence of such a problem. Therefore, campaigns aiming at increasing customer awareness must be clearly distinctive from other campaigns. Two examples of socially responsible online campaigns illustrate how companies can show the foolishness of users or the fatal consequences of online negligence: the strategies of mBank and du.

The leading retail bank in Poland, mBank, decided to focus its campaign *"Nie robisz tego w realu? Nie rób tego w sieci!"* ("Not doing it in real life? Do not do it on the Net!") on the foolishness of Internet users (WirtualneMedia 2015). The campaign targeted people who perform banking transactions on computers and smartphones. Using the hashtag #nieróbtegowsieci, mBank attempted to increase knowledge of the threats that banking customers may encounter in the network (Grey Wizard 2015; Duszczak 2015). Its concept was based on emphasizing the analogy between behaviors on the Internet and non-Internet.

The campaign likewise utilized television to spread awareness of cybersecurity. One of the spots portrayed a man dressed in a beige trench coat, with his lapels tilted, as if in an act of exhibitionism, after he visualizes people laughing (mBank 2017). The final scene of the advertisement depicts the same man *en face*, with a plaque hanging around his neck, revealing his customer ID, password, PIN number, and his personal ID. At the conclusion the campaign motto is revealed: "Not doing it in real life? Do not do it on the Net!" In this regard mBank was willing to underscore how non-Internet, security-related behaviors could appear suspicious and that customers should not treat them differently than activities on the web. Marketer+ nominated this campaign for the 2015 Social Campaign of the Year award in the category of Corporate Campaigns and Firm Foundations.

A mobile operator from the United Arab Emirates, du, tackled online negligence in its push to educate the public on cybersecurity. In November 2016, it launched the digital campaign "Be Safe" with the hashtag #PostWisely (du 2017). The company relied on unsettling material from real-life events. Occurring in the UAE and abroad, these narratives provided target audiences with a glimpse into the minds of cyber criminals: How do cyber criminals operate, and how can seemingly innocent social media posts lead to life-threatening crimes like kidnapping, child abuse, and burglary? (Clark 2016).

Both campaigns, regardless of their approach or tone, have companion websites. These informative sites focus on the types of cyber threats, their consequences, possible prevention methods, and proposed actions if an issue were to occur.

Conclusion

Despite the multitude of cyber-attacks that occur every year, consumers are not fully aware of the importance of cybersecurity (PricewaterhouseCoopers 2018; Verizon 2018; International Telecommunication Union (ITU) 2017; AMEinfo Staff 2016; Fidelis Cybersecurity 2016; ICDL Arabia 2015, 2016; Pew Research Center 2015; Bada et al. 2015; Centrum Badania Opinii Społecznej (CBOS) 2015; Eurobarometer 2015; Smith 2014; Paullet and Pinchot 2012). They do not recognize the importance of prevention or the disastrous consequences of a cyber-attack. Moreover, Internet users overshare on social media, willingly disclose sensitive data in exchange for free apps, and trust open WiFi networks. They suffer from identity theft, phishing, snooping, spying, and child predators. They expose themselves to cyber criminals from the repetitive use of password sets, usually based on easy combinations of birth dates. They avoid using anti-virus software on their computers and passwords and fingerprint recognition on their mobile devices. They eagerly click on links from untrusted sources.

The increasing cost of regular cyber-attacks cannot be measured simply in terms of monetary loss. Cyber insecurity can inflict wounds as deep as a loss of reputation, bullying, and even suicide. Adding to this is the unsupervised Internet access of children, who may later encounter serious digital security problems as adults.

CSR should not only focus on sustainability, corporate accountability, and shared values creation. Rather, it must also confront social issues through cyber threats education. One solution is to educate online consumers through digital campaigns, as exemplified by mBank and du. In this regard, CSR will help companies compete in branding and positioning and improve their business ethics and responsible management. More importantly, though, CSR will guide customers on how to proactive in their own lives, as the prevention of a problem is better than a cure.

References

AccountAbility (2017). *AccountAbility Standards*. Available from https://www.accountability.org/standards/. Accessed 22 Jan 2017.
Agger, B. (2015). *Oversharing: The Eclipse of Privacy in the Internet Age*. Available from https://doi.org/10.1016/B978-0-08-097086-8.64122-3.
AFP. (2017). *Japanese Researchers Warn of Fingerprint Theft from 'Peace' Sign*. Available from https://phys.org/news/2017-01-japan-fingerprint-theftpeace.html. Accessed 11 Jan 2017.
AMEinfo Staff. (2016). *Cybercrime Alert: Nearly Half of UAE Users Add People They Don't Know*. Available from http://ameinfo.com/technology/it/social-media-facebook-cyber-threat. Accessed 23 Nov 2016.
Antonucci, D. (2017). *The Cyber Risk Handbook: Creating and Measuring Effective Cybersecurity Capabilities*. Hoboken: Wiley.
Arabian Marketer. (2016). *UAE Tops Middle East List for Most Employee Data Leaks: Report*. Available from https://arabianmarketer.ae/uae-tops-middle-east-list-for-most-employee-data-leaks-report/. Accessed 3 Oct 2016.
Awan, I., & Blakemore, B. (Eds.). (2012). *Policing Cyber Hate, Cyber Threats and Cyber Terrorism*. London: Routledge.
Bada, M., Sasse, A. M., & Nurse, J. R. C. (2015). Cyber Security Awareness Campaigns: Why Do They Fail to Change Behaviour? In *1st International Conference on Cyber Security for Sustainable Society* (pp. 118–131). Nottingham: Sustainable Society Network.
Bałdys, P. (2014). Życie na widoku. Nowe media a kultura transparencji. *Media I Społeczeństwo, 4*, 42–55.
Breach Live Index. (2018). *2017: A Record Year for Stolen Data*. Available from https://breachlevelindex.com/. Accessed 12 Sept 2018.
Brenner, S. W. (2009). *Cyberthreats: The Emerging Fault Lines of the Nation State*. New York: Oxford University Press.

Centrum Badania Opinii Społecznej (CBOS). (2015). *Bezpieczeństwo w Internecie, CBOS Report 109/2015*. Warszawa: Centrum Badania Opinii Społecznej.

Chekalov, V. (2018). *Awesome Cyber Security Facts*. Available from https://itedgenews.ng/2018/07/27/awesome-cyber-security-facts/. Accessed 27 July 2018.

Clark, J. F. (2016). Growing Threat: Sextortion. *Cyber Misbehavior, 64*(3), 41–44.

Cohen-Almagor, R. (2015). *Confronting the Internet's Dark Side: Moral and Social Responsibility on the Free Highway*. New York: Cambridge University Press.

Dewey, C. (2015). *What the Offensive Tweets of Jeb Bush's New Aide Say About Growing Up in the Oversharing Age*. Available from. https://www.washingtonpost.com/news/the-intersect/wp/2015/02/10/what-the-offensive-tweets-of-jeb-bushs-new-aide-say-about-growing-up-in-the-oversharingage/. Accessed 14 Feb 2015.

Diehl, S., Karmasin, M., Mueller, B., Terlutter, R., & Weder, F. (Eds.). (2017). *Handbook of Integrated CSR Communication*. New York: Springer.

du. (2017). *Be Safe*. Available from http://www.du.ae/personal/helpandsupport/mobile/besafe. Accessed 10 Nov 2017.

Duszczak, P. (2015). *Internetowe grzechy Polaków*. Available from http://www.networkmagazyn.pl/internetowe_grzechy_polakow. Accessed 13 Nov 2015.

Eurobarometer. (2015). *Special Eurobarometer 423 Cyber Security Report*. Available from http://ec.europa.eu/public_opinion/archives/ebs/ebs_423_en.pdf. Accessed 1 Feb 2015.

Fereira, O. (2016). *The Dangers of Social Media and Oversharing*. Available from http://singlegadget.com/the-dangers-of-social-media-and-oversharing/. Accessed 30 Nov 2017.

Fidelis Cybersecurity. (2016). *CyberEdge Group: 2016 Cyberthreat Defense Report*. Available from https://www.fidelissecurity.com/resources/cyberedge-group-2016-cyberthreat-defense-report-0. Accessed 20 Nov 2017.

George Washington University. (2017). *Cybersecurity by the Numbers*. Available from https://security.online.gwu.edu/blog/cybersecurity-by-the-numbers. Accessed 12 May 2017.

Gharibi, W., & Shaabi, M. (2012). Cyber Threats in Social Networking Websites. *International Journal of Distributed and Parallel Systems (IJDPS), 3*(1), 119–126.

Grey Wizard. (2015). *Internetowe grzechy Polaków*. Available from https://infowire.pl/generic/release/303737/internetowe-grzechy-polakow/. Accessed 13 Nov 2015.

Griffor, E. (Ed.). (2016). *Handbook of System Safety and Security: Cyber Risk and Risk Management, Cyber Security, Threat Analysis, Functional Safety, Software Systems, and Cyber Physical Systems*. Cambridge: Syngress Publishing.

Harthorne, M. (2017). *Flashing the Peace Sign Can Get Your Identity Stolen*. Available from http://www.newser.com/story/236719/researchers-warnfingerprints-can-be-stolen-from-selfies.html. Accessed 12 Jan 2017.

ICDL Arabia. (2015). *Cyber Safety Report: Research into the Online Behaviour of Arab Youth and Risks they Face*. Dubai: ICDL Arabia.

ICDL Arabia. (2016). *Social Media: Influencing Young Minds*. Dubai: ICDL Arabia.

Ihlen, Ø., Bartlett, J., & May, S. (Eds.). (2011). *The Handbook of Communication and Corporate Social Responsibility*. Hoboken: Wiley.

International Telecommunication Union (ITU). (2017). *Global Cybersecurity Index (GCI) 2017*. Geneva: ITU.

Internet World Stats. (2017). *World Internet Usage and Population Statistics*. Available from https://www.internetworldstats.com/stats.htm. Accessed 27 Feb 2018.

Kupczyk, P. (2016). *Użytkownicy nie dbają o prywatność na portalach społecznościowych*. Available from http://di.com.pl/uzytkownicy-nie-dbaja-o-prywatnosc-na-portalach-spolecznosciowych-54106. Accessed 7 Jan 2016.

Leiter, M. (2016). *How to Choose Social Media Platforms*. Available from http://www.melissaleiter.com/blog/how-to-choose-social-media-platforms. Accessed 6 Apr 2016.

mBank. (2017). *Uważni w sieci*. Available from https://www.mbank.pl/uwazniwsieci/page/o-kampanii/. Accessed 21 Jan 2017.

McKean, J. S. (2014). *Customer's New Voice: Extreme Relevancy and Experience Through Volunteered Customer Information*. Hoboken: Wiley.

Oxford English Dictionary. (2018). Available from https://en.oxforddictionaries.com/definition/cyberthreat. Accessed 7 Mar 2018.

Paullet, K., & Pinchot, J. (2012). *Cybercrime: The Unintentional Effects of Oversharing Information on Facebook*. In 2012 Proceedings of the Conference on Information Systems Applied Research v5 n2231, pp. 1–7, New Orleans, Louisiana: ISCA.

Pew Research Center. (2015). *Teens, Social Media & Technology Overview 2015*. Available from. http://www.pewresearch.org/wpcontent/uploads/sites/9/2015/04/PI_TeensandTech_Update2015_0409151.pdf. Accessed 9 Apr 2015.

PricewaterhouseCoopers. (2018). *21st CEO Survey the Anxious Optimist in the Corner Office*. Available from https://www.pwc.com/gx/en/ceo-survey/2018/pwc-ceo-survey-report-2018.pdf. Accessed 9 Mar 2018.

SAI (2017). *SA8000® Standard*. Available from http://www.sa-intl.org/index.cfm?fuseaction=Page.ViewPage&PageID=1689. Accessed 21 Jan 2017.

Shambler, T. (2017). *UAE Is Most at Risk for Employee Data Leaks in the Middle East*. Available from http://www.arabianbusiness.com/uae-is-most-at-risk-for-employee-data-leaks-in-middle-east-647029.html. Accessed 4 Dec 2017.

Smith, A. (2014). *Half of Online Americans Don't Know What a Privacy Policy Is*. Available from http://www.pewresearch.org/fact-tank/2014/12/04/half-of-americans-dont-know-what-a-privacy-policy-is/. Accessed 4 Dec 2017.

Sophos. (2017). *Cyber-Security*. Available from http://blog.titania.com/cyber-security-hereford-worcestershire-business-manifesto-2017/. Accessed 20 Aug 2018.

Symantec. (2015). *2015 Internet Security Threat Report*. Available from https://www.symantec.com/content/en/us/enterprise/other_resources/21347933_GA_RPT-internet-security-threat-report-volume-20-2015.pdf. Accessed 1 Apr 2015.

Tarabasz, A. (2017). *Cyber Threat Awareness in Digital Marketing Campaigns: Comparative Analysis of UAE and Poland*. Available from https://doi.org/10.13140/RG.2.2.32736.69127.

Trim, P., & Lee, Y. (2014). *Cyber Security Management: A Governance, Risk and Compliance Framework*. New York: Routledge.

Twenge, J. M., & Campbell, W. K. (2013). *The Narcissism Epidemic: Living in the Age of Entitlement*. New York: Atria Paperback.

Ulsch, M. (2014). *Cyber Threat! How to Manage the Growing Risk of Cyber Attacks*. Hoboken: Wiley.

Verizon. (2018). *2017 Data Breach Investigations Report: Executive Summary*. Available from https://www.knowbe4.com/hubfs/rp_DBIR_2017_Report_execsummary_en_xg.pdf. Accessed 2 Sept 2018.

Visser, W., Magureanu, I., & Yadav, K. (2015). *The CSR International Research Compendium – Volume 3: Society*. London: Kaleidoscope Futures.

WirtualneMedia. (2015). *„Nie robisz tego w realu? Nie rób tego w sieci!"- mBank ostrzega przed cyberprzestępcami (wideo)*. Available from https://www.wirtualnemedia.pl/artykul/nie-robisz-tego-w-realu-nie-rob-tego-w-sieci-mbank-ostrzega-przed-cyberprzestepcami-wideo. Accessed 17 Dec 2015.

Zaharia, A. (2016). *10 Alarming Cyber Security Facts that Threaten Your Data*. Available from https://heimdalsecurity.com/blog/10-surprising-cyber-security-facts-that-may-affect-your-online-safety/. Accessed 12 May 2016.

14

Integration and Coordination of Care and Social Services as a Responsible Way of Handling Psychiatric Disability

Annie Bartoli, Christelle Perrin, and Jihane Sebai

Introduction and Research Question

In the field of healthcare, the feeling of failure facing compartmentalized organizations and services has brought about legislative and regulatory consideration as well as political concerns regarding the problems of coordination and integration (Leutz 1999). The latter can be categorized, in particular, through the work of multidisciplinary teams, organization in divisions or networks, governance, responsibility, and shared information, with problems related to the coordination of human and management resources (Miramon 2010). Different organizational designs of coordination and integration have been developed in order to assure, most particularly, cooperation among the medical, clinical, and social components of patient care.

The concept of case manager (Hofmarcher et al. 2007) appeared in the United States during the 1970s and, at first, concerned social workers and then nurses. Even though their methods may vary, case management is now

A. Bartoli (✉)
University of Versailles, Versailles, France

Georgetown University, Washington, DC, USA
e-mail: agb39@georgetown.edu

C. Perrin • J. Sebai
University of Versailles, Versailles, France
e-mail: christelle.perrin@uvsq.fr; jihane.sebai@uvsq.fr

© The Author(s) 2019
A. Bartoli et al. (eds.), *Responsible Organizations in the Global Context*,
https://doi.org/10.1007/978-3-030-11458-9_14

widespread in the United States, Great Britain, and Canada and is expanding in Europe. In France, the topic of case management appeared in 2008 within the sphere of care of the aged through the national Alzheimer's project. However, it is still a relatively new professional area within the sector of mental health, which aims to produce a better interface between healthcare and social activities. In the objective of side-stepping the fragmentation of services (medical and social) and in optimal adjustment of responses to the needs of people suffering from severe mental difficulties, case management has appeared as a new form of charge taking, including encouragement for the patient as well as multi-dimensional and progressive support in his/her regular life. For the patient then, the concept of integration of services is used in order to assure ubiquitous care (by participants in medical, health, and social areas) and by subscribing, within the timeline, to continuity of care. For the professional participants, case management allows for the reinforcement of ability to assess the level of intervention required for the patient, as well as for the ability to obtain appropriate services (Petitqueux-Glaser et al. 2010). On the societal level, this approach may be considered to be a more responsible way to approach the issues of mental health, for it looks beyond institutional and organizational divides in order to deal with the question as a whole.

Case management can correspond to two types of objectives: on one side, clinical objectives translated in terms of quality of life for the patients and the caregivers (Vickrey et al. 2006; Callahan et al. 2006), and, on the other side, medico-economic objectives in terms of the organization of health and social resources (Bass et al. 2003; Weinberger et al. 1993). Whatever the prioritized and researched objective, and the variability of professional practices categorized under the term case management, the majority of the analyses concur with the necessity of a universal approach to taking charge of the sick person, as well as to the importance of articulation between the world of care and that of social facilities. In addition, even if the potential impacts are generally recognized in terms of improvement in quality and efficiency,[1] and of response to a problem of public health, its operational declination and translations remain multiform and often a source of confusion.

In this chapter, we endeavor to underline the potential input of different facets of comprehensive and responsible mental health patient care. In particular, four levers are emphasized: integration of care and services; coordina-

---

[1] Case Management Society of America's Standards of Practice for Case Management. Revised January 2010. Available from www.cmsa.org.

tion among stakeholders; case management; and empowerment (viewed as growth of the capacity of patient action). We propose to unite these four sectors in a pattern of analysis and action, titled from the acronym of the four levers: "ICCE framework."

We are particularly interested in the innovative French structure that specializes in the care of young schizophrenics (Prepsy). With this case, we attempt to shed light on the feasibility of this pattern and to underline the social responsibility of the involved structure to respond to the needs of its patients in order to make an impact in society. In particular, we study the role of responsibility among "case managers" in the improvement of patients' path of life (Gozlan 2016; Frankel and Gelman 2011). In order to accomplish this, it is first necessary to clarify the basic outlines of the four active levers and to show the necessity of their interaction within a scenario of broad intervention in the service of responsible care of psychiatric handicap.

Exploration of Primary Concepts and Theoretical Frameworks

Our research relies on the perspective of four innovative concepts in the management of mental health: integration, coordination, case management, and empowerment, which form a group we call the "ICCE framework" (Fig. 14.1).

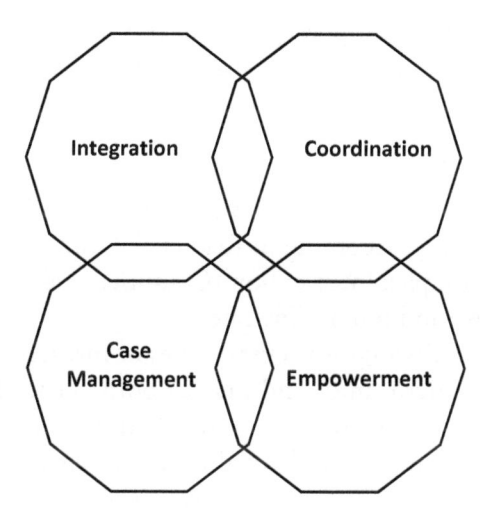

Fig. 14.1 ICCE framework. (Source: Authors)

Integration

The concept of integration is polysemic. In the area of mental health, it is often used to translate the necessary articulation among professional action: medical, health, and social activity for comprehensive patient care. In view of professional areas of specialization, as well as institutional divisions, this articulation is not straightforward, and its effective implementation has become a major challenge. In France, since the 1996 Juppé Ordinances, the 2009 Couty Report, and, more recently, the Laforcade Report of 2016, the nation's political climate and regulation regarding mental health are particularly influenced by this objective of integration.

As such, integration consists of connecting the health system to a team of services (social and/or medico/social) in the perspective of an increase in quality of care and patient satisfaction (Leutz 1999). For the patient, integration means seamlessness in the upgrade of care and an ease of navigation (WHO 2008) resulting in better continuity of services (OMS 2000). It is this idea of continuity of care which has been most stressed in specialized academic journals (Armitage et al. 2009; Sebai 2016). According to (Somme 2008; Somme et al. 2013), integration has, as its goal, the improvement of continuity in intervention with people suffering a loss of autonomy. It consists of the establishment of organizational measures and clinical tools aimed at informational transmission and interior coordination among health sectors and medico-social and social areas (Kodner and Kyriacou 2000). "The object of coordination which plays out from this intended integration cannot, therefore, be reduced either to a single clinical dimension, be it professional action composed for a user, or to the single organizational dimension, for norms and rules of the establishment, organization of work, or the distribution of resources[2]" (Couturier et al. 2011). The integration of services must, therefore, deal as much with the clinical side of all medical practice (management continuity, according to Reid et al. 2002), as with the organizational side of all complex intervention (Couturier et al. 2011), in order to assure comprehensive and responsible care.

Shaw et al. (2011) distinguish several types of integration that play out on different levels (micro, mid, and macro) both vertically and horizontally. Integration is considered to be "vertical" if it connotes different levels of care (e.g. a hospital referral) or different levels of decision-making

---

[2] Translation by the authors.

(e.g. in France, regional health agencies and "councils-general"). Integration is said to be "horizontal" if it performs at the same level of care (e.g. professionals of primary healthcare) or at the same level of decision-making. Recent literature highlights five principal dimensions of the integration procedure:

- Clinical integration: Defined as informational coordination of services and relations among health professionals (Kodner 2009); also touches on the articulation of care (Contandriopoulos et al. 2001) at the heart of procedures (Shaw et al. 2011). It can, for example, concern advanced practices, protocols, and inter-professional groups.
- Integration of services: Defined as a group of techniques and organizational models formed to ensure transmission of information, inner coordination and collaboration, and among health and social services, administrative and financial services (Kodner and Kyriacou 2000; Ham et al. 2011).
- Functional integration: Defined as the alignment of support functions and budgetary and financial systems at the heart of a shared structure (Field 2011).
- Normative integration: Covering the development of values, culture, and shared visions throughout organizations, professional groups, and individuals, aimed at the development of mutual objectives of integration, or identification and correction of deficits of communication (Shaw et al. 2011).
- Systemic integration: Concerns the consistency of legislation, politics, and organizational procedures coherently implemented on every level of organizations (Curry and Ham 2010).

Even though the terms "integration" and "integrated care" are often interchanged, it is interesting to distinguish them. Actually, integration without coordination of care cannot lead to integrated care. Integrated care is the end result of integration (Shaw et al. 2011), and the rationale of integration is equally inseparable from coordination. The two concepts of coordination and integration are often interchanged and complimentary. While coordination seeks to assure articulation among participants in an organization, in order to address deficiencies of service functioning, integration is understood to go beyond: it inclines toward in-depth modification of organizational function so that together they find solutions to the gaps in continuity experienced by the patients. Thus, the logic of integration cannot, in any case, be the "ownership" or the "mission" of a single participant or organization; by nature, it corresponds to a collective project supported by a partnership (Somme et al. 2013). Therefore, the two procedures are complimentary and synergistic in so much as each allows the maximization of the effects of the other: to work on the articulations and maximize the effect of reorganization and role reversal. Coordination can be considered a stage or a necessary, actually indispensable, way to integration, even if it is not specifically its formalized goal. However, coordination is not necessarily aimed at formulating integration (Somme et al. 2013). In other words, one can consider that coordination is to organizations what continuity of care and service is to the patient. Coordination engages strategies of functional integration, where continuity puts professionals to the test of their strategies of clinical integration.

Integration is particularly associated with patient needs in complex therapeutic situations. For these people integration must allow for the development of specific and personalized responses leading to the concept of "case management" (Challis et al. 2001). Thus, case management can insert itself as a dimension of integration, but not as a distinctly complementary technique (Dubuc et al. 2011; Somme et al. 2012). The emergence of the concept of case management—its contours and specificities—will be addressed in the next paragraph.

Coordination

One of the major conditions of comprehensive and responsible caregiving to patients with psychiatric difficulties rests on the coordination of care and service. The concept of coordination is part of the classical concept of organizational management, its potential supports being regularly emphasized. It may be defined as "an organizational process of interactions between various participants and activities, toward the end of attaining a result which could not be achieved with the addition of isolated actions" (Bartoli and Gozlan 2014).

In France, the Couty Report on mental health (2009) demonstrated the need for "a level of agreement of an area […] assuring effective cooperation and coordination of various participants particularly concerned with the stake: elected officials, caregivers, social workers, those responsible for housing and employment, etc." The author stresses that necessary care coordination collides with professional and institutional reflexes and that only certain individual initiatives, which must be encouraged, can run counter to these. Coordination of these activities seems to indicate participatory cooperation among stakeholders, which can no longer function indifferently to other participants. As to coordination, it is considered to be essential, for the recognition of others that cannot be limited either at their discretion or blow-by-blow action (Jaeger 2010). It is a dual objective: on one side, one must overcome the relative limits of partition and the fragmentation of health systems and, on the other side, avoid recourse of too frequent hospitalizations (Cameron et al. 2014). It involves responding to the multiple medical and social needs of patients with chronic pathologies (Thiel et al. 2013), who often encounter difficulties in coherent articulation of their care in the transitions among different services and structures (Oliver et al. 2014).

In the area of mental health, the issue of coordination between care and services is particularly strong given the complexity of pathologies and their frequency in the population (World Health Organization 2010). An additional challenge is that of integration that can be seen as a procedure aimed at "coordinating interdependences" (Contandriopoulos et al. 2001) for the implementation of a collective project.

Case Management

Case management has its roots in the vast movement of "deinstitutionalism" underway in the United States in the early 1950s. It was realized that the multiplication and fragmentation of services, as well as the lack of coordination among the different service participants (medico-social and social), did nothing to promote the social reintegration of the individual (Intagliata 1982; Schwartz et al. 1982). Chronically ill psychiatric patients can suffer serious malfunctions in social communities. It is within this context that case management developed; from the beginning, it was in a relatively limited sense conceived as a way of connection of the patient with service geared toward diagnosed needs. At that time case management had, above all, an objective to plan services (Bachrach 1979). Although introduced as a reactive model, its initial concept did not actually allow for true clinical and organizational implementation among different participants. It was even able to identify a significant number of lost follow-ups (Petitqueux-Glaser et al. 2010).

Later on, case management saw its role evolve significantly within a wider field of application. Exceeding its goal of connection among services, other dimensions joined the trend: the dimension of therapy (Lamb 1980; Petitqueux-Glaser et al. 2010) and the resolution of problems of daily life (Intagliata 1982). From the case management of connection, it went through a case management scenario of readjustment, founded on the concept of the individual strengths of the patient (Rapp and Goscha 2006), with intensive team follow-up called assertive community treatment, or ACT. The philosophy of this approach is to favor, on behalf of the patient, a progressive care aimed at the reestablishment of the individual within ordinary life, in collaboration with his/her immediate circle. More and more, one speaks of treatment within the community (Test and Stein 1978) and the teaching of life skills (Wallace et al. 1980). This type of intervention developed in the United States along different lines. To the case manager can be added other credentialed individuals: therapeutic case manager, specialist case *manager*, generalist case manager, care manager (Hofmarcher et al. 2007), and disease manager (Kodner 2009; Shifren-Levine and Fleming 1985).

For some years, developments in the area of psychiatric rehabilitation have significantly influenced the approach of case management. Thus, the teaching of social skills within normal circumstances is increasingly augmented (Anthony and Liberman 1986).

The acquisition of authorized personnel is assumed to play out in a normal setting, as suggested by Test and Stein (1978), but a normal network could also be used with greater efficiency (Harris and Bergman 1985). It is, henceforth, a marriage between the model of case management and the approach of necessary rehabilitation (Goering et al. 1988), even if its actual implementation remains rare.

In addition, another objective of case management is to assist and support people in their negotiations with the different services that they want to receive or which they need. The point of departure is, then, no longer the service but the individual. As such, case management, which initially had a function based on the distribution of services (administrative and unilateral), became a mode of practice in mental health, recognizing the importance of the integration of bio-psycho-social dimensions of treatment, that is, a clinical and communal approach.

Generally, the role of case manager plays out in six principal dimensions: (1) facilitation of patient access to appropriate services, (2) help for the patient to develop his basic skills, (3) offering of practical assistance to the patient via therapy, (4) intense use of diagnostic screening, (5) improvement of the patient's quality of life, and (6) access to clinical intervention where indicated (Bachrach 1989; De Cangas 1994). Universality and continuity of patient care are thus assumed to offer more responsible management of the patient, only possible by the alignment of certain conditions (Bachrach 1979), in particular the following:

- thoroughness of connections between the patient and professionals involved in follow-up

- individualization of response to the needs of the patient and his family
- totality of patient care and services
- adaptability of service offerings geared to the evolution of the situation
- relational dimension, encompassing relational mutual confidence
- accessibility (temporal, special, financial, cultural, etc.), corresponding to the necessity of dealing with obstacles and obtaining needed services and care
- communication among the participants working with the patients and among those close to them
- patient participation in the definition of his individualized plan (empowerment)

Empowerment

In prioritizing the framework that encourages patients to activate their resources to take charge of their future, case management is moving resolutely toward education in the development of the capacity to act (*empowerment*). Despite the haziness which surrounds the option of empowerment, one generally recognizes the importance of involved individuals to participate and reinforce their capacity to influence their reality (Le Bossé 2003) and mobilize useful resources (personnel, relational, material, informational) to take charge of their own destiny (ibid.). This automation "ideal" is, in fact, only possible if the patient is already in a "zone approaching autonomy" (Zittoun 2006, p. 169[3]), allowing him to choose the best part of the system created for him. However, certain researchers recall that it is not necessary to fall into a "contradictory ordinance" (Duvoux 2009), for the practice also demonstrates the difficulty of an individual to extract the best part of the intended program designed for him. Certain researchers do note how the requirement of independence puts the transformation of a "paradoxical injunction" at risk (Duvoux 2009), and the practice also demonstrates the difficulty of taking the concept to its logical conclusion in certain specific clinical situations.

---

[3] The notion of proximal zone of development was introduced by Vygotsky and refers to the gap between the present capacity of the patient to deal with what happens to him in his life and that which he would have if he were under medical care. This gap offers possible autonomation whereby the patient would be able to appropriate and reinvest the enhancement of experienced autonomy in a situation of support.

Coordination, integration, case management, and empowerment thus form a set of essential and complementary levers for responsible management of mental health. According to convention, we will call this "the ICCE scheme" (or "ICCE framework"). Its implementation within classical institutional structures is difficult in that these levers rest precisely on cutting care and social or medical services. However, certain innovative devices among organizations do exist and can provide responses where structural or sociopolitical systems are sometimes powerless. One of these devices, established in France, will be examined in order to elucidate certain conditions, limits, and more responsible impacts of caregiving for the patient's mental health in the pattern of ICCE.

Empirical Research: Case of an Innovative Organization in Mental Health

Presentation of the Studied Organization

The main case studied in this research is Prepsy in Paris. It deals with personalized multidisciplinary medical-social support services[4] of varying intensities, both collaborative and multidisciplinary, all aimed at young adults from 18 to 25 years of age. These patients suffer from chronic psychiatric problems that cause general dysfunction in their personal, familial, academic, or professional lives. Intervention focuses on a return to autonomy by limiting handicaps encountered in daily life, providing better access to services offered by the group, and developing better lines of contact among the many professionals and organizations available to help patients eligible for mental health care (attending physicians, private or hospital psychiatrists, psychologists or psychotherapists, social workers, social administrators, administrative services, academic institutions, professional organizations, families, friends, etc.).

The Prepsy structure may be considered an organizational innovation in the comprehensive care of mentally handicapped patients. Its uniqueness is particularly apparent in the implementation of case management that supports a new practice of mental healthcare among young schizophrenic patients.

---

[4] The institutional structure of Prepsy is based on Service d'Accompagnement Médico-Social pour Adultes Handicapés (SAMSAH), a medico-social support service for handicapped adults.

Empirical Approach

The adopted method is multifaceted, qualitative, and rooted in empiric reality (Glaser and Strauss 1967). It rests on the principles of case study as research data. According to Yin (2009), a case corresponds to concrete reality (body, event, phenomenon, or action) and becomes research material when implemented by conditions and stages of a scientific approach that allows for the yielding of theoretical results. Our epistemological position is "adductive" (Peirce 1931), in the sense that comprehension of observed phenomena is constructed from an iterative approach between observation of facts over time and the use of theoretical concepts and frameworks to aid in their interpretation.

Empirical research is first based on semi-directive interviews lasting between an hour and an hour and a half. The sample of 24 interviewees represented the following categories of personnel:

- Personnel of the studied structure: specialized educators, nurses, medical doctors, administrators, ergonomists, directors, etc.
- Some patients and their families.
- Institutional professionals identified as stakeholders in the functioning of Prepsy.
- National experts working in the area of coordination or of integration in mental health.

The interviews relied on discussions concerning the concepts, practices, and baselines involved in their practices. They centered, on one side, on the concepts and representations of participants concerning the above-analyzed ideas (coordination, integration, case management, empowerment) in the area of mental health, and, on the other side, descriptions of practical evidence concerning the structures of universal patient care.

These interviews were conducted on voluntary basis following a commitment to confidentiality and anonymity. With interviewee authorization, a recording was made for the assurance of the greatest possible fidelity to the discussion. The gathered data was handled according to qualitative research methodologies, specifically with the use of anonymous transcripts secondary data and thematic encryption from Nvivo 11 software and manual code. The data was structured to allow for the ease at data interpretation.

Additionally, the written data was gathered from reports, detailed reporting, and internal documents from the company.

Synthetic Analysis and Interpretation of Results

Highlighting of the Efficiency of the Concepts

The four concepts at the base of ICCE are present in varying degrees, according to the representations and testimony of interviewed participants.

Procedures of Integration

In the operational plan, Prepsy first demonstrates strong clinical integration of structure targeting the offer of integrated services based on prevention and personalized help to patients. In France, the operational linking of health and social sectors is not easy, given the administrative, political, and institutional cuts already in place. Also, Prepsy's challenge to seek augmentation was that of integration in the heart of its professions and key skills necessary to this interaction of the medical and social fields. So, professions such as that of the ergonomist charged with the evaluation of physical handicaps have been integrated in the area of employment of physicians, nurses, social workers, educators, and so on.

In addition, in the area of the integration of services, empirical research underlines the importance of articulating different areas of care. This is based on the patient, begins at the first contact with him or her, and throughout concerns of his/her path of communication about his/her case and mutual understanding of therapeutic needs, skills, and resources to mobilize and respond. Integration of services is, then, in place throughout the participation of work groups and consultations necessary to encourage, by networking of abilities and reciprocal action of each, continuity of follow-up and diminution of isolation and risks of re-hospitalization. This leads to internal multiprofessional cooperation but also to external multidisciplinary cooperation with various professional and institutional participants whose involvement seems indispensable to the path of the patient.

Furthermore, Prepsy created a physical and space-specific organization so that the representatives of different professions can speak easily on a daily basis and that communication among internal participants is as easy as possible. According to interviewed personnel, oral culture and provision of "open space" offices contribute to this fluidity. In addition, informal exchanges and coordinative multi-professional meetings are organized every week. Additional meetings are also implemented according to the complexity of the situation.

Also revisited is the concern of consensus on organizational objectives (development of common values) and the creation of a common identity (a "we") in the activity (Somme et al. 2013), regarding the normative integration described above. Finally, the objective of comprehensive and responsible integration within Prepsy seems to depend on a procedural approach (contact, communication, cooperation, consensus, and cohesion based on mechanisms of confidence, mutual comprehension, and co-responsibility). Thus represented, ubiquitous integration at the heart of Prepsy seems to illustrate the model of Demers et al. (2005), which brought to life a study on the integration of services to the aged who have lost their autonomy.

Implementation of Coordination Processes

Empirical research confirms that Prepsy is working with a large network of professionals, who deal with the areas of health, social spheres, academics, associations, and the economy. This network is non-restrictive so that each new patient can bring with him new stakeholders or designate the specific needs which will lead him to link with new participants. Cooperation among participants cannot exist without the proactive approach from Prepsy, which functions with partners or regular contacts and which maintains continued contact with multiple professionals in order to present to them the approach and the role they played in patient support. Prepsy thus endeavors to weave a culture of exchange and communication with patients and with other health professionals in an atmosphere that is normally geared to autonomous development. Prepsy, therefore, confirms itself as the role of coordinator.

Case Management

Even if the understanding of the terminology of "case management" is variable, according to the interviewees, most of the responses closely converge on the ideas and examples of the role of case manager and the necessary skills for this position. Within Prepsy, almost all the members of the team are capable of filling the role of case manager, whatever their basic profession. They are usually nurses, social workers, or educators who are responsible for formulating a plan of individualized and coordinated intervention for monitoring the patient and providing support and connection with the family. The case manager is defined by how his abilities line up with the primary needs of the patient. In addition to his listening and communication skills, as well as his synthesis and adaptive abilities, the choice of case manager rests on the specific abilities to respond to the clinical or social needs expressed by the patient at the moment. This involves gathering useful information for the individualized plan and describes the short- and mid-term objectives, approaches, and interventions required to bring patient goals to fruition. He contacts outside professionals who are essential to the plan of action for the patients and, with them, designs their path forward. Certain outside speakers, as well as contact with family members of the patient, underline this interaction.

From the first contact, the engagement of the case manager is a major criterion of the success of the care. In fact, at the time of the patient's admission, a situation report is made. Depending on his clinical situation and expectations (to pursue or renew his studies, have satisfying work, enjoy a normal social life, etc.), he is assigned a case manager from the team. The team has the ability to reinforce connections among social, medical, and health activities, linking administrative, educational, and professional services with the patient, and to coordinate among the various participants. Benefitting from this coordination, the case manager seeks to participate in the compartmentalization of the system but, above all, from a proactive rather than reactive approach, with the goal of assuring continuity of care, as under index in the literature (Leavitt 1983). The objective of the case manager is, thus, to accompany and support patients in their negotiations with the various services that they would like to receive and which they need. They try to offer support or backing aimed at the remediation of certain defects: lack of basic knowledge, absence of a training, being a school dropout, conflict in family relations, insecurity of living conditions, substance dependence, and/or insufficient personal and social skills to tackle the job market efficiently.

The role of the case manager is also that coordinatior of services and social rehabilitation. The case manager is the active representative of the patient and works to shorten the delay between the appearance of psychological problems and access to specialized and coordinated support. Indeed, he or she attempts to minimize the impact of the illness in its acute stages or its remission. He or she will intervene in order to reduce the symptoms and diminish subjective distress while simulatenously helping the patient with medication or by intervening in times of crisis. This process reinforces clinical integration.

Empowerment

At the heart of Prepsy is the feeling of empowerment—the added value of the team that supports young people in the difficult transition from school to job (Soulet 2005). The care practices are, indeed, integrative and flexible depending on the level of necessary help (Leutz 1999) and contribute to the reestablishment and progressive control of the patient over his/her own decision-making (Fig. 14.2).

The process of empowerment is mainly formed within the normal milieu of the patient (i.e. to stay at his/her home most of the time), which places the case manager within physical and emotional proximity to the patient. The relation that forms between the patient and the case manager is based on mutual confidence and plays out as an individualized approach to services linked with respect to the expectations and needs expressed by the individual. Besides intervention in the patient's natural milieu, customization of the relationship represents the second value added to this care. Actually, the individualization of proposed services allows for the adaptation of the case manager's intervention in the process of the evolving the patient's needs during the process of social reintegration.

Prepsy has chosen not to organize group meetings among the patients, as that can sometimes be arranged in other contexts, particularly in hospital settings where they are invited to participate in different sports and cultural activities. According to the members of the team, these collective dynamics have a positive and stimulating effect in certain cases but can also cause devastating consequences to certain patients, where self-esteem can be very fragile and where any failure (whether in sports or in other comparisons with others) can be negative. Prepsy has made the choice of individualized care centered on each person, with variable intensity. The care is progressive and adapted to the patient's progress.

The Prepsy team leads the patient, little by little, to find ways to feel empowered and to take his life in his own hands. Prepsy works likewise with the implementation of demonstration apartments where patients could assess

Motivation → Engagement → Oriented Action →
Responsibility in self-care
= **Empowerment**

Fig. 14.2 Process of patient empowerment. (Source: Authors)

themselves in relation to everyday circumstances. In that same dynamic Prepsy benefits from the contribution of a "peer help." For instance, an elderly person who has become a member of the team can represent the reflection of a patient years after a successful integration in the work world.

Challenges and Difficulties Encountered

Despite inputs by the innovative structure of Prepsy concerning patients, families, and institutional partners, the case study also reveals several limits and obstacles.

In particular, even if it is true that concentration and coordination, both intra- and inter-institutional, are necessary, they remain difficult to apply in response to the needs of people who are psychiatrically chronically ill. Indeed, even though it is an innovative and atypical organization within the mental health sector, Prepsy is not immune to certain institutional restraints. Initially, the team had difficulty in establishing itself in a system of highly institutionalized public psychiatry, marked by relative lack of understanding of broad integration by public institutions. The limited understanding of Prepsy's role as a coordinating body completely different from other medico-social support services for the handicapped has made it difficult for Prepsy to cooperate and collaborate with other professionals (psychiatrists, specialized centers, hospitals, etc.) in the region, who rely on pivotal players in the French mental healthcare system.

Accordingly, one of Prepsy's challenges remains to seat itself and reinforce its legitimacy in an area traditionally marked by institutional structures (hospital services, medico-psychiatric facilities, etc.). Within this context the attainment of legitimacy is a constant struggle. The direction of Prepsy is highly sensitive to this challenge and strives to become known and recognized via a form of active lobbying and systematic networking. Furthermore, the territorial dynamics of the French health system limit Prepsy's outreach past a certain geographic area unless it duplicates the organization. It is to this point that certain political participants cognizant of the interest of this innovative organization take broad charge care of mental health patients. In addition, the road is long to "scatter" this type of structure in other places.

In the area of personnel, young employees who lack work experience, even though being an opportunity in terms of motivation and dynamism, often represent a challenge for the company. While they often are part of the team leaning toward an innovative work method, their inexperience makes it difficult for them to consider the gap with old school methods and activities.

In addition, as opposed to the top-down model commonly known in this type of area, the Prepsy case managers benefit from a quite wide autonomy as to the methods of patient care. Although the perimeter of operation may be set and well-focused, this autonomy sometimes represents a source of discomfort for the personnel, particularly for those whose Prepsy experience represents their first professional job. This constraint may result in a significant turnover of professionals or a certain loss of motivation translated by a weaker involvement. The youth of the structure and the turnover of employees cause a specific challenge. A dynamic of integration can only be efficacious by weaving a relationship of trust that would succeed over time. Therefore, the objective to create inter-organizational, rather than interpersonal, relations with external participants is not easy.

On the clinical level, the approach centered on the patient, as much as to the unique person, collides with the practice in varying resistance. Actually, it implies respect and needs of patient expectations. However, certain patients, given the complexity of their case, are not always in touch with what they want or how to express it, and sometimes the expectations turn out to be variable and unstable. In this type of pathology the patient cannot recognize himself as being ill and finds difficulty in assessing his specific expectations and needs as identified by those close to him and by professionals.

Finally—and this is not limited to Prepsy—the poverty of financial resources, as well as difficulties of obtaining them from public funding, causes serious obstacles to improvement, development, and deployment of innovative tools of this type.

Discussion and Conclusion

With regard to the theoretical structure mobilized along with gathered empirical results, the responsible role of the innovative structure of Prepsy, in the overall and individualized care of young patients with discernible psychiatric problems, looks clear. The developed procedures endeavor to fight for those who are repressed dysfunctionality in traditional forms of care, specifically regarding access to benefits; cutoffs from medical, social, and sanitation services; and an overly systematic path to hospitalization.

Throughout the approach of case management, the internal and external coordination of the diverse facets of integration, and the facets of empowerment that have been implemented, the studied structure distinguishes itself by a comprehensive patient care system whose impacts are potentially social by nature but likewise emphasize the larger role of the economic and medical fields. In placing each patient at the heart of the care facility (Armitage et al. 2009), as well as mobilizing medical, medico-social, and social services in an attempt to respond to the patient's specific needs, the structure thus fulfills a mission of comprehensive care.

Its pertinence could be approached specifically in terms of patient satisfaction regarding their support system (family, guardians, teachers, etc.) and by statistics concerning their return to employment or school. It rests on several levers, such as individuation of care, integration of social and medical services in organizational coordination, participation of case managers, and development of the capabilities of patient action. This pertinence is also recognized by experts who consider this case to be a model of the genre and by the institutions which envisage its spreading over French territory. Across the formalization of the "ICCE framework," research has highlighted four key interrelated levers that foster widespread patient care in mental health: coordination of care and services, integration (considered as clinical, functional, cultural, and systemic), case management, and patient empowerment.

Limits and constraints are equally present and strongly bound to the isolated and pioneering character of this organization, which has difficulty in obtaining recognition and necessary support for its future. Furthermore, the considerable efforts demanded for the deployment of such a facility represent sources of difficulty in matters of management of human resources and also requires all the more of managerial involvement.

This research is, however, ongoing and will not arrive at certain full conclusions given particular limits. The empirical method is based essentially on the disadvantage of a reduced external validity and cannot lead to a generalization. In addition, the specificity of the French environment could be compared to other cases of comprehensive care of patients with mental troubles in various countries in order to gain more significant findings.

Moreover, it appears that complementary levers could be introduced in the ICCE framework, such as the detection and early intervention procedures mentioned by several interviewees and certain international experts (McGorry et al. 2001). Actually, the risk of physical handicaps becoming chronic, resulting from delayed action, would lead to less efficient care. In facilitating coordinated access to health services, and to nearby social support with the involvement of a "case manager," the integrated and personalized approach, particularly when instituted following early detection, seems to contribute to obtaining better clinical results by limiting institutionalization and certain avoidable hospitalizations (Eklund and Wilhelmson 2009; Martínez-González et al. 2012).

Further investigation must be conducted as far as possible in so much as the issue of comprehensive approach in mental health seems significant: first from the human viewpoint toward patients and their families but also in terms of social and economic costs for society as a whole.

References

Anthony, W. A., & Liberman, R. P. (1986). The Practice of Psychiatric Rehabilitation: Historical, Conceptual, and Research Base. *Schizophrenia Bulletin, 12*(4), 542–559.

Armitage, G. D., Suter, E., Oelke, N. D., & Adair, C. E. (2009). Health Systems Integration: State of the Evidence. *International Journal of Integrated Care, 9*(2), 1–11.

Bachrach, L. L. (1979). Planning Mental Health Services for Chronic Patients. *Hospital and Community Psychiatry, 30*(6), 387–393.

Bachrach, L. L. (1989). Case Management: Toward a Shared Definition. *Hospital and Community Psychiatry, 40*(9), 883–884.

Bartoli, A., & Gozlan, G. (2014). Vers de nouvelles formes hybrides de coordination en santé mentale: entre conformité et innovation. *Management & Avenir, 68*(2), 112–133.

Bass, D. M., Clark, P. A., Looman, W. J., McCarthy, C. A., & Eckert, S. (2003). The Cleveland Alzheimer's Managed Care Demonstration: Outcomes After 12 Months of Implementation. *The Gerontologist, 43*(1), 73–85.

Callahan, C. M., Boustani, M. A., Unverzagt, F. W., Austrom, M. C., Damush, T. M., Perkins, A. J., Fultz, B. A., Hui, S. L., Counsell, S. R., & Hendrie, H. C. (2006). Effectiveness of Collaborative Care for Older Adults with Alzheimer Disease in Primary Care: A Randomized Controlled Trial. *JAMA, 295*(18), 2148–2157.

Cameron, A., Lart, R., Bostock, L., & Coomber, C. (2014). Factors That Promote and Hinder Joint and Integrated Working Between Health and Social Care Services: A Review of Research Literature. *Health & Social Care in the Community, 22*(3), 225–233.

Challis, D., Darton, R., Hughes, J., Stewart, K., & Weiner, K. (2001). Intensive Care-Management at Home: An Alternative to Institutional Care? *Age and Ageing, 30*(5), 409–413.

Contandriopoulos, A. P., Denis, J.-L., Touati, N., & Rodriguez, R. (2001). Intégration des soins: dimensions et mise en oeuvre. *Ruptures, revue transdisciplinaire en santé, 8*(2), 38–52.

Couturier, Y., Belzile, L., & Gagnon, D. (2011). Principes méthodologiques de l'implantation du modèle PRISMA portant sur l'intégration des services pour les personnes âgées en perte d'autonomie. *Management & Avenir, 47*(7), 133–146.

Couty, E. (2009). *Missions et organisation de la Santé mentale et de la psychiatrie*. Paris: Ministère des Solidarités et de la Santé.

Curry, N., & Ham, C. (2010). *Clinical and Service Integration. The Route to Improved Outcomes*. London: The King's Fund.

De Cangas, J. P. C. (1994). Le "Case management" affirmatif: une évaluation complète d'un programme du genre en milieu hospitalier. *Santé Mentale au Québec, 19*(1), 75–91.

Demers, L., Saint-Pierre, M., Tourigny, A., Bonin, L., Bergeron, P., Rancourt, P., Dieleman, L., Trahan, H., Caris, P., Barrette, H., Hébert, A., & Lavoie, J. (2005). *Le rôle des acteurs locaux, régionaux et ministériels dans l'intégration des services aux aînés en perte d'autonomie*. Québec: École nationale d'administration publique, Université du Québec.

Dubuc, N., Dubois, M. F., Raîche, M., Gueye, N. R., & Hébert, R. (2011). Meeting the Home-Care Needs of Disabled Older Persons Living in the Community: Does Integrated Services Delivery Make a Difference? *BMC Geriatrics, 11*(67), 2–13.

Duvoux, N. (2009). Les assistés peuvent-ils être autonomes ? Sociologie compréhensive des politiques d'insertion. *Lien social et politiques, 61*, 97–107.

Eklund, K., & Wilhelmson, K. (2009). Outcomes of Coordinated and Integrated Interventions Targeting Frail Elderly People: A Systematic Review of Randomised Controlled Trials. *Health & Social Care in the Community, 17*(5), 447–458.

Field, S. (2011). *NHS Future Forum: Summary Report on Proposed Changes to the NHS*. London: Department of Health & Social Care.

Frankel, J., & Gelman, S. R. (2011). *Case Management: An Introduction to Concepts and Skills* (3rd ed.). New York: Oxford University Press.

Glaser, B. G., & Strauss, A. L. (1967). *The Discovery of Grounded Theory: Strategies for Qualitative Research*. London: Weidenfeld and Nicolson.

Goering, P. N., Wasylenki, D. A., Farkas, M., Lancee, W. J., & Ballantyne, R. (1988). What Difference Does Case Management Make? *Hospital and Community Psychiatry, 39*(3), 272–276.

Gozlan, G. (2016). Le case management en santé mentale. In S. Trosa & A. Bartoli (Eds.), *Les paradoxes du management par le sens* (pp. 27–35). Rennes: Presses de l'EHESP.

Ham, C., Imison, C., Goodwin, N., Dixon, A., & South, P. (2011). *Where Next for the NHS Reforms? The Case for Integrated Care*. London: The King's Fund.

Harris, M., & Bergman, H. C. (1985). Networking with Young Adult Chronic Patients. *Psychosocial Rehabilitation Journal, 8*(3), 28–35.

Hofmarcher, M. M., Oxley, H., & Rusticelli, E. (2007). *Improved Health System Performance Through Better Care Coordination*. Paris: OECD.

Intagliata, J. (1982). Improving the Quality of Community Care for the Chronically Mentally Disabled: The Role of Case Management. *Schizophrenia Bulletin, 8*(4), 655–674.

Jaeger, M. (2010). Introduction. *Vie sociale, 1*(1), 9–12.
Kodner, D. L. (2009). All Together Now: A Conceptual Exploration of Integrated Care. *Healthcare Quarterly, 13*(sp), 6–15.
Kodner, D. L., & Kyriacou, C. K. (2000). Fully Integrated Care for Frail Elderly: Two American Models. *International Journal of Integrated Care, 1,* 1–19.
Lamb, H. R. (1980). Therapist-Case Manager: More Than Brokers of Services. *Hospital and Community Psychiatry, 31*(11), 762–764.
Le Bossé, Y. (2003). De l'"habilitation" au "pouvoir d'agir": vers une appréhension plus circonscrite de la notion d'*empowerment*. *Nouvelles pratiques sociales, 16*(2), 30–51.
Leavitt, S. S. (1983). Case Management: A Remedy for Problems of Community Care. In C. J. Sanborn (Ed.), *Case Management in Mental Health Services* (pp. 17–41). Binghamton: Haworth Press.
Leutz, W. N. (1999). Five Laws for Integrating Medical and Social Services: Lessons from the United States and the United Kingdom. *The Milbank Quarterly, 77*(1), 77–110.
Martínez-González, N. A., Berchtold, P., Busato, A., & Egger, M. (2012). *Effectiveness of Integrated Care Programmes in Adults with Chronic Conditions: A Systematic Review*. Bern: Institute for Social and Preventive Medicine, University of Bern.
McGorry, P. D., Yung, A. R., & Phillips, L. (2001). Ethics and Early Intervention in Psychosis: Keeping Up the Pace and Staying in Step. *Schizophrenia Research, 51*(1), 17–29.
Miramon, J.-M. (2010). La coordination ressources humaines organisation management: Un défi majeur pour la cohérence d'un fonctionnement institutionnel. *Vie sociale, 1*(1), 59–74.
Oliver, D., Foot, C., & Humphries, R. (2014). *Making Our Health and Care Systems Fit for an Ageing Population*. London: The King's Fund.
Organisation mondiale de la Santé. (2000). *Rapport sur la santé dans le monde, 2000 – Pour un système de santé plus performant*. Geneva: OMS.
Peirce, C. S. (1931–1935). *Collected Papers*. Cambridge: Harvard University Press.
Petitqueux-Glaser, C., Acef, S., & Mottaghi, M. (2010). Case Management: Quelles compétences professionnelles pour un accompagnement global et un suivi coordonné en santé mentale. *Vie sociale, 1*(1), 109–128.
Rapp, C. A., & Goscha, R. J. (2006). *The Strengths Model: Case Management with People with Psychiatric Disabilities* (2nd ed.). Oxford: Oxford University Press.
Reid, R., Haggerty, J., & McKendry, R. (2002). *Defusing the Confusion: Concepts and Measures of Continuity of Healthcare*. Ottawa: Canadian Health Services Research Foundation.

Schwartz, S. R., Goldman, H. H., & Churgin, S. (1982). Case Management for the Chronic Mentally Ill: Models and Dimensions. *Hospital and Community Psychiatry, 33*(12), 1006–1009.

Sebai, J. (2016). Une analyse théorique de la coordination dans le domaine des soins: application aux systèmes de soins coordonnés. *Santé Publique, 28*(2), 223–234.

Shaw, S., Rosen, R., & Rumbold, B. (2011). *What Is Integrated Care?* London: Nuffield Trust.

Shifren-Levine, L., & Fleming, M. (1985). *Human Resource Development: Issues in Case Management*. Rockville: Center for State Human Resource Development, Community Support and Rehabilitation Branch, National Institute of Mental Health.

Somme, D. (2008). *Filières de soins, intégration, gestion de cas et maintien de l'autonomie des personnes âgées* [thèse]. Reims: Université de Reims-Champagne Ardenne.

Somme, D., Trouvé, H., Dramé, M., Gagnon, D., Couturier, Y., & Saint-Jean, O. (2012). Analysis of Case Management Programs for Patients with Dementia: A Systematic Review. *Alzheimer's & Dementia, 8*(5), 426–436.

Somme, D., Trouvé, H., Passadori, Y., Corvez, A., Jeandel, C., Bloch, M.-A., Ruault, G., Dupont, O., & De Stampa, M. (2013). Prise de position de la société française de gériatrie et gérontologie sur le concept d'intégration. *Gérontologie et société, 36*(145), 201–226.

Soulet, M. H. (2005). Vers une solidarité de responsabilisation. In J. Ion (Ed.), *Le travail social en débat(s)* (pp. 86–103). Paris: La Découverte.

Test, M. A., & Stein, L. I. (1978). The Clinical Rationale for Community Treatment: A Review of Literature. In L. I. Stein & M. A. Test (Eds.), *Alternatives to Mental Health Hospital Treatment*. New York: Plenum Press.

Thiel, V., Sonola, L., Goodwin, N., & Kodner, D. L. (2013). *Developing Community Resource Teams in Pembrokeshire, Wales: Integration of Health and Social Care in Progress*. London: The King's Fund.

Vickrey, B. G., Mittman, B. S., Connor, K. I., Pearson, M. L., Della Penna, R. D., Ganiats, T. G., Demonte, R. W., Jr., Chodosh, J., Cui, X., Vassar, S., Duan, N., & Lee, M. (2006). The Effect of a Disease Management Intervention on Quality and Outcomes of Dementia Care: A Randomized, Controlled Trial. *Annals of Internal Medicine, 145*(10), 713–726.

Wallace, C. J., Nelson, C. J., Liberman, R. D., Aitchison, R. A., Lukoff, D., Elder, J. P., & Ferris, C. (1980). A Review and Critique of Social Skills Training with Schizophrenic Patients. *Schizophrenia Bulletin, 6*(1), 42–63.

Weinberger, M., Gold, D. T., Divine, G. W., Cowper, P. A., Hodgson, L. G., Schreiner, P. J., & George, L. K. (1993). Social Service Interventions for Caregivers of Patients with Dementia: Impact on Health Care Utilization and Expenditures. *Journal of the American Geriatrics Society, 41*(2), 153–156.

World Health Organization (WHO). (2008). *Integrated Health Services: What and Why?* Geneva: WHO.
World Health Organization (WHO). (2010). *Programme d'action: combler les lacunes en santé mentale (mhGAP)*. Geneva: WHO.
Yin, R. K. (2009). *Case Study Research: Design and Methods* (4th ed.). Thousand Oaks: SAGE Publications.
Zittoun, T. (2006). *Insertions. A quinze ans, entre échecs et apprentissage. [Insertions. Being fifteen, from failure to apprenticeship]*. Berne: Peter Lang.

15

Postface and Conclusion: Current Challenges and Forward-Thinking Perspectives on Responsibility in Organizations

Mile Terziovski

Introduction

The traditional economic paradigm of the organization is often interpreted narrowly in the context of corporate social responsibility (CSR). The purpose of an organization was not to be externally focused for the benefit of society but rather to simply make a profit. According to de Jong and van der Meer (2017, p. 71), "Society nowadays expects organizations to be socially engaged. Almost every modern organization is in one way or another involved in corporate social responsibility (CSR) activities." Recent research suggests that CSR is widespread amongst global corporations, although there is no agreed upon definition amongst researchers. According to Bice (2017, p. 17), "Studies remain heavily focused on making a business case for CSR, despite its widespread acceptance into business practice." Bice goes on to examine CSR from an institutional perspective, arguing that institutionalism is well placed to address the core challenges of CSR. Similarly, Haski-Leventhal et al. (2017) develop an Employee Social Responsibility and Corporate Social Responsibility Congruence Model, which appears to be a unique model to address both companies and employees, hence adding to the single-level CSR typology. This book goes a step further by synthesizing a broader paradigm of CSR by looking through the lens of institutional, international, and professional perspectives.

M. Terziovski (✉)
Swinburne University of Technology, Hawthorn, VIC, Australia
e-mail: mterziovski@swin.edu.au

- Institutional perspective—Examining both commercial businesses and public or non-profit organizations, Part I provides discussions on ethics and human resources management as key parts of organizational responsibility, and Part II examines the role of communication and reputation related to social responsibility.
- International perspective—Analyses made in different countries, Part III provides representations and practices of responsibility in the European context.
- Professional perspective—Combining the outlooks of researchers and practitioners, Part IV provides new forms of responsibility to address societal challenges.

Ethical behavior is a critical imperative of leadership theory such as transformational leadership and authentic leadership (Bedi et al. 2016). An extension of these theories, responsible leadership assumes responsibility for organizational outcomes as well as for the processes and people with which they work, as well as the effects on society and the environment. In the following section, the chapters of this book are aligned with each of the perspectives and grouped in Parts I–IV. Key issues that Responsible Organizations are likely to face in the managerial, ethical, cultural, and socio-economic domains are identified from each chapter.

Various Perspectives of Responsibility

Institutional Perspective

The institutional perspective looks at both commercial businesses and public or non-profit organizations. Part I provides discussions on ethics and human resources management as key parts of organizational responsibility, and Part II examines the role of communication and reputation related to social responsibility. In Chap. 2, McCabe discusses several issues such as due process for non-unionized employees, procedural justice, employee voice systems, ethics, and employee rights in the employment relationship. The concept of due process is explained as "the rights of employees to have impartial third parties such as peer panels or arbitration to review the personnel decisions that may adversely affect them." The author argues that organizational decisions must be fair and align themselves with procedural justice and ethical due process. The author concluded that a Responsible Organization should have policies and practices in place to increase employee morale. Overall, this chapter argues that a "Responsible Organization" creates an environment that encourages employees to raise their grievances to management. The author concludes that "a just, fair, and legitimate open-door" culture is one in which executives are committed to their employees and make them feel comfortable, "without fear of retribution."

Duckworth in Chap. 3 discusses continuous improvement concepts based on the total quality management (TQM) philosophy, as applied to organizational responsibility, arguing that many organizations struggle with resources to apply to social and environmental responsibility. The author explains how continuous improvement for social responsibility (CISR) can be integrated into existing Lean Six Sigma or Operational Excellence improvement programs. However, the author emphasizes the need for Standard Operational Excellence methods to be aligned with social responsibility targets, such as "…sustainable profitability, people, and planet are the end goal…ensuring that all leaders speak the language of responsibility… [and] that CSR leaders are speaking the language of business objectives."

Ben Mlouka and Hefaiedh in Chap. 4 discuss the critical role of employee commitment and survival during crisis, using the 2011 Tunisian Revolution. The authors examine how CSR practices influenced employees' commitment to allow company survival during the crisis period. A qualitative method based on four case studies with a thematic content analysis was conducted. According to the authors, "The results show that employees play a dual role in the societal pressures faced by companies…It appears that the nature of CSR practices dedicated to employees influence their behavior in terms of organizational commitment." Globalization and radical change have created instability and widespread crisis in many countries. Organizations are challenged with the commitment and behaviour of their employees, during periods of instability and crisis, making their commitment a strategic issue for Responsible Organizations.

Part II explores the challenges and opportunities and how they relate to communication and reputation related to CSR.

Glass and Cahn in Chap. 5 classify ethics codes using natural language processing. The authors argue that business ethics scholars have varied opinions of corporate ethics codes, stating, "Many advocate them as a way to contribute to an organizational environment in which ethics will be a regular consideration in the decision-making process." The authors develop a model which indicates that ethics codes may be differentiated from each other based on their terminology using NLP models as a tool to identify which companies' ethics codes are different. The authors conclude that ethics codes in companies classified as "Ethical" were found to be different from large corporations, stating that "…the codes of these 'Ethical' companies can serve as models on which to base writing of an ethics code." The authors recommend future research by using ethics codes and financial data to test the relationship between CSR and corporate performance.

Goxe and Viegas Pires in Chap. 6 critically analyze diversity of the multinational company L'Oréal, demonstrating that L'Oréal's definition of diversity is based on three sociodemographic characteristics: gender, disability, and origins.

The authors present results which show that different discursive frameworks coexist in multinational organizations. For example, the three types of discourse are interlocked in corporate communication, which reinforces the customer orientation of the organization. The authors argue, "This orientation, as well as other aspects of rationalistic discourse, also contribute to create a sense of legitimacy for shareholders and other stakeholders that might be preoccupied with the economic performance of the firm." The societal dimension of diversity discourse positions the firm within broad societal challenges and contributes to reputation building in the eyes of civic stakeholders.

Bargenda in Chap. 7 discusses the role of aesthetic CSR communication from a global perspective on organizational art collections. This chapter critically discusses aesthetic artifacts, such as artwork and art collections, and argues that they enhance CSR by satisfying social and environmental standards, stating "…the pluralistic uses of aesthetics within the broader scope of corporate sustainability (CS) delineate the major relevance of arts-based initiatives for global finance organizations." The author concludes that "…aesthetic artifacts achieve synergies between context-specific factors and global issues of sustainability." However, arts-based CSR initiatives may not be solely driven by organizational outcomes, according to the author, who proposes further research to explore varying motivational factors, for example, executive motivations.

Petit in Chap. 8 argues that law, and specifically "soft law," can consolidate the approach of CSR in its questioning of companies' reputations. The author examines the multinational corporations' awareness of their social responsibility law vs. reputation, stating, "Designed primarily as a moral responsibility, corporate social responsibility (CSR) is a privileged basis from which to question the reputation of multinational companies, and thereby to act on their ability to create economic opportunities…Law can reappear in the foreground of the levers that are available to our societies in order to ensure that multinational companies satisfy social and public interests." Petit argues that CSR should not be confined to definitions and explanations; it must also include "co-construction of the standards of compliance." The author concludes that compliance can lead to internalizing the organizational control system and helps companies to structure themselves to meet the standards of compliance. Overall, meeting CSR goals can lead to an integrated culture of conformance and performance.

International Perspective

The international perspective provides practices of responsibility internationally.

In Chap. 9, Bouterfas, Raytcheva, and Rouet provide a discussion on CSR in Europe. The developments in this chapter show that theoretical, social, and political approaches can always be different, from one country to another, particularly across the Atlantic. The authors state, "Some multinational firms are applying a new managerial paradigm integrating CSR. It is no longer (or not only) a marketing or communication argument." This chapter concludes that "corporate philanthropy, partnerships, and humanitarian activities are particularly characteristic of a new proactive orientation."

In Chap. 10, Marasova, Vallušová, Vasileva, and Philip de Saint Julien present results of a comparative study of CSR practices of Veolia in France, Slovakia, and Bulgaria. Based on an examination of documents of the Veolia Group on the application of CSR in three countries, interviews with managers, questionnaire surveys, and the media reveal that "the level of CSR approach, largely determined by the European standards, is approximately the same in these countries." However, the authors found that the approaches to CSR differ only in methods used to meet the standards. For example, unlike France, management of Veolia in Slovakia and Bulgaria needs to focus more intensively on communication about the importance of the central distribution of heating and water and protecting the environment. The authors conclude that "communication to employees, town authorities, and municipalities, as well as to the wider society, still has some aspects in which improvement is necessary."

In Chap. 11, Faucheux, Gans Combe, Kuszla, and O'Connor, based on a study in Europe, examine social costs of non-responsible research. This chapter addresses (1) research misconduct of persons and organizations directly engaged in the practice of scientific research and (2) responsible research, or the activities of discovery and innovation respectful of wider societal values.

Based on results from the European DEFORM Project, the authors clarify the distinction between and the inter-relations of the two concepts in (1) and (2). The authors look at the phenomenon of research fraud to highlight misconduct relative to "internal" standards of good science. The authors argue,

"New conventions of reciprocal accountability are required…But this cannot be obtained by inward-looking processes; rather there must be transparency in the engagement of accountability from each stakeholder toward the others." The authors conclude that the quality of the relationships is of critical importance.

Professional Perspective

The professional perspective in Part IV provides new forms of responsibility to address societal challenges by combining the outlooks of researchers and practitioners.

In Chap. 12, Assens and Bouchez examine corporate governance in social networks and communities in three settings: self-governed networks, lead organization-governed networks, and network administrative organizations. The authors argue that governance based on "altruism in partnerships, equal decision-making power and equity in the sharing of relational benefits is distorted." According to the framework based on the three forms of governance, the authors concluded that "…the network and community are not always untarnished examples of good governance that are unwaveringly respectful of democratic principles." According to the authors, the rules of exchange are established through conventions and based on a balance of bargaining power, largely dependent on the member's position within the network. On the other hand, member's location is less important, which "reflects his influence over others as an intermediate or a pilot." Indeed, "the true limits of a network or a community are often intangible; they are based on a sense of belonging to a club, with specific rules of co-optation and control."

In Chap. 13, Tarabasz examines CSR in times of internet insecurity. The author discusses the growth of the internet users and social narcissism. Furthermore, the author argues that cyber threats are exacerbated by the enormous growth of social networking and lack of knowledge related to awaiting cyber threats, which are also favored by personable identifiable data (PID) being voluntarily revealed by digital users themselves. Increasing attacks on social media accounts, stolen online identities, ransomware strikes, and excessive trust in open WiFi all lead to tremendous data breaches. The author provides evidence from market reports that the "…greatest threats to companies' online security are not third-party hackers but departing employees." The author concludes that a proactive approach is needed to educate digital customers in terms of cyber threats.

In Chap. 14, Bartoli, Perrin, and Sebai present results from a research project that focuses on the management and coordination of patient care processes in the field of mental health. The authors state that "…mental health pathologies are among the most complex diseases, especially because they are multi-symptomatic and often become chronic." This chapter examines how to integrate and coordinate care and social services as a responsible way of handling psychiatric disability, particularly in the comprehensive and societal consideration of the patient's needs, which goes beyond the creation of networks of experts and independent key players. The authors conclude that coordination and integration need to be implemented in the context of case management and empowerment.

Key Issues That Responsible Organizations Are Likely to Face in the Future

The key ideas studied in the chapters of this book and perspectives for the future regarding the issues that Responsible Organizations are likely to face in managerial, ethical, and socio-economic domains are synthesized below within the institutional, international, and professional perspectives framework.

Institutional Perspective

The institutional perspective identified ethics and human resources management (HRM) as key parts of organizational responsibility. The role of communication and building reputation is related to social responsibility. Bice (2017, p. 22) defines an institution as "frameworks of rules; proscriptive actions; patterns in repetitive interactions; customs; governance structures; special arrangements which minimize transaction costs; sets of norms, rules or principles; or directly or indirectly agreed roles combined with conventions." The definition recognizes the social phenomena of institutions that emerge as social patterns shaped by cultural norms, as synthesized from Chaps. 1, 2, 3, 4, 5, 6, and 7.

- Leadership and human resources management practices would encourage employees to raise their grievances to management. This would require policies, procedures, and management practices to increase employee morale through role clarity and job satisfaction. This would likewise require a more flexible organization that would be less bureaucratic and more efficient to deal with complaint in a timely manner and demonstrate duty of care. This finding is consistent with a meta-analytic review of ethical leadership outcomes and moderators conducted by Bedi et al. (2016), who found that "ethical leadership is related positively to numerous follower outcomes such as perceptions of leader interactional fairness and follower ethical behavior."

- Continuous improvement concepts, principles, tools, methods, and techniques are adapted by Responsible Organizations, which lead to social and environmental responsibility performance improvement such as commitments to environmental management standards and reductions of waste and defects. This is supported by Campbell et al. (2016, p. 274) who state that "…the establishment of internal control can guide an organization to achieve several specific objectives including effectiveness and efficiency of operations, reliability of financial reporting, and compliance with applicable laws and regulations."
- Better internal controls also allow the Responsible Organization to communicate relevant and accurate information to the external stakeholders, which enhances their confidence and trust that the organization is implementing its vision and mission underpinned by ethical principles and practices.
- Globalization, instability, and widespread crisis: Responsible Organizations would be challenged with the behavior of their employees during a crisis, toward their work and their company. Senior management would need to have a corporate crisis plan in place making employee commitment a strategic issue. For example, according to Hernandez Bark et al. (2016, p. 475), "Motivation is a primary driver of human behaviour; it forms the direction, the intensity, and persistence of human's actions."
- Sustainable profitability, people, and planet are the end goal: ensuring that all leaders speak the language of responsibility and not just economic goals is imperative. On the other hand, Responsible Organizations need to ensure that CSR leaders understand the business objectives. A study by Cai et al. (2016, p. 587) concludes the following: "Our study demonstrates that environmental initiatives are generally associated with lower levels of firm risk for a company, a stance that scholars of finance, management, and environmental studies would see as a positive influence."

- Ethics codes: Anecdotal evidence shows there is a positive relationship between "ethical" organizations and financial performance. Companies classified as "ethical" were found to be different from large corporations in how they articulate their ethics codes and can serve as role models for how to write ethics codes. The authors recommend future research by using ethics codes and financial data to test the relationship between CSR and corporate performance. There is also the opposite view as expressed by Walker et al. (2017, p. 53), stating that "although many organizations around the world have engaged in corporate social responsibility (CSR) programing[sic], there is little evidence of social impact.
- Walker et al. (2017) found that when consumers believed an organization deployed CSR strategically, the initiative negatively influenced organizational attitudes." The authors argue that to reverse such negative attitudes, it is imperative for organizations to have their programs evaluated through third-party program evaluations.
- Discourse on diversity of a multinational company like L'Oréal reinforces the importance of the creation of a customer-oriented culture. This orientation can also contribute to the creation of a sense of legitimacy for stakeholders that have "tunnel vision" when focusing on the economic performance of the firm. The Responsible Organization would prioritize the societal dimension of diversity discourse. This would raise organizational reputation and be seen as responsible in the eyes of civic stakeholders. Audi et al. (2016, p. 551) conclude that "…trust is both ethically important and essential for business but difficult to measure. Contrary to what one might think, firms with a strong trusting culture frequently use audit and control-type words and that trust is positively linked with subsequent share-price volatility."
- Aesthetic CSR: Responsible Organizations through aesthetic artifacts, such as artwork and art collections, would enhance their corporate social responsibility (CSR) image by satisfying social and environmental standards. However, the motivation behind arts-based CSR initiatives may not be driven by organizational outcomes alone.

International Perspective

This perspective analyzed the opportunities and challenges for "Responsible Organizations" in different countries:

- Responsible multinational firms have embarked on a new managerial paradigm within the concept of Responsible Organizations, integrating dimensions of CSR with corporate philanthropy, partnerships, and humanitarian activities that are characteristic of a new non-marketing orientation. CSR is also integrated with internal management processes, such as the quality of human resource policies and leadership skills that are seen as key assets for global performance. The literature supports the synergy between the interests of diverse stakeholders—employees, shareholders, government, customers, partners, sponsors, communities, and society, all underpinned by the Employee Social Responsibility and Corporate Social Responsibility Congruence Model discussed earlier (Haski-Leventhal et al. 2017).
- Compliance law, and specifically "soft law," is an important lever that is available to societies to ensure that multinational companies satisfy social and public interests. "Soft law" helps companies internalize their organizational control system to meet the standards of compliance and to create an integrated culture of conformance and performance. According to Thorne et al. (2017, p. 85), "A firm's national institutional context, which includes legal, regulatory, and professional structures, influences the firm's responsiveness to CSR."
- Approaches to CSR differ among countries only in methods used to meet the standards. For example, unlike France, management of Veolia in Slovakia and Bulgaria needs to focus more on the communication of CSR to employees, town authorities and municipalities, and to society. According to Thorne et al. (2017, p. 85), "…cross-national differences in CSR arising from cross-national variations in stakeholder pressure may lie in the nature of respective countries' institutional framework."
- New conventions of reciprocal accountability: Responsible Organizations have outward-looking processes and are transparent in the engagement and communication of accountability toward stakeholders. Responsible Organizations develop competence and responsibility through the development of relationships and collaboration through informal networks.

Professional Perspective

This perspective provides a new form of responsibility to address societal challenges.

- Networking and community sense of belonging to a club: Responsible Organizations can be characterized with five interacting features—net-

worked, flat, flexible, diverse, and global. Governance issues within these interacting features are dependent on the "rules of exchange" that are established through conventions and based on a balance of bargaining power, for which a member's position within the network is more important than their location.
- CSR in times of internet insecurity: The biggest threat for Responsible Organizations in the twenty-first century is online security. A CSR culture would focus on educating digital customers about cyber threats. The major problem within and outside the organization is the oversharing of information on social media, with individuals willingly disclosing sensitive data in exchange for free applications. Notwithstanding the fact that big data and digital tools are beneficial to individuals and organizations, Responsible Organizations will be confronted with the challenge of questioning the meaning of privacy in our society.
- Integration and coordination of care and social services: Responsible Organization would be "game changers striving to defy outmoded business models and design tomorrow's enterprises" (Osterwalder and Pigneur 2010). For example, mental health pathologies are among the most complex diseases; they are multi-symptomatic and often become chronic. A Responsible Organization would be able to demonstrate an innovative way of handling psychiatric disability. Furthermore, coordination and integration would need to be implemented along with case management and empowerment.

Conclusion

Several dimensions have emerged as key issues that Responsible Organizations are likely to face in the future, such as internal management processes, continuous improvements, human resource policies, and leadership skills. Also, the rapid development of digital technology and the emergence of big data have enabled the interests of employees, shareholders, governments, customers, partners, communities, and society to be interconnected with the aim of achieving global corporate performance.

However, these developments have raised new questions regarding ethics and responsibility. Whilst positive benefits are obtained from big data and digital tools, Responsible Organizations will have to come to terms with the meaning of privacy in our society and the risk of a single-minded focus on profit maximization instead of focusing on stakeholders' interests, as evidenced by the global financial crisis. Heimans and Timms (2018) in their book *New Power* have summed up the challenge for Responsible Organizations: "The future will be won by those who can spread their ideas better, faster, and more durably."

References

Audi, R., Loughran, T., & McDonald, B. (2016). Trust, But Verify: MD&A Language and the Role of Trust in Corporate Culture. *Journal of Business Ethics, 139*(3, December (II)), 551–561.

Bedi, A., Alpaslan, C. M., & Green, S. (2016). A Meta-analytic Review of Ethical Leadership Outcomes and Moderators. *Journal of Business Ethics, 139*(3), 517–536.

Bice, S. (2017). Corporate Social Responsibility as Institution: A Social Mechanisms Framework. *Journal of Business Ethics, 143*(1, July (II)), 17–34.

Cai, L., Cui, J., & Jo, H. (2016). Corporate Environmental Responsibility and Firm Risk. *Journal of Business Ethics, 139*(3, December (II)), 563–594.

Campbell, S., Li, Y., Yu, J., & Zhang, Z. (2016). The Impact of Occupational Community on the Quality of Internal Control. *Journal of Business Ethics, 139*(3, December (II)), 271–285.

de Jong, M. D. T., & van der Meer, M. (2017). How Does It Fit? Exploring the Congruence Between Organisations and Their Corporate Social Responsibility (CSR) Activities. *Journal of Business Ethics, 143*(1, June (II)), 71–83.

Haski-Leventhal, D., Roza, L., & Meijs, L. C. P. M. (2017). Congruence in Corporate Social Responsibility: Connecting the Identity and Behavior of Employers and Employees. *Journal of Business Ethics, 143*(1, June (II)), 35–51.

Heimans, J., & Timms, H. (2018). *New Power: How Power Works in Our Hyperconnected World- and How to Make It Work for You* (pp. 1–325). Sydney: Macmillan Australia.

Hernandez Bark, A. S., Escartin, J., & Scuh, S. C. (2016). *Journal of Business Ethics, 139*(3, December (II)), 473–483.

Osterwalder, A., & Pigneur, Y. (2010). *Business Model Generation*. Hoboken: Wiley.

Thorne, L., Mahoney, L. S., Gregory, K., & Convery, S. (2017). A Comparison of Canadian and US CSR Strategic Alliances, CSR Reporting, and CSR Performance: Insight into Implicit-Explicit CSR. *Journal of Business Ethics, 143*(1, June (II)), 85–98.

Walker, M., Hills, S., & Heere, B. (2017). Evaluating a Socially Responsible Employment Program: Beneficiary Impacts and Stakeholder Perceptions. *Journal of Business Ethics, 143*(1, June (II)), 53–70.

Index[1]

A

Accountability, 6, 7, 10, 13, 48, 57, 66, 68, 144, 217, 233, 234, 247, 280, 284
Accountable, 1, 4, 51, 215n9
Aesthetic, 117–130, 278, 283
Africa, 183, 239
Amazon, vii, 9
America, *see* United States (US)
Apple, vii, 9
Arbitration, 21, 25–26, 30, 36
Art, 85, 117–130, 165, 181
Art collections, 117–130, 278, 283
Awareness, 8, 22, 36, 61, 66, 162, 164, 175, 178, 185, 188, 195, 238–240, 245, 278

B

Behavior, vii, viii, 2, 9, 41, 45, 48, 49, 51, 52, 55, 58, 60, 61, 63, 65, 66, 68, 69, 79–81, 83, 84, 91, 94, 101, 102, 105, 120, 134–136, 138, 140, 142, 142n4, 145, 145n6, 153, 158, 168, 178, 185, 194, 208, 211, 217, 227, 229, 241, 245, 246, 276, 277, 282
Big data, vii, 6–10, 285
Bulgaria, 175, 176, 189–195, 279
Business, v–ix, 1, 3–11, 13, 22, 23, 26, 30, 37, 40, 43–47, 49, 58, 66, 68, 79, 90n1, 99, 108–110, 113, 117, 119, 120, 122, 125–127, 129, 134, 138, 142, 143, 145, 154, 156–159, 163, 165, 167, 170, 171, 181, 183–189, 193–195, 202, 208, 210, 215, 217, 223, 225, 238, 244, 247, 275–277, 282, 283, 285
Business ethics, vi, 6, 7, 117, 141, 158, 247, 277

C

Care, 67, 163, 167, 185, 186, 194, 208, 281, 282
Care and social services, 251–269, 281, 285

---

[1] Note: Page numbers followed by 'n' refer to notes.

© The Author(s) 2019
A. Bartoli et al. (eds.), *Responsible Organizations in the Global Context*,
https://doi.org/10.1007/978-3-030-11458-9

Index

Case management, 251–253, 256–261, 263–264, 267, 268, 281, 285
Case study, 22, 39, 59, 60, 63, 211, 216, 238, 261, 266, 277
Challenges, vii, viii, 2, 4, 9, 11–13, 30, 40, 43–44, 55, 110, 111, 113, 118, 129, 135–137, 141, 156, 160, 163, 191, 200, 210, 217, 224, 225, 243, 254, 257, 262, 266–267, 275–286
Change, v, 9, 12, 25, 26, 30, 33, 41, 43–45, 47–49, 51, 58, 80, 90n2, 101, 118, 122, 128, 129, 138, 156–158, 161, 163, 165, 166, 176, 178, 180, 182, 193, 226, 277
China, 183
Citizenship, vi, 10, 55, 64, 65, 155, 158
Classification, 80, 88, 90, 93–94, 158, 224
Codes of conduct, 3, 79, 83, 135, 137, 138, 157, 178
Commitment, 51–72, 120, 121, 123, 124, 137n1, 138–140, 159, 161, 162, 164–167, 169, 176, 179–181, 183, 185, 261, 277, 282
Communication, 11, 12, 39, 44, 55, 57, 63, 65, 66, 68, 91n4, 98, 101, 103, 105–108, 111–113, 117–130, 142, 142n4, 143, 157, 159, 161, 167–171, 179, 181, 185, 191, 192, 195, 212, 225, 238, 243, 245, 255, 259, 262–264, 276–279, 281, 284
Community, 6, 11, 13, 34, 56, 57, 61, 62, 64, 66, 85, 90n2, 101, 105, 110, 119–121, 125, 128, 142n4, 154, 157, 161–166, 169, 178, 179, 181, 182, 186, 189, 193–195, 201, 202, 215, 223–234, 257, 258, 280, 284, 285
Company, vii, 1, 21, 42, 51, 80, 98, 119, 133, 153, 175, 195, 204, 224, 238, 275

Competition, 4, 61, 160, 165
Compliance, vii, 7, 80–82, 85, 142, 144–146, 144–145n6, 157, 162, 163, 170, 183, 195, 209, 210, 234, 278, 279, 282, 284
Conduct, 24, 30, 53, 54, 79, 81, 90n4, 136, 139, 178, 179, 191
Continual improvement (CI), 39–49, 57, 245, 277, 282, 285
Cooperation, 184, 187, 189, 195, 251, 256, 262, 263
Coordination, 2, 24, 27, 140, 251–269, 281, 285
Corporate, vi–viii, 2–4, 6, 10, 11, 13, 27, 29, 34, 35, 55–57, 59, 79–83, 87, 88, 90n3, 91, 93, 98, 99, 101, 103–106, 108, 111–113, 120, 121, 124, 126–129, 134, 158–160, 163, 164, 166, 171, 175, 177, 179, 181, 184, 185, 190, 193, 195, 214, 238, 240, 244, 245, 247, 277–280, 282–285
Corporate social responsibility (CSR), v, vi, viii, 2–6, 12, 13, 39, 40, 43–45, 48, 49, 51–72, 80, 83, 84, 90n3, 94, 101, 102, 117–130, 133–137, 137n2, 140–146, 153–171, 175–195, 202, 210, 237–247, 275, 277–280, 282–285
Corporate sustainability (CS), 60, 118–121, 278
Corporation, v–ix, 1, 9, 33, 79, 94, 97, 102, 103, 113, 129, 133–146, 189, 226, 228, 275, 277, 278, 283
Country, viii, ix, 2, 4–6, 12, 13, 56, 59, 62, 63, 110, 125, 142n4, 154–157, 161, 163, 170, 171, 175–195, 205, 206, 207n6, 268, 276, 277, 279, 283, 284
Crisis, 51–72, 159n5, 213, 215, 264, 277, 282

Culture\cultural, viii, ix, 3, 5, 9, 13, 41, 42, 44, 45, 48, 55, 62, 64–67, 69, 90n4, 101, 102, 105, 106, 110, 112, 119, 120, 124–129, 139, 153, 156, 163, 164, 169–171, 175, 178, 181, 185, 195, 202, 215, 225, 255, 259, 262, 263, 268, 276, 279, 281, 283–285
Cyber, 237–242, 244–247, 280, 285
Cybersecurity, 238–240, 244–246

D

Danone, 3, 159–160, 166, 176
DEFORM project, 200, 206, 211, 215n9, 279
Democracy, v, 28, 34, 137n1, 140, 185, 224, 231–234, 280
Digital, 8, 10, 11, 13, 223, 226, 230, 231, 237, 238, 240, 242, 243, 246, 247, 280, 285
Digitalization, 8
Discourse, 49, 97–113, 129, 138, 153–171, 182, 190, 209, 210, 278, 283
Diversity, 5, 10, 11, 13, 91n4, 97–113, 121, 153, 162, 165, 176, 179, 181, 182, 278, 283
Due process, 21–37, 276

E

Employee, vii, 2, 6, 7, 10, 21–37, 39, 44, 45, 48, 51–69, 79–83, 85, 90n2, 90n4, 98, 105, 107, 109, 113, 119, 120, 122, 123, 125, 128, 129, 134, 154, 155, 158, 159, 161–164, 166, 168, 170, 176, 178, 179, 181, 183–188, 194, 195, 213, 214, 232, 238, 239, 267, 275–277, 279, 281, 282, 284, 285
  commitment, 51–72, 277, 282
  handbook, 29–32, 36, 37
  voice, 21–37, 276
Empowerment, 253, 259–261, 265–268, 281, 285
Engagement, 46, 49, 119, 120, 167, 169, 201, 209, 211, 212, 217, 225, 264, 280, 284
Environment, 2, 36, 37, 39, 51, 56, 58, 61, 64–67, 69, 71, 79, 108, 113, 117–119, 121–123, 125, 127–129, 133, 141, 154, 161–163, 165, 170, 175, 176, 178, 181–183, 186, 188, 189, 191, 192, 194, 195, 199, 212, 225, 238, 268, 276, 277
Equity, 4, 34, 57, 224, 233, 234, 280
Ethics, 6–8, 12, 21–37, 53, 55, 67, 68, 79–94, 109, 118, 123, 134, 135, 147, 153, 158, 160, 161, 166, 177, 210, 217, 276, 277, 281, 285
Ethics codes, 79–94, 277, 278, 283
Europe, v, 3, 13, 103, 106, 125, 153–171, 177, 187, 194, 207, 207n6, 208, 214, 230, 239, 252, 279
European context, 67, 276
European Union (EU), vii, 10, 141, 157, 189–191, 193, 208
Excellence, 39, 40, 157, 160

F

Facebook, vii, 9, 10, 226, 237, 242, 244
Finance sector, 129
Firm, v–viii, 8, 31, 32, 34–36, 80, 97, 98, 102, 110, 111, 113, 117, 119–121, 142n4, 171, 177, 187, 189, 195, 214, 226, 228, 246, 278, 279, 282–284

France, 3, 5, 12, 103n1, 123, 141, 163, 166, 167, 175–177, 180, 182–185, 187, 191, 195, 252, 254–256, 260, 262, 279, 284

Fraud, 7, 8, 178, 200, 203–209, 205n2, 206n4, 207n6, 212–214, 216, 279

G

Global, v, vii, ix, 1–13, 43, 103, 108, 113, 117–130, 141, 144, 145n6, 153, 155, 160, 166, 169, 170, 179, 182, 183, 190, 194, 237, 275, 278, 284, 285

Global context, v, ix, 1–13, 118

Globalization, v–ix, 1, 5, 8, 52, 189, 277, 282

Google, vii, 9, 10

Governance, vi–ix, 103, 179, 184, 199, 200, 202, 203, 210, 216, 217, 223–234, 251, 280, 281, 285

Government, 3, 5–8, 11, 12, 56, 144n6, 155, 156, 164, 168, 179, 190, 210, 217, 224, 239, 284, 285

H

Health, 37, 44, 51, 61, 71, 154, 159, 165, 176, 178, 179, 181, 182, 192, 199, 201, 202, 210, 211, 232, 252–258, 260–264, 266, 268, 269

History, v, viii, ix, 9, 67, 91, 122–124, 127, 176, 186, 224n1, 237

Holistic, viii, 3, 13

Human, vi, 2, 5, 7, 27, 36, 37, 71, 80, 84–86, 112, 113, 133, 155, 157, 159, 176, 179–182, 188, 199, 201, 208, 210, 238, 269, 282

Human resources (HR), 6, 26–28, 30, 39, 57, 67, 182, 183, 191, 208, 213, 268, 284, 285

I

Inclusion, 8, 10–11, 91, 105, 111, 112, 122, 136, 159, 164, 194, 207n6

Inclusive, v, vi, ix, 2

India, 183

Innovations, 11, 40, 41, 43, 44, 47, 49, 109, 122, 126, 129, 156, 159, 161–165, 167, 178, 180–181, 184, 186, 193, 200–202, 209–213, 217, 260, 279

Institution, 1, 10–12, 32–33, 52, 102, 110, 111, 123, 127, 137n2, 140, 157, 164, 179, 185, 190, 192, 193, 195, 201–203, 207, 208, 212, 215, 224, 243, 260, 266, 268, 281

Institutional perspective, 6, 275–279, 281–283

Integration, 5, 22, 54, 129, 157–159, 194, 233, 251–269, 281, 285

International, vii, 4–8, 12, 13, 35, 53, 61, 97, 110, 111, 119, 124, 125, 127, 137n2, 140, 145n6, 155, 164, 179, 184, 186–188, 190, 191, 205, 206, 268, 279–280, 283–284
competition, 4
perspective, 6, 275, 276, 279–281, 283–284

Internet, vii, 11, 182, 190, 237–247, 280, 285

Internet insecurity, 237–247

J

Justice, 21–37, 55, 56, 58, 65, 68, 79, 81, 137, 207, 209

L

Language, vi, viii, 40, 79–94, 98, 101, 102, 113, 138, 168, 217, 277, 282

Law, 3, 5, 7, 8, 66, 83, 103n1, 119, 133–146, 162, 178, 183, 186, 206, 214, 278, 282, 284
Leader, 2, 10, 39, 40, 43–46, 48, 49, 66–68, 112, 154, 158, 159, 162, 166, 230, 231, 233, 277, 282
Leadership, viii, 6, 45, 48, 49, 55, 57, 66–68, 160, 162, 169, 276, 281, 282, 284, 285
Legitimacy, vi–ix, 51, 52, 66, 98, 102, 111, 113, 125, 127, 129, 135–141, 145, 147, 155, 158, 170, 224, 227, 231–233, 266, 278, 283
L'Oreal, 97–113, 160–162, 166

M

Management, 1, 21–37, 40, 41, 55, 57, 90n4, 98–103, 118, 134, 154, 175, 176, 178, 195, 210, 223, 237, 251, 252, 263, 277
Manager, 1, 7, 26, 27, 29, 30, 32, 35, 36, 41, 53, 66–69, 82, 90n1, 97, 98, 118, 121, 123, 128, 138, 164, 170, 179, 181, 183, 184, 188, 189, 194, 195, 214, 217, 229, 231, 251, 258, 263–265, 279
Mental health, 252–254, 256–258, 260–261, 266, 268, 269, 281, 285
Michelin, 154, 162–163, 167
Microsoft, vii
Misconduct, 144, 200, 203–205, 205n2, 207, 211, 212, 279
Modern corporation, v, vi, viii
Motivation, 52, 62, 64–66, 119, 129, 158, 163, 192, 195, 267, 278, 282, 283
Multinational, 8, 9, 59, 67, 98, 103, 106, 112, 113, 133–146, 153, 155, 156, 164, 170, 171, 175, 177, 189, 190, 194, 195, 278, 279, 283, 284

N

Natural language processing (NLP), 79–94, 277
Network, 8, 124, 127, 180, 183, 189, 191, 223–234, 237, 238, 241, 242, 245, 246, 251, 258, 263, 280, 281, 284, 285
NGOs, *see* Non-Governmental Organizations
Non-Governmental Organizations (NGOs), vii, 110, 155, 156, 164, 180, 184, 192, 231
Non-profit, 2, 6, 12, 183, 276
Non-responsible research, 199–217, 279
Nonunion, 21, 23–36

O

Organization, viii, 1–13, 21–37, 39–49, 52, 80, 97, 117–130, 134, 154, 155, 177, 186–187, 195, 211, 224, 229–232, 239, 251, 260, 275
Organizational responsibility, 1, 2, 5, 12, 13, 39–49, 276, 277, 281
Organizational structure, 44–45
Origins, viii, 3–5, 53, 59, 60, 64, 66, 105, 106, 112, 124, 127, 155, 278

P

Participation, 10, 32, 49, 56, 81, 102, 155, 167, 213, 259, 262, 268
Participative management, 31, 36
Partnership, 90n3, 110, 111, 127, 164, 165, 171, 177, 179–180, 183, 193, 210, 255, 279, 280, 284
Patient, 41, 251–269, 259n3, 281
People, 4, 8–11, 37, 40, 45, 48, 61–63, 67, 84, 98, 99, 106–108, 110, 112, 122, 127, 139, 144, 161–163, 166, 168, 177, 182–184, 186, 187, 189, 193, 202, 204, 206, 212, 215n9, 237, 240, 243–245, 252, 254, 256, 258, 266, 276, 277, 282

Performance, vi, 4–6, 35, 39–49, 51, 52, 56, 67, 68, 83, 84, 90n2, 94, 97, 100, 109, 113, 120, 123, 124, 141, 155, 158, 159n3, 160, 162–164, 166, 176, 179, 180, 184, 188, 201–203, 210, 213, 215, 216, 230, 278, 279, 282–285

Philanthropy, 3, 90n2, 120, 126, 128, 129, 171, 193, 279, 284

Poland, 238, 243, 245

Policy, v, 2–6, 11–13, 22, 24, 26, 28–32, 36, 61, 63, 65, 80, 82, 98, 99, 102, 103, 105, 109–112, 118, 120, 121, 124, 128, 129, 157, 158, 160, 165, 166, 170, 171, 181–184, 189–194, 201, 205, 210, 211, 213, 242, 243n1, 276, 281, 284, 285

Politics, 9, 127, 255

Power, vi–ix, 82, 83, 98, 100–103, 119, 128, 133, 139, 139n3, 141, 155, 168, 183, 199, 210, 211, 223–227, 232, 234, 280, 285

Practices, 2, 22, 42, 52, 79, 98, 117, 142, 153–171, 175, 199, 252, 275

Prepsy, 253, 260–263, 260n4, 265–267

Procedural justice, 31–32, 81, 276

Procedure, 3, 21–36, 137, 137n1, 144, 145, 158, 178, 200, 202, 206, 208, 211, 215–217, 255, 257, 262–263, 267, 268, 281

Process, viii, ix, 2, 4, 6, 8, 10, 12, 21–37, 39–44, 46–48, 54, 79, 81, 85, 97, 98, 100, 105, 113, 119, 121, 126–128, 137n1, 137n2, 138–140, 146, 154–158, 162, 166, 171, 176, 178, 184, 201, 202, 207–211, 216, 217, 227, 231, 238, 239, 245, 256, 263, 265, 276, 277, 280, 281, 284, 285

Professional communities, 223–234

Professional perspective, 6, 275, 276, 280–281, 284–285

Profit, 7, 8, 11, 37, 40, 143, 155, 165, 245, 275, 285

Protection, 3, 10, 11, 33, 61, 65, 66, 134, 154, 155, 160, 178, 180, 182, 185, 188, 189, 192, 195, 202, 240, 244

Psychiatric disability, 251–269, 281, 285

Psychiatry, 251–269

Public, 2, 4, 6, 7, 11–12, 49, 52, 58, 62, 98, 102, 120, 128, 133, 134, 140–143, 145n6, 147, 164, 165, 169, 170, 175, 179, 182, 186, 189–192, 195, 202, 206n5, 208–210, 212, 214, 217, 224, 232, 242–246, 252, 266, 267, 276, 278, 284
   management, xviii, xix
   organizations, 4, 11–12
   sector, 66, 202, 210, 215, 232

Q

Quality, 6, 25, 40–44, 49, 55, 56, 68, 83, 84, 94, 126, 140, 159, 168, 169, 178, 180, 183, 186, 187, 192, 193, 199–203, 210, 215–217, 252, 254, 258, 280, 284

R

Regulation, vi, viii, ix, 5, 7, 24, 25, 28, 53, 56, 58, 82, 142n4, 144–146, 145n6, 155, 157, 162, 163, 184, 186, 254, 282

Relation, 34, 35, 63, 66–68, 91, 188, 216, 238, 265

Relationships, v–ix, 1, 4, 13, 21, 32–34, 36, 37, 47, 48, 52, 53, 62, 66–68, 82, 83, 101, 117, 123, 125, 126, 128, 136, 139n3, 141, 143, 147, 156, 161,

163–165, 169, 176, 180–183, 187–189, 193, 217, 223, 225, 226, 229, 242–244, 265, 267, 276, 278, 280, 283, 284
Reputation, vii, 12, 51, 90n3, 117, 120, 133–146, 155, 160, 165, 179, 183, 208, 214, 240, 247, 276–278, 281, 283
Research, v, 12, 21, 52, 80, 97, 118, 171, 177, 199–217, 223, 242, 251–253, 275
Responsibility, vi, 1–13, 26, 39–49, 51, 82, 102, 125, 133–146, 199, 224, 240, 251, 275
Responsible management, 5, 6, 247, 258, 260
Responsible organization, ix, 4–7, 10–13, 21–37, 121, 276, 277, 281–286
Rights, 2, 5, 7, 21, 23, 27, 31, 33, 40, 56, 58, 64, 79, 80, 90n2, 113, 133, 142, 157, 176, 179, 181, 182, 189, 209, 211, 231, 232, 276

S

Security, 9, 84, 128, 237–247, 280, 285
Shareholder, 3, 6, 8, 9, 113, 125, 158, 164, 168, 170, 178, 179, 214, 217, 245, 278, 284, 285
Six Sigma, 39–43, 46, 49, 277
Slovakia, 175, 176, 185–190, 195, 279
Social, v, 1, 39, 52, 82, 98, 118, 133–146, 153–171, 176, 199–217, 223–234, 237, 238, 240–244, 246, 247, 251–269
 costs, 199–217, 279
 network, 223–234, 241, 242, 280
 relationships, 223

responsibility, viii, ix, 2–4, 12, 39, 43–49, 52, 56, 67, 90n3, 133–147, 155, 183, 185, 209, 212, 253, 275–278, 281, 284
Society\societal, v–ix, 2–6, 8, 12, 13, 31, 42, 51, 53, 58, 61–65, 67–69, 98, 108–111, 113, 119, 123–125, 127, 129, 133, 135, 136, 146, 154–159, 163, 164, 176, 178, 179, 181–184, 192, 195, 199–203, 207, 209–212, 215–217, 238, 245, 252, 269, 275–281, 283–285
Soft law, 133, 135–137, 139n3, 141, 278, 284
Stakeholder, 2–8, 12, 39, 43, 45–48, 51–53, 58, 59, 64, 68, 79–81, 85, 98, 111, 113, 119, 121, 125, 126, 128, 130, 134, 135, 140, 153–157, 160, 161, 164, 166, 168–171, 175, 177–180, 182–185, 193, 201, 202, 208, 209, 215–217, 215n9, 245, 253, 256, 261, 263, 278, 280, 282–285
Standards, vii, 11, 12, 42, 43, 49, 54, 57, 61, 65, 79, 88–93, 90n1, 121, 135–142, 137n1, 137n2, 139n3, 145n6, 146, 153, 156, 159, 170, 171, 178, 179, 188, 194, 195, 200, 203, 212, 233, 245, 278, 279, 282–284
Strategic management, 4
Strategy, viii, 3, 8, 40, 45–47, 57, 60–64, 67–69, 101–103, 109, 110, 118, 121, 125, 127–129, 137n2, 141–146, 153–169, 171, 175–177, 181–182, 184, 186, 190, 210, 213, 238, 244, 245, 256

Structure, 44–45, 58, 82, 84, 86, 101, 134, 145n6, 146, 158, 187, 188, 227, 228, 231, 232, 234, 253, 255, 257, 260–262, 260n4, 266–268, 279, 281, 284
Survival, 51–72, 165, 277
Sustainability, vi, 39, 44, 48, 117, 118, 120, 124, 145, 161, 181, 200, 209–211, 217, 247, 278
Sustainable development, 4, 61, 120, 155, 156, 158–161, 163–167, 176, 177, 179, 180, 183, 186, 192, 195
System, v, 4, 7, 8, 10, 21, 22, 24–28, 30, 33–37, 42, 43, 45, 47–49, 55, 84, 85, 119, 120, 138, 145, 145n6, 146, 155, 158, 163, 167, 189, 192, 193, 195, 213, 215, 217, 238, 239, 241, 254, 255, 257, 259, 260, 264, 266, 268, 276, 279, 284

Trade union, 56, 62, 63, 157, 179, 183
Transparency, 7, 43, 48, 165, 180–181, 185, 217, 224, 233, 280
Trust, 81, 85, 90n4, 127, 134, 143, 145, 147, 158, 161, 162, 215, 223, 225, 228, 229, 246, 267, 282, 283
Tunisia, 51–72

UAE, 238, 242–244, 246
Unions, 24, 56, 62–64, 66, 157, 164, 179, 183
United States (US), 31, 91, 97, 99, 103n1, 108, 109, 125, 142, 143n5, 154, 177, 205, 212, 251, 252, 257, 258
User, 10, 229, 237–246, 254, 280

Values, vi, vii, 2, 3, 41, 48, 54–56, 61, 64–65, 67, 68, 79–82, 84, 85, 90n3, 97, 100, 105, 109, 117, 120–122, 124, 127–129, 134, 136, 138, 139, 146, 153, 155–159, 161–165, 167, 169, 171, 175, 178–180, 182, 186, 189, 195, 199, 200, 202, 203, 209–214, 247, 255, 263, 265, 279
Veolia, 154n1, 163–165, 167, 171, 175–195, 279, 284

Working conditions, 3, 58, 61, 63, 65–66, 68, 155, 162, 179, 182, 186, 192